Celebration

A Portrait Of Hawai'i Through The Songs Of
The Brothers Cazimero

Celebration

A Portrait Of Hawai'i Through The Songs Of The Brothers Cazimero

Written by Ronn Ronck
Designed by Bill Fong and Leo Gonzalez

Mutual Publishing of Honolulu

This book is dedicated to Maʻiki Aiu Lake (1925–1984).
She taught everyone she touched to live life as a
celebration and contributed more to the perpetuation
of Hawaiian culture than many who
have lived far longer.

"Tomorrow's a new day."

First Edition, September, 1984
Second Edition, November, 1984

Library of Congress catalogue card number 84-060783
ISBN: 0-935180-11-7

Produced by Bennett Hymer

Mutual Publishing of Honolulu
2055 N. King Street
Honolulu, Hawaiʻi 96819

Song Acknowledgments

We would like to thank the following composers, publishers, and agencies for granting permission to use their songs (copyright dates indicated when provided by copyright owner).

ACCADIA MUSIC COMPANY: Mai Lohilohi Mai Oe by Lena Machado; E Kuʻu Baby Hot Cha Cha by Lena Machado © 1962; Holo Waʻapa by Lena Machado © 1971.

HELEN DESHA BEAMER MEMORIAL HAWAIIAN MUSIC SCHOLARSHIP FUND, KAMEHAMEHA SCHOOLS: Ke Aliʻi Hulu Mamo by Helen Desha Beamer; Na Kuahiwi ʻElima by Helen Desha Beamer.

COLUMBIA PICTURES PUBLICATIONS: My Hawaiian Souvenir by Johnny Noble © 1937 (renewed 1964), Miller Music Corporation. All rights assigned to CBS Catalogue Partnership. All rights controlled and administered by CBS Miller Catalog. International copyright secured. All rights reserved. Used by permission.

Waikiki Hula by Isaac Keola © 1929 (renewed 1957), Miller Music Corporation. All rights assigned to CBS Catalogue Partnership. All rights controlled and administered by CBS Miller Catalog. International copyright secured. All rights reserved. Used by permission.

Kuwiliwili Iʻho Au by Henry Berger © 1929 (renewed 1957), Miller Music Corporation. All rights assigned to CBS Catalogue Partnership. All rights controlled and administered by CBS Miller Catalog. International copyright secured. All rights reserved. Used by permission.

CRITERION MUSIC CORP. Hawaiian Hula Eyes by Wm. Harbottle, Randy Oness © 1945 (renewed 1972); Pua Maeʻole by John Kamana © 1954 (renewed 1982); He Punahele by Albert Nahalea © 1962; Maui Waltz by Bob Nelson © 1969–1978.

ATLANTIC MUSIC CORP: Waikiki by Andy Cummings © 1947 (renewed 1973).

continued on page 224

Contents

List of Songs

Foreword

*D*uring the past decade my work with Robert and Roland Cazimero has been quite rewarding, personally as well as professionally. The overwhelming success of the Brothers Cazimero is noteworthy in itself but our association means considerably more than that, reaching into that realm of brotherhood that few people ever get the chance to experience.

We met first in 1975, almost immediately after Robert and Roland had parted ways with Peter Moon and the Sunday Manoa. Music of Polynesia (a record company owned by my father, Jack de Mello) signed them up and began to develop the combination of talents which is today known as the Brothers Cazimero. After I took over their management we talked about career objectives and set goals. We changed the overall direction and focus, with an aim to expanding the entire dimension of Hawaiian music and dance.

Roland and I were close from the beginning. We talked endlessly about ideas and music. Robert was more cautious. He wasn't anxious to commit himself until he found out more about this new individual in his life. Gradually the three of us became a team and, as we explored our new musical terrain, the magic was apparent.

There is, of course, a very difficult growth period in any relationship of this kind. Obstacles, which sprung up at every angle, were overcome only by a total commitment to art. All of us felt like giving up at times but the foundation we gradually built is now one of the tightest knit and most respected in the industry.

Some people close to the Brothers Cazimero look at me as the motivator but Robert and Roland are neither lazy nor afraid of change. They have an uncanny ability to create their own momentum and follow their own destiny. When I'm feeling down and out they also can motivate me.

Don Ho, the entertainer who put contemporary Hawaiian music on the world map, once told me that the Brothers Cazimero have perpetuated the Hawaiian culture another two or three hundred years. His reference to culture, and not just to music, made me view their achievement in an entirely new light. It made me more aware of the leadership responsibility they have to the entire Hawaiian community.

We made the decision, early on, to restructure Robert and Roland's approach to Hawaiian music in terms of the traditional 'ohana. Their combined talents, both as recording artists and concert performers, are nurtured and supported by their extended family.

A concert by the Brothers Cazimero, therefore, involves more than two musicians who get up in front of an audience and sing songs. It is a cooperative project. Many people work behind the scenes to make sure when the show goes on that my stage setting is the best possible showcase for Robert's quick wit, Roland's deadpan humor, and 'Ala's strength and beauty.

Celebration, the book you are about to read, is also a team effort. It was created through unity, love, and the efforts of people inspired by the Hawaiian music that is so uniquely performed by the Brothers Cazimero. So up with the lights. Sit back, turn the pages, and enjoy!

Jon de Mello

Preface

The Brothers Cazimero have helped set the direction of contemporary Hawaiian music. Both in their live performances and on record albums they have established a professional standard that few other groups have matched.

During the early 1970s, Robert and Roland, along with Peter Moon, were the Sunday Manoa. *Guava Jam,* their first album, was released in 1972. Two others, *Cracked Seed* and *The Sunday Manoa 3* followed before the group disbanded in 1975. Their music enjoyed such tremendous popularity that it is often credited with spearheading a cultural revival in Hawaiian music, art, literature, and dance.

Reorganized later into a duo, the Brothers Cazimero continued their contribution to this "Hawaiian Renaissance" in a number of significant ways. Robert's *halau,* Na Kamalei, was the first all-male hula group to perform at the Merrie Monarch Festival in Hilo. Roland's cycle of songs for *Pele,* the volcano goddess, merged music and myth to create a modern masterpiece. His *Warrior* suite, inspired by Kamehameha the Great, showed that he was almost as much a risk taker as the Hawaiian kingdom's first king.

Together, Robert and Roland Cazimero continue to be the two most innovative and imitated Hawaiian performers of their generation. This book, which includes a selection of their favorite recorded song lyrics, explores their Hawai'i through biography, landscape, and the major themes that have influenced their music.

Celebration, like most books, was created with the help of friends. At the top of the list, of course, is Robert Cazimero and Roland Cazimero. It was their music that inspired this project and their enthusiasm that kept it rolling. Jon de Mello and Leah Bernstein of The Mountain Apple Company provided hours of guidance and administrative support.

Special thanks also goes to all of Hawai'i's songwriters, especially those whose work appears in *Celebration.* These Islands have been abundantly blessed by their talents and music.

Photographers contributing to *Celebration* include Douglas Peebles, Jim Haas, Dennis Callan, Allan Seiden, Frank Salmoiraghi, Greg Vaughn, Ron Jett, David Davis, Linny Morris, Philip Spalding III, Gil Gilbert, Carl Shaneff, Tom Brown, and Chris McDonough. Historical photographs were generously provided from the Baker/Van Dyke Collection by Robert E. Van Dyke and Gladys R. Van Dyke. Artists contributing to the book include Herb Kawainui Kane, Dietrich Varez, Martin Charlot, B. Kliban, Ralph Kagehiro, and Renee Iijima. Individual page-by-page credits for these photographers and artists can be found at the end of the book.

Others who gave their time, suggestions, and energy to *Celebration* are Amelia Lucero, Donald P. Holmes, Jay Hartwell, Sarah Magalotti, Galyn Wong, Kanoe Cazimero, Lein'ala Kalama Heine, Dana Washofsky, John Charlot, Wayne Harada, June Gutmanis, Terence Barrow, Roger G. Rose, Willis H. Moore, Rocky K. Jensen, Lucia Tarallo Jensen, Pierre Bowman, Mary Jane Knight, Leonard Lueras, Edward Joesting, Elizabeth Tatar, Greg Bloch, and Barbara Dunn. Larry Lindsey Kimura provided English translations for a number of songs from the Hawaiian. Thanks, too, to all my colleagues at the *Honolulu Advertiser* for their encouragement and support.

The final names on this list belong to the designers of *Celebration,* Bill Fong and Leo Gonzalez of The Art Directors, Inc., and Bennett Hymer of Mutual Publishing of Honolulu. Without them there would be nothing to celebrate.

Ronn Ronck

Opposite page: 'uli'uli (gourd rattle) used in hula.

A Musical Family

So many choices
in life to be made
So many things to do
So many hills
to climb to the top
As we move along
singing our songs
As we walk this land—
hand in hand
As we spread
the warmth of our love

The Warmth Of Our Love
Roland Cazimero

Questions to answer
truths to be told
Realizations
as we now grow old
So many hills
to climb to the top
As we move along
singing our song
As we walk this land—
hand in hand
As we spread
the warmth of our love

It is significant that the Brothers Cazimero have titled one of their albums *Proud Family.* Anyone who attends their nightclub or concert performances can readily see that Robert and Roland draw a tremendous amount of strength from their friends and relatives.

"We define our family or *'ohana* very broadly," says Robert. "It may have begun with our parents and brothers and sisters but it now includes hundreds of people who give us the support necessary for our creative endeavors.

"To carry this thought even further we like to think that our family extends to each and every one who buys our records or comes to see us in person. Without them one fact is certain. There would be no Brothers Cazimero."

Roland was once asked during a radio interview to name the song he'd like to have sung at the end of his life on earth. He chose one that he'd written himself, "The Warmth of Our Love," which the Brothers Cazimero recorded on their album, *Waikiki, My Castle By the Sea.*

The song tells of having "many choices in life" and "hills to climb." Of two brothers who walk the land of Hawai'i, hand in hand,

singing their songs and spreading "The Warmth of Our Love."

"When we die," Roland told the interviewer, "this should be the song played for us. It is exactly how we have lived our lives."

Hopefully, for both the Brothers Cazimero and their fans, the end is a long ways off. It is time now to talk about beginnings.

Robert and Roland grew up in Kalihi, on the island of O'ahu, but the roots of the Cazimero *'ohana* are firmly planted on the Big Island. Elizabeth "Betty" Meheula, their mother, was born in Hawi while their father, William "Bill" Cazimero, was born in Niuli'i—two neighboring districts in Kohala.

Bill, the second of 12 children, grew up on a farm in this North Kohala town and taught himself to play several musical instruments. As a teenager he could switch easily between the bass fiddle, trumpet, tenor sax, and steel guitar.

While continuing his interest in music, Bill worked as an overseer with the Kohala Sugar Company. In 1930, he put together a nine-piece band, known simply as Bill Cazimero's Orchestra.

The group included three of his brothers, Manuel, Louis and Joe, along with five of their friends. They performed first at dances in Niuli'i but soon their popularity was drawing assignments throughout the Big Island.

Meanwhile, in Hawi, Betty was also being raised in a musical family. Her father, Paul Meheula, was a talented musician who played the mandolin, 'ukulele, and violin at private parties.

Betty learned to play the guitar and 'ukulele from her father and often joined he and her sister Helen as a musician. Betty became a popular singer in the community with a wide range of Hawaiian, Japanese, and Filipino songs.

Kohala was a small enough place for Bill and Betty to have known each other as teenagers but each eventually married someone else and started a family of four children each. In later years, when Betty was divorced and Bill a widower, they struck a closer friendship and fell in love.

They left the Big Island for O'ahu in 1940 and were married on Dec. 9 of that year in Kawaiaha'o Church. Both Bill and Betty took jobs in Honolulu in hopes of building a new future for themselves and for the children that had been left in Kohala in the care of other family members.

Bill worked temporarily for the Inter-Island Drydock Company and then as a special duty policeman. Later he got a civilian job with the Naval Shipyard Public Works Center and remained there for nearly 25 years. Betty got employment at the Bank of Hawaii and later at Liberty House.

Neither Bill nor Betty gave up their music. They lived simply at the old Pali Hotel, working day jobs, and playing music at night. With the advent of World War II they performed with Emilio "Big Aunty" Guerreiro at U.S.O. shows. Betty, meanwhile, and her sister Helen formed one of the first modern all-female groups in the Islands. When Betty became pregnant soon afterwards she knew that the future was about to arrive.

Their first child, Rodney or "Tiny," was born in 1942. Resettling in Honolulu made raising Tiny difficult but Betty's mother and stepfather, Heloki Moʻokini, took immediately to Tiny, and he was raised in Kohala in the Hawaiian adoption custom of *hanai*.

In 1943 their marriage expanded into a musical union. Together with other local musicians they played on the military bases as well as an assortment of popular nightspots in downtown Honolulu and Waikiki. Betty would still perform from time to time with her female group and Bill continued to freelance with other musicians, including the Bill Werner Combo and Band.

By 1948 Bill and Betty had worked hard enough to purchase a new house and within a year nearly all the children were brought to Honolulu and into the new home on Palena Street in Kalihi. On March 20, 1949, Robert was born and on September 6, 1950, Roland was born along with his twin sister, Kanoe. By this time there were enough children to help at home and the three older sisters, Geri, Jean, and Joyce took care of the younger Cazimeros while Bill and Betty continued their daily jobs and musical careers.

Robert and the twins had a normal childhood in Kalihi while the oldest brother, Rodney, was raised on the Big Island by Betty's father. The three Oʻahu children all attended the Wonderland Play Garden Playschool. Kanoe and Roland later went to Fern Elementary School while Robert was enrolled at the Hongwanji Mission School. He rejoined the twins at Fern in the third grade.

"We fondly remember our childhood, "Robert says. "There was no such thing as half-brothers and half-sisters and everybody got along well and loved each other. We weren't rich but we never thought of ourselves as poor. Mama and Daddy were always there when we needed them and gave us what was important."

During the early 1950s, Bill and Betty regrouped and started their own band and Polynesian show. "Betty and Her Leo Alohas" was formed with Aunty Loving Gomes on piano and Uncle Danny Camacho on bass. Betty recruited cousins and nieces for dancers and soon their Polynesian shows were a four-to-five nights a week routine. Thursday nights were regular rehearsal nights on Palena Street and although put to bed early Robert, Roland and Kanoe were avid listeners.

Musical talent seemed to come natural to the Cazimero children. Robert remembers the three of them singing in bed when they were around seven or eight years old. On one Thursday night their rendition of "Singing Bamboo" brought cheers and applause from the rehearsing family in the living room.

"We did three-part harmony. Roland and I took the parts and gave Kanoe the lead because it was hard for her to sing parts. I took the high part while Roland sang low."

Preceding pages: an early portrait of the Cazimero family; and Betty Cazimero holds her twins, Kanoe and Roland, as Robert stands. At left: Betty and Bill Cazimero, Mama and Daddy. Above: Betty and Bill perform.

Another memory that has stayed with Robert and Roland is that of "Boat Days." Since the early years of this century the great passenger ships had carried passengers back and forth from California and their dockings at Honolulu Harbor were gala social events. The end of these "Boat Days" came in 1970 when the fourth Lurline, a Matson Liner, departed on its last voyage.

"During the 1950s and 60s," Roland says, "our parents often played for the arriving passengers on the Lurline and other ships. Sometimes we'd go out on the tugboats and accompany the ships into the harbor.

"Bands played, people sang, and streamers were waving everywhere. Sometimes confetti was thrown from the upper decks. It was quite a celebration. Although there are now new passenger ships sailing in Hawaiian waters the excitement of the past has gone forever."

Of the two brothers it was Roland who first started playing professionally. He had a natural "ear" for music and at the age of nine began playing the stand-up bass in the family band.

"Before I joined them," Roland explains with a laugh, "there was a female bass player. She was a good musician but Mama didn't get along with her too well because she was always smiling at Daddy. So she left and I took over. I stood on a chair and played the upright bass. My coat was several sizes too big but everybody thought I was quite cute."

The family band played various civilian and military clubs around O'ahu. Some Hawaiian songs were played but the popularity of the group rested on its dance music. Rhumbas, sambas, and foxtrots added to the variety.

While Roland was playing in the band, Robert and Kanoe were taking piano lessons. The family bought a brown stand-up piano for them to practice on. Kanoe eventually lost interest because, as she explains, "Robert played better than me and, besides, he insisted that it was his piano and never got off the stool. I hardly ever got enough time to practice."

Looking back, she also says that her interests seldom strayed beyond the day's more popular tunes. "Robert was great at everything. He could memorize complex classical pieces and at the same time play the latest pop song 'by ear.' "

Kanoe finally got her parent's permission to drop piano lessons and, like many young local girls during the late 1950s, she attended countless Parks and Recreation Department sponsored hula classes. Later she studied under a cousin, Lorainne Johnson, and John Pi'ilani Watkins. She developed into an excellent dancer and in hula discovered a world free of direct competition with her brothers.

"In those days," Robert says, "Kanoe and I felt closer together, even though she and Roland were twins. Looking back now it was probably because we always stayed behind when Roland left at night to play in the band."

For his part, Roland says he was always a little jealous. "I didn't like Robert having all the fun. He got to go play while I had to put on my coat and go play in the band."

At the age of 10, Kanoe joined her parent's band as a hula dancer. Robert came aboard at age 13 to play piano. All got child labor clearances and were signed up for the Musician's Union.

Roland, meanwhile, had received his first formal musical instruction at Kalakaua Intermediate School. Here, in the school's band class, he finally learned how to read music and play guitar.

"I also learned the tuba," he says. "There were a lot of Japanese students in the band class and they all seemed to get the popular instruments. Nobody wanted to play the tuba so I did and got in the band that way."

At left: Boat Day at Honolulu Harbor, where the Royal Hawaiian Band and outrigger canoes welcomed passengers arriving on Matson Navigation Co. ocean liners. Above: a young Kanoe Cazimero dances in her family's show at a military club.

*I try to speak of things so real
To convey with love
How I act and feel
Turn away the hurt
Turn away the pain
Just don't stand alone in tears of rain*

Our Song

Robert Cazimero
Roland Cazimero

*But try to speak of things more real
To convey with love
how you act and feel
Then the hurt may cease
And the pain may go
And the simple truth we all will know
is "you care"*

Both Robert and Roland continued their musical explorations at Kamehameha Schools. Robert was accepted for the 7th grade and during his prep school years he was able to pursue voice and a more formal piano training. Four years later Roland and Kanoe (by then nicknamed "Tootsie") entered Kamehameha Schools.

Robert was already part of the Concert Glee Club, the Hawaiian Ensemble, and student musical director. Roland, too, joined the Glee Club and also performed as a musician with the Hawaiian Ensemble, a group of 20 members organized by Winona Beamer. Beamer also taught her students the hula and both Robert and Roland studied the dance with her.

"When we started at Kamehameha Schools," Robert explains, "the place was very un-Hawaiian. There was no push to learn the Hawaiian language and even the hula was only done sitting down. Nona Beamer and maybe a couple other teachers were all alone in their efforts to reawaken a pride in our Hawaiian heritage."

The year 1967 was a pivotal one for Robert and Roland. Through their sister, Kanoe, they met dancer Leina'ala Kalama Heine, or "'Ala," who would eventually find a permanent place on stage in their live performances. Later they also got to know Kanoe's teacher, Ma'iki Aiu Lake, a *kumu hula* who helped spark the contemporary hula revival.

Kanoe was then dancing Wednesday nights in the Na Kapuna Night shows at the Moana Hotel. Pua Alameida was in charge of the musicians, Bill Kaiwa was the featured singer, and Ma'iki was the lead dancer. Kanoe was in the line with Dianna Livingston.

"'Ala," recalls Kanoe, "was our group's comic hula dancer. Everybody loved her. One evening Robert drove me down to the Moana and came inside to watch the show. I introduced him to 'Ala and they've been the closest of friends ever since."

Shortly thereafter Ma'iki was invited to Kamehameha Schools by Robert's music class to talk about Hawaiian music and her own compositions. When a classmate asked her to sing one of her songs, "Aloha Kaua'i," it was Robert who volunteered to accompany her on piano.

"She asked me later," Robert says, "if I wanted to learn *kahiko* hula from her but I foolishly declined. At the time both Roland and I were thinking more about 'rock 'n roll.' Mama and Daddy said we could leave their band and we went out to spread our new wings."

They joined a rock band, with Robert playing piano and organ and Roland on guitar or bass. They played regularly at school dances and various other social affairs around town. When not playing rock music they would often head down to Steamboats in Waikiki where they were sometimes asked to play behind well-known Hawaiian performers like Genoa Keawe and Pauline Kekahuna. They were also frequently guest musicians on "Waikiki After Dark," a program that was broadcast live from various nightclubs over KCCN radio.

A short time after graduation (Robert in 1967 and Roland in 1968), their friend, Peter Ahia, asked them to sing the background voices for an album that Bill

The Brothers
Catzimero

At left: in this Kamehameha Schools' photograph, Roland plays the bass, while Robert plucks the 'ukulele. Above: "The Brothers Catzimero," by B. Kliban.

Kaiwa was about to record. It was at the first rehearsal that the Brothers were introduced to guitarist Peter Moon. Moon had already picked a bass player for the recording but after hearing Roland play he made a quick substitution.

Robert and Roland kept in contact with Moon and on another occasion they joined up again to record instrumental tracks for Don McDiarmid, Jr. on his Hula label. Their resulting album, credited to the Maile Serenaders, also featured Gabby Pahinui. This record was the beginning of the "sound" that eventually found its way into the mature Sunday Manoa.

The original Sunday Manoa group consisted of Moon and Cyril Pahinui (one of Gabby's sons) on guitars, Albert "Baby" Kalima, Jr. on bass, and Palani Vaughan doing vocals. Their first album was called *Meet Palani Vaughan and the Sunday Manoa.* Following this debut Vaughan left the group to start a solo career and Bla Pahinui replaced his brother Cyril. The new trio cut a second album, *Hawaiian Time.*

After more personnel changes another trio emerged, this time consisting of Peter, Robert, and Roland. This group, with Kanoe as a solo dancer, made its formal opening at the Outrigger Canoe Club.

Sunday Manoa's first album, *Guava Jam,* was released on Hula Records in 1972 and its tremendous success is sometimes used to mark the beginning of what's been termed the "Hawaiian Renaissance" in contemporary local music. Their follow-up album, *Cracked Seed* (with Gabby Pahinui) came out a year later.

"After *Cracked Seed* was released," Roland says, "we started playing with Peter at the Primo Gardens in the Ilikai Hotel and then at the Prow Lounge in the Sheraton-Waikiki Hotel. I can't think of a show run that we've ever enjoyed more than that."

The group's third album, *The Sunday Manoa 3,* was recorded both in Hawai'i and on the Mainland. A

Home In The Islands
Henry Kapono Ka'aihue

*The road's gone far away from home
And we've been lonely, missing you only
When we are away a sunny day
Is not quite the same as the ocean blue*

*At home in the islands, at home in the islands,
At home — in the middle of the sea*

*We're two happy guys, beneath tropic skies
Living the life of the gypsy musician
And it's hard on our heads
when the lady of our hearts
is miles and miles and miles away*

*At home in the islands, at home in the islands
At home — in the middle of the sea*

*There's no other place that I'd rather be
Than home in these islands
in the middle of the sea
There's no other place that we'd rather be
Than home in the islands
in the middle of the sea
Keeping real close to a family of friends
Taking it easy in the tropical breezes*

*At home in the islands, at home in the islands
At home — in the middle of the sea*

chorus from Kamehameha Schools was used as well as a California string section. Robert and Roland believe this is the best Sunday Manoa album in terms of song selection and feeling.

Robert had difficulty, though, with one song, "Hawaiian Lullaby," with its haunting line of "Where I Live, There Are Rainbows." It was supposed to be recorded on the Mainland and Robert found it especially hard to sing about Manoa Valley while camped out in a small L.A. studio.

"I was going to give up," he explains, "when one morning everybody showed up at the studio wearing aloha shirts and leis. Flowers were put around the room and when I closed my eyes I could almost smell

*Above: the Sunday Manoa with Roland, Peter Moon, and Robert.
At right: one of the Moku Lua islands off Lanikai, O'ahu.
Following pages: Roland, Leina'ala Kalama Heine, and Robert; and
Jack de Mello, the Brothers Cazimero's first manager.*

the islands. I pretended I was standing on Round Top and looking down on Manoa. The song got done and it turned out beautiful."

While playing with Sunday Manoa, Robert met up again with Ma'iki Aiu when he visited her *halau* on Keeaumoku Street. Aunty Ma'iki was just beginning her first *kumu hula* class in *kahiko* and Robert joined the group. In 1973, he graduated as a *kumu hula* with 27 other students.

Shortly thereafter, Robert and his good friend, Wayne Keahi Chang, decided to form their own all-male *halau.* Chang was a graduate of Aunty Ma'iki's second *kumu hula* class and the two young men asked her for a name. She chose Na Kamalei o Lilihua which they eventually shortened to Na Kamalei.

'Ala had also studied the hula with Aunty Ma'iki and sometimes, during the Sunday Manoa's live performances, she would be asked to dance on stage. Later, as a duo, Robert and Roland would invite 'Ala to join them as a regular dancer.

Despite the popularity of Sunday Manoa, the trio fell apart in 1975. Moon's decision to break up the group was taken hard by the Brothers but they managed to bounce back with the help of family and friends. They were soon introduced to Jack de Mello, a Mainland-born composer, arranger, and conductor.

In 1958 the multi-talented de Mello had founded Music of Polynesia, a publishing and recording company that had produced over 200 albums. He had heard the Sunday Manoa albums and was curious about how the Cazimeros would sound as a duo.

"Our first meeting with Jack," Robert says, "was at the Musicians Union. There was already a piano in one of the rooms and we brought along a bass. We told him the story of our lives and played all the familiar songs."

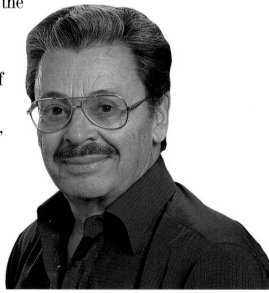

e Mello liked what he saw and heard. Almost immediately he put Robert and Roland into a studio to record an album and then arranged for a nightclub engagement to give his new clients public exposure.

Needing a name for the duo, both de Mello and the brothers went home one evening to think about it. They next day everybody returned with the same choice: *The Brothers Cazimero.* This also became the title of their celebrated debut album, released in 1976.

"The decision to dissolve Sunday Manoa," de Mello wrote for the album's liner notes, "created many reactions. But with every ending there is a new beginning and Robert and Roland, the Brothers Cazimero, are perfect mirrors for one another. For their first album, we chose to present them within all of their musical dimensions."

De Mello's words were prophetic. This was indeed a new beginning for Robert and Roland and the songs they chose for their first album savored old directions and pointed to new ones. Included was "Aloha Tower," a song which brought back memories of the great white passenger liners which used to dock in its shadow. Another was "Royal Hawaiian Hotel" and farther down the road this "Pink Palace" on Waikiki Beach would provide the Brothers Cazimero a nightclub home in its famous Monarch Room.

Among the traditional favorites was "Kilakila 'O Haleakala," a volcanic salute to Maui's Mount Haleakala. The album's hit turned out to be "Morning Dew," a thoughtful musical poem to the quiet early morning hours. The lyrics were written by Larry Lindsey Kimura, poet and Hawaiian language teacher at the University of Hawai'i, and the music composed by Eddie Kamae, the leader of his own group, the Sons of Hawai'i.

ust before the release of their first album, the Brothers Cazimero opened at the Territorial Tavern in downtown Honolulu. Roland, dressed in what he now describes as Kama Sutra pants (wide-legged trousers with slits on one side), sat like a Cheshire cat on a white oversized cube. They hired a hula dancer, Lokelani Hew Len, who descended from the second floor raft and danced down the stairs to the stage. "She was a very beautiful dancer," Robert remembers today. "When she came down the stairs the audience went wild."

The Territorial Tavern show gave the Brothers Cazimero a chance to establish an identity beyond the former Sunday Manoa group. They downplayed the songs they had recorded with Peter Moon and concentrated on the material they had introduced with their first album.

While working at the Territorial Tavern, Robert and Roland also developed the on-stage formula that still marks their public appearances today. Robert, with his quick wit and flair for comedy, stands behind the upright bass and delivers the vocal patter. Roland sits while playing his guitar and projects a more serious image. His presence reflects a strong Hawaiian consciousness.

The Brothers Cazimero work from a written script but leave room to improvise. No two acts are ever exactly the same. Cues are taken from the audience reaction.

"Music comes from the heart and the mind," Robert once told *Honolulu Star-Bulletin* entertainment editor, Pierre Bowman. "I am in charge of the talking and the slow songs. Roland is in charge of all the rhythm and the fast songs."

Roland concurs but says "it's only a pattern in the act. A fast song, a slow song. We have an idea of what songs we'll do, but no idea of how it will happen.

My Hawai'i,
My beautiful Hawai'i
How I long to be with you
My Hawai'i,
My beautiful Hawai'i
On an island paradise

My Beautiful Hawai'i

Solomon "Sonny" Kamahele

All the stars that shine so bright
Holding hands at night
Making all my dreams come true
My Hawai'i
My beautiful Hawai'i
How I long to be with you

The feedback from the audience tells us what we're going to do next." Robert added that "I love to make them feel so good and laugh, and right after that, bring them to tears."

Are the Brothers Cazimero the same off stage as they are on? Kanoe says they aren't. "When the spotlight goes out," she explains, "their personalities are exactly the opposite. Robert can be shy and meditative. He leads a fairly quiet and cultured life at home. Roland, who plays the straight part on stage, is much more active. He likes jokes, kids, and parties. He fools around and goes out drinking with the boys."

By the end of 1976 the boys had a brand new

album, *The Brothers Cazimero Vol. II* and a new show at the Prow Lounge in the Sheraton-Waikiki Hotel. It was a triumphant return to the scene of their happiest days with Peter Moon and the old Sunday Manoa.

Wayne Harada, the entertainment editor of the *Honolulu Advertiser,* called the Prow Lounge opening show "the most uncanny display of *mana* I've ever encountered in Hawai'i. Indeed, it was more than a mere nightclub opening: it was a Major Happening . . ."

On stage the Brothers Cazimero were joined by dancer Leina'ala Kalama Heine, now recognized as one of Hawai'i's finest comic hula dancers, and members of Robert's highly acclaimed Halau Na Kamalei. The *halau* was spotlighted on "Waika," a song based on the chant "Hole Waimea" with new music by John Spencer.

"When I graduated as a *kumu hula,*" Robert explains, "my chant was 'Hole Waimea.' It worked well in the show and we included it in our second album. Every hula student in Hawai'i went out and bought it because of that song."

Roland's *Hokule'a* album appeared in February of 1977 and was followed later in the year by *"The Brothers Cazimero In Concert."* During the summer the Brothers Cazimero did a moonlight concert at the Waikiki Shell. Close to 8,500 tickets were sold.

As the year ended the Brothers Cazimero had a new manager, Jon de Mello, and a new record label, The Mountain Apple Company. Jon had the time to give Robert and Roland more personal attention and, being of the same age, found it easier than his father to establish a one-to-one working relationship.

The de Mellos also have Big Island connections. Jon's great-grandfather came to Hawai'i in the first wave of Portuguese immigrants and raised his family near Captain Cook on the Kona Coast. His grandfather sought new horizons and went to California. Jack de Mello was born in Oakland.

Not all hula is serious. Here, 'Ala performs a comic hula.
Following pages: Roland and Robert with manager Jon de Mello in his
Tantalus house that includes a recording studio used by the group.

On one of his frequent trips back to the Islands, Jack met Penelope Wassman, a Roosevelt High School graduate then singing at the now vanished Lau Yee Chai restaurant in Waikiki. They were married in 1946 and Jon was born a year later in Honolulu.

Jon attended a variety of O'ahu schools and in 1966 graduated from Kalani High School. He then went to Berkeley to study painting at the California College of Arts and Crafts. After graduating in 1970 he returned to Honolulu and joined his father's music publishing and recording business. He remained there until 1976 when he branched off on his own to form The Mountain Apple Company.

Over the years Jon also continued to grow as a fine artist. Today he is an accomplished painter and printmaker in addition to the musical talents which have earned him recognition as one of the Hawai'i's leading talent managers, concert organizers, and record producers.

Robert says that without Jon the Brothers Cazimero would likely not be around today. He has kept the duo working together through the hard times as well as the good and is given the credit for transforming the Brothers Cazimero from backyard luau performers into the state's leading contemporary Hawaiian group.

"We work as a team," Jon says, "but Robert and Roland set the course. They have a great sense of where they are and where they want to go. I just keep a close watch on their progress and try keep the train from falling off the track." ■

May Day Is Lei Day In Hawai'i

I lei 'oe no ku'u kino nei
I lei 'oe me ke onaona ē
Pau'ole ka'u 'i'ini eia i ku'u pu'u wai
Ho'i mai, lawe mai, kou aloha ia'u nei
I lei 'oe i wili 'ia me ka nani
'O kou mino 'aka mai
Eia ho'i au no nā kau a kau
I lei 'oe no Hawai'i nei

I Lei 'Oe
Robert Cazimero

You are the lei of my person
You are the lei of sweetness
Never ending is my desire
Here in my heart
Return bring your love to me

You are the lei I entwine
With the beauty of your smile
Here I am forever
You are the lei of Hawai'i

One of the first things that Jon de Mello did after taking over the career management of the Brothers Cazimero was to search around for another concert opportunity. He found what he was looking for in Lei Day.

"For over half-a-century," de Mello explains, "the celebration of Lei Day has been an important tradition in Honolulu. We decided to add a little spice to it by staging the first Brothers Cazimero Lei Day concert at the Waikiki Shell in 1978. In the beginning we were only thinking about a single concert but it was such a success that we've returned to the Shell every Lei Day since."

Because the Brothers Cazimero have become so closely identified with Lei Day and its emphasis on the natural beauty of Hawai'i, their songs frequently make reference to flowers and the custom of lei making, giving, and wearing. One of Robert's best received compositions is the lovely and gentle "I Lei 'Oe" ("You Are The Lei"), a song that he sang solo on the Brothers Cazimero's 1979 album, *Waikiki, My Castle By The Sea.*

The first Lei Day celebrations that Robert can remember were at Fern Elementary School which he attended with Roland and Kanoe. Their parents always

made leis for them to wear to class and added another for the teacher. Fern School, like most elementary schools in Hawaii, had a Lei Day pageant each year for parents and Robert says the three kids always enjoyed "showing off" for mom and dad.

"My greatest moment came in the sixth grade," Robert explains. "That's when I was chosen to be the king of the school's Lei Day program. My queen was Lynette Palama who now works for the Department of Public Safety. That's about as close to being royalty as either of us is ever going to get."

Roland says that Lei Day became especially important to Robert and himself during their days at Kamehameha Schools. If May 1 fell on a weekend the entire family would meet for lunch somewhere in Waikiki and then walk together over to Kapiʻolani Park. Here they would listen to the Hawaiian music and look at the winning entries in that year's lei making contests.

"If we had any grand plans for the evening," he says, "we'd also stop at the lei stands and buy leis for our friends. We wanted to see everybody wearing flowers.

"After Robert and I played our first Lei Day concert," he adds, "we decided that this was something we wanted to do year after year. We were

*Preceding pages: May Day 1984 with the Brothers Cazimero at
the Waikiki Shell and Diamond Head in the background; four views of
Lei Day wearers and makers. Above: the Brothers Cazimero rise
above the Shell's stage in their 1984 Lei Day concert.
At near right: the Brothers at the Shell in 1982. At far right:
Marlene Sai sings with the Brothers in 1984.*

still celebrating Lei Day with the family. The only real difference was that our family had gotten larger."

The Brothers Cazimero and Jon de Mello begin planning their Lei Day concert about mid-March and start practicing for it around the second week of April. Because of their busy schedule, however, many elements are left to the last few days. There is seldom time for a full dress rehearsal and, because the Shell is also rented by other groups, the stage setting is often not completed until the afternoon of the concert.

"It's a good thing," Jon says, "that the public never gets to see the work we put in behind stage before the Lei Day concert. It's far from being glamorous. On concert day itself we're usually at the Shell from dawn to dusk.

"We do the final fixing of the stage, check the lighting, and place the flowers. There are leis to be made, costumes to fit, dance routines to go over, and final musical arrangements to work out with our guest artists."

Each year the Brothers Cazimero pick an overall theme for their Lei Day concert. In 1982 it was "May Day Magic," and de Mello hung banners from the Shell roof that turned the setting into a monumental fan. The Brothers occupied a large rising saucer covered with strands of green maile and white gardenia flowers.

For 1983 the Lei Day theme was "Hawaiian Rainbow." Robert and Roland performed on a stage beneath a hand-crafted rainbow of real flowers and artificial blooms. The backdrop was highlighted by a giant orchid and bird of paradise.

The 1984 theme was "Song of Old Hawai'i," a title that reflects an emphasis on classic Island melodies. This Lei Day concert also featured the most spectacular entrance for the Brothers that de Mello has yet devised. Robert and Roland emerged from behind a white two-panel drape perched high above center stage on a Condor "cherrypicker"

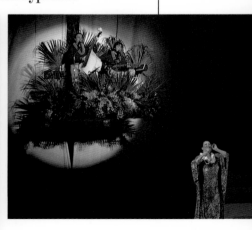

29

platform. The Brothers, held in place by safety harnesses underneath their shirts, sang from the flower-covered platform most of the night, sometimes rising 60 feet up into the air. "We're the Flying Cazimeros," Roland joked to the surprised crowd below.

For the finale Robert and 'Ala brought on their respective *halau hula* members to perform a jazzy Hollywood hula spectacular. The bare-chested men of Na Kamalei pounded on jungle drums while the women of Na Pualei O Likolehua wore tight hot pants, brightly-colored scarves, and feathered hats. 'Ala danced among them in a bouncing cellophane skirt.

"It gets harder each year," de Mello says, "to present the Lei Day concert. This is because we don't want to repeat ourselves. We have to come up with fresh ideas. Lei Day is the year's biggest challenge to our creativity."

One common thread that has run through all of the Brothers Cazimero Lei Day concerts is the inspiration of Don Blanding, sometimes called the "Father of Lei Day." The Brothers' 1982 concert opened with a special tribute to the now legendary Blanding.

The origins of Lei Day go back to early 1928 when Blanding, a talented young artist who wrote and illustrated his own books of light verse, suggested in a guest newspaper editorial that Hawai'i needed a holiday of its own. "Why not," he asked, "have a Lei Day?"

"Let everyone wear a lei and give a lei," Don Blanding wrote in *Hula Moons*, his 1930 book of memoirs. "Let it be a day of general rejoicing over the fact that one lived in a Paradise. Let it be a day for remembering old friends, renewing neglected contacts, with the slogan 'Aloha,' allowing that flexible word to mean friendliness on that day."

Blanding, a transplanted Oklahoman, saw that leis were given to arriving or departing friends—and on various important occasions—but were seldom seen around the Islands otherwise. Only the older Hawaiians still made leis simply for the pleasure of wearing something beautiful.

In presenting his Lei Day idea, Blanding said he wanted "to bring out the aloha that is expressed in the lei. Everywhere in the world the color, romance and glamor of Hawaii is associated with the lei. In recent years the custom has been allowed to decay and the special day is intended to bring it into prominence again."

Blanding's suggestion of a Lei Day was seconded by *Honolulu Star-Bulletin* writer Grace Tower Warren who recommended that May Day (which was also her birthday) be celebrated as Lei Day in the Islands. By April the newspapers were full of encouraging letters of response and plans went ahead for the celebration.

Honolulu's first Lei Day, May 1, 1928, centered around the lobby of the downtown Bank of Hawaii at King and Bishop streets. Crowds packed the exhibit area where the centerpiece was a fountain turned into a Maypole decorated with maile. Bina Mossman and her group provided the music and Blanding crowned the first Lei Day Queen, 19-year-old Nina Bowman, a University of Hawai'i student.

Much of the interest, of course, was shown the lei contest entries. The bank had provided $225 in gold to be divided among the winners in several

30
Above: three views of leis. At right: strands of pikake, 'ilima, and pua kenikeni await Lei Day necks backstage at the Shell with Maynard "Gramps" Hoapili. Far right: Don Blanding.

Ku'u pu'a ku'u pu'a mae' o le
Nou mau ko'u li'a 'ana
He no he'a Oe i ku'u ma ka la
A no na kau a kau

Na ni he u'i kawa hine la
A he lei we' hi no na kupu na

Pua Maeóle
John "Squeeze" Kamana

Ku'u pu'a ku'u pu'a mae' o le
Nou ku'u me le nei

My darling, never fading flower
You're my constant desire
And your loveliness will be in my heart for you
For you alone, my sweet

Beautiful and gorgeous
the lovely maiden
And the garland is to be kissed.

My darling never fading flower
This is my song for you

different categories. Princess Abigail Kawananakoa presented the prizes. Nobody was happier, of course, than Blanding. He had always loved being the center of attention.

Donald Benson Blanding was born November 7, 1894, in Kingfisher, Oklahoma Territory. His father was a judge who had raced in the opening of the Cherokee Strip and he spent his youth in nearby Lawton, graduating from Lawton Intermediate School. At the age of 15 he left this prairie town behind and began traveling around North America and Europe.

Blanding loved to sketch and he gradually developed skills as an artist. He spent a summer

Soft Green Seas

R. Alex Anderson/Leonie Weeks/Ted Fio Rito

Soft green seas, a mass of leis,
Flaming trees and lazy days;
Fragrant nights of song and flowers,
Melting lights and dream filled hours;
Smiles and glances, steel guitars,
Hula dances, laughter, stars!
And then to haunt this soul of mine,
Someone, someone, left behind.

drawing the wonders of Yellowstone National Park and then spent the years 1913 to 1915 sharpening his craft at the Chicago Art Institute. He also had quite a talent for writing verse and enjoyed composing imaginative and clever poems about the many fascinating places he visited.

During a 1916 stop in Kansas young Blanding decided to pass the time by boarding a streetcar to see the sights. Along the way the streetcar passed a playhouse that was presenting a stage production of "The Bird of Paradise." The actress Lenore Ulrich had the starring role.

Since the matinee was about to begin Blanding got off the streetcar, bought a ticket, and went inside. The popular stage play, with its haunting chants and hypnotic drum beats, worked its magic.

"In those two hours," he wrote in *Hula Moons*, "Hawaii put her spell everlastingly upon me. Through the illusion of the stage I lived in a land of music and laughter where flower-crowned, amber-fleshed people invoked a fierce goddess of lava and fire, through a ritual of furious dancing and the staccato rattle of dried gourds filled with hard seeds.

"A girl danced. With arms and hands undulant as restless waves, her body supple as a swaying vine, her bare feet moving with caressing lightness, she danced against an exotic background of trailing, tangled *lianas* and tall, sky-rocketing palm trees.

"All the dreamer in me responded. Anyone who saw Lenore Ulrich in the part of Luana can understand. I had found my Islands of Delight and was committed to the voyaging."

When the 21-year-old Blanding subsequently inquired about transportation to Hawai'i he was told that tickets were $90 for a   five-day trip by ship from San Francisco. He was in California a week later and soon aboard a steamship bound for Honolulu.

Upon his arrival in Hawai'i he went through a variety of odd jobs, as a manager of an amateur theater and as a cartoonist on the *Honolulu Advertiser*. He also spent a couple years in the Army, primarily at Ft. Shafter and Schofield Barracks.

Terence Barrow, an internationally-known Pacific scholar and author, is currently doing research for a book about Blanding. In a preliminary article for the *Advertiser* he wrote that "Don Blanding became much attached to his Hawaiian friends and they adopted him. He was given the Hawaiian name of 'Aloha Lani,' meaning 'brilliant light from the sky.' Blanding was a tall, handsome fellow and solidly built; he was never without a smile. He reveled in living with Hawaiians and was welcomed by them. What little money he needed he made by selling sketches and paintings."

At one point he and a partner, painter Frank Moore, opened up Cross-Roads Studio, a gallery near the 'Iolani Palace grounds and opposite the old Pacific Club. They exhibited the work of other local artists as well as their own. Later, Blanding worked for George Mellen's advertising agency as a copywriter.

One of Blanding's clients was the Japanese company which produced the soup seasoning, Aji-No-Moto. Needing a gimmick, he started to illustrate and write verse for a series of ads that ran daily in the *Star-Bulletin* for two years. Readers especially enjoyed the poems because he included references to local people and events.

Having now established a local reputation as both artist and poet, Blanding combined both talents in a booklet entitled *Leaves from a Grass House,* which was printed by his friends at the *Star-Bulletin* in 1923. Two-thousand copies were sold almost immediately and a second edition was brought out by the Patten Company in Honolulu.

Following on this success came *Paradise Loot* (1925) and *Flowers of the Rainbow* (1926). From 1926 to 1928 he worked in the advertising department of the *Star-Bulletin* where he created a regular feature entitled "Don Blanding's Page."

The best poems—Blanding liked to call them "word-pictures"—from his first three books, along with more of his stylish pen-and-ink silhouette sketches, were subsequently collected in *Vagabond's House.* This book, which brought Blanding overnight success and the unofficial title of Hawai'i's poet laureate, was published by Dodd, Mead and Co. of New York in that historic first Lei Day year of 1928.

"Early on the morning of May First," Blanding wrote in *Hula Moons*, "I turned out and walked from the studio in King Street to board a downtown street car. A big truck lumbered by. A voice hailed me. I saw a Hawaiian boy that I knew, pointing excitedly to his hat and grinning broadly. A yellow ilima lei, three strands wide, encircled his hat like a triple chain of gold, and a loop of red hibiscus swung jauntily over the radiator cap. When the streetcar came by it resembled a florist's delivery wagon. Motormen, conductor, and passengers were laden with garlands. Japanese, Chinese, Philippine and white faces beamed over bright blossoms. Street workers rivaled the garden shrubs in brilliant blooming. School children, housewives, milkmen and vegetable vendors celebrated with leis . . . It was estimated that a hundred thousand people wore the badge of friendliness that day."

Lei Day was made a territorial holiday in 1929 and the University of Hawai'i started to schedule its own pageant to coincide with the excitement downtown. In 1930 the Bank of Hawaii shared the spotlight with the Alexander & Baldwin and Davies and Company buildings. Then a year later, Honolulu's mayor, George Fred Wright, offered the lobby of Honolulu Hale for the festivities.

Eventually the festivities were moved outside between Honolulu Hale and the Mission Memorial building. Steel bleachers were erected for the spectators. In 1940 movie actress Dorothy Lamour presented that year's queen with a carnation lei from California.

And what of the man who started it all? Don Blanding took his royalties from *Vagabond's House* and in 1929 set up his own Vagabond's House Studio in New York City. A couple of years later he was in New Mexico, then in California where he established still another Vagabond's House at Carmel-by-the-Sea.

He was always a popular lecturer and spoke frequently around the country on Hawai'i and other subjects. The books of poems also continued: *Songs of the Seven Senses, Let Us Dream, Memory Room, The Rest of the Road,* and *Drifter's Gold.* His illustrations were used on greeting cards, on fabrics for shirts and dresses, and even on a line of dinnerware.

Even with his spreading fame, however, Blanding remained in touch with the islands. As Lei Day approached in 1939 he sent the following poem, "The Friendly Day," to the editor of the *Star-Bulletin* and it was subsequently published in the newspaper.

The Friendly Day

Hawaiian years are like great
golden leis,
Hawaiian days are like
bright tropic flowers,
The hours are the petals of
these days,
The minutes are the pollen
of the hours.

Our tears are only gentle
soothing rain,
Aloha is the perfume of
these tears,
And Lei Day is the clasp that
links the chain
To make a joyous garland
of the years.

36   *Above: lei sellers at Honolulu Harbor in the 1930s before Matson's ocean liner arrives. At right: leis of orange 'ilima, whose blossom was once reserved for royalty, and kou.*

E ku'u ipo o ke aumoe
'Auhea lā 'oe e maliu mai
I neia leo a ke aloha
He ho'oheno kēia, nou wale nō

'Auhea ke ahi o ku'u kino
Ku'u hoa mahana a ka 'i'ini
Anu ho'i au i ka pō mahina
Ho'i mai nō 'oe, e pili hemo 'ole

Pā kolonahe a ke ahe makani
Hō mai ana i kou 'ala
He lei liko o ko'u pu'uwai
Ka pilina ho'i, na'u ia lei

Hā'ina 'ia mai ana ka puana
E ku'u ipo o ke aumoe
'Auhea lā 'oe e maliu mai
He ho'oheno kēia nou wale nō

Ku'u Ipo O Ke Aumoe

Charles Warington Jr./Malia Craver

O my sweetheart of the midnight hour
Listen, pay attention
To this voice of love
This I dedicate to you alone

Where is the fire of my body
My darling companion of desire
I am cold in the moonlight night
Come back to me and remain never to part

A soft wind blows its gentle caresses
Carrying your fragrance to me
You are a leaf bud lei of my heart
A union for me to adorn

Sing my dedication
My sweetheart of the midnight hour
Listen, pay attention
This I dedicate to you alone

landing remained in California until 1940 when he moved to Florida. That year he also married Dorothy Binney Putnam, the divorced wife of publisher George Putnam who later married Amelia Earhart. Blanding's book *Floridays* was published in 1941.

He left Florida in 1948 (the marriage didn't last) and returned to California. A new book, *Mostly California*, also published in 1948, celebrated this experience.

Over the years Blanding often traveled back to Hawai'i to make appearances at the annual Lei Day activities. In 1953 he read poetry from *Vagabond's House* at a concert with the Honolulu Pops Orchestra. Blanding's last book was published in 1955. It contained both new poems and old and was appropriately titled *Hawaii Says Aloha*.

"The end came to his earthly life," Barrow explained, "on June 10, 1957, when he died of a heart attack while in Los Angeles. Due to the fact that Don desired to be buried at sea, his close friend and trustee, Frank S. Lindsay, told me that he and his wife, Lily Doris, also a close friend of Don, flew to Hollywood to bring back Don's ashes.

"Then on July 5 of the same year, beachboy friends of Blanding conveyed a party of six or seven outrigger canoes out from Waikiki Beach. *Kahuna* David 'Daddy' Bray was among those in the group.

"Before the canoes departed for sea, a large gathering of friends attended a service performed by the Rev. Charles M. Simon of the Church of Religious Science, and a Hawaiian service by Daddy Bray. Then the lei-draped canoes set out near sunset; once beyond the reef, the ashes were scattered by Lindsay as he recited the 23rd Psalm just as the sun dropped below the western horizon."

Don Blanding, artist and poet, the author of nearly two dozen books and the father of Lei Day, had come home to Hawai'i. Today, due to the work of Barrow and other enthusiasts, the books of Don Blanding are enjoying an upswing in popularity. Collectors search out the rarest of editions and second-hand bookstores have trouble keeping even the basic titles in stock.

"One of my regrets," Robert Cazimero says, "is that I never met Don Blanding. He had tremendous energy and talent and his books are little treasures that mean more to me with each passing year. My favorite is *Hula Moons*, a long prose poem that paints a very romantic picture of Hawai'i during the 1920s. I read a short section of it during our 1982 concert."

oday the heart of Honolulu's yearly Lei Day celebration is in Kapi'olani Park. In addition to the Hawaiian music, the lei sellers, and traditional craft exhibits, a lot of attention is given to the Department of Parks and Recreation's annual lei-making contest. The city has sponsored this lively competition for over a half-century and the winning entries are hung in portable galleries.

There is a Mayor's Grand Prize for the best overall lei as well as separate awards for the most "typically Hawaiian lei," the best "hat lei," and the various color leis which are made up of flowers which are "red," "blue," "green," "pink," and "yellow." In 1984 a special "silver" category was added in honor of the year being Hawai'i's Silver Anniversary of statehood.

Hawai'i's master lei makers take their art quite seriously. The grand prize winner for 1984 was Ray Wong, a social studies teacher at Kaimuki High

School. He entered his first contest in 1971 and has been back each year since. His Mayor's Grand Prize entry was for a "blue lei" consisting of salvia, statice, pa'iniu, blue moss cypress, dendrobium, ola'a beauty, alyssum, Persian violets, dusty miller, petunia, and silver tree.

Wong, who also picked up 11 other awards, practically danced around the park when told of his prizes. Although a Hawaiian only in spirit, Wong told a *Star-Bulletin* reporter that Pele and all the rest of Hawai'i's gods "must know how I feel. I know this art is something that has to be perpetuated, so I don't think they will be against me. I think they go for me. There's always that love, win or lose."

According to Wong, once he has the materials at hand each of his leis takes about two hours to make. Each lei is special and can never be duplicated. "I know when one is right and when one is wrong. When it doesn't flow, you start all over, no matter how much work you've done."

Ray Wong—champion lei maker: "this art must be perpetuated;" and leis entered in Honolulu's annual contest can take up to two hours to weave.

All of the eight major Hawaiian Islands have their own representative lei. Except for Niʻihau, which has a tiny sea shell, these island symbols are flowers and plants. In addition to being strung on leis they are often subjects for Hawaiian arts and music.

Oʻahu's flower is the tiny ʻilima blossom, an orange-to-yellow colored flower that is strung into a soft rope-like lei. Hundreds of the round silky flowers, each about an inch in diameter, are used for a single strand. Because the blossoms are difficult to collect and string, ʻilima leis are prized by those fortunate to receive one. In an earlier age ʻilima leis were only worn by Hawaiian royalty.

The Big Island's official flower is the lehua, a scarlet blossom of the ʻohiʻa tree or shrub. A dark red hardwood, the ʻohiʻa-lehua tree grows well on the Big Island's volcanic slopes and may grow to over a hundred feet tall. Lehua flowers are delicate tufts which can resemble a lei of feathers and are often bound with ferns. The lehua is sacred to Pele, the goddess of the volcanoes.

Maui's flower is a small pink rose, actually two small roses that are not native to Hawaiʻi but were introduced during the 1800s, possibly by the missionaries. The Damask rose and the China rose quickly became favorites of the Hawaiians who named them collectively as roselani or "heavenly rose." Because the early Hawaiians did not pronounce the "r" or the "s" their name for the sweetly scented flowers was pronounced lokelani.

Kauaʻi's lei flower is really not a flower but the seed or berry of the mokihana plant. The purple mokihana grows on a scraggly little shrub that is a native to the island's forests. These fragrant seed capsules seeds are strung like beads and are usually woven with strands of maile, an aromatic vine-like shrub with glossy green elliptical leaves. In old Hawaiʻi maile was sacred to Laka, goddess of the hula.

Molokaʻi's flower is the tiny white kukui or candlenut tree blossom. The kukui is also the official state tree of Hawaiʻi. Lei makers usually string the five-petaled flowers together with the tree's silvery-gray downy leaves. The nuts of kukui are also polished and strung as leis.

Lanaʻi's flower is the Kaunaʻoa, a rusty-orange vine with thread-like stems. There are sometimes tiny pointed flowers but no leaves. Kaunaʻoa is a parasitic plant and grows wild in fields and along the roadside. It clings to shrubs and other plants, wrapping itself

ʻO ke ʻala o kou lei maile lauliʻi
Ke kono mai nei iaʻu
E honi kāua e ka hoa
O ka uka pua lehua

E hele ana nō au i laila
ʻO kāu pane ia iaʻu
I loko o ka mahina
ʻAe aku wau hele nō

ʻO ka pāpale kau paʻa ma ke poʻo
Hoʻomanaʻo ʻia au i kahi kiʻi
No loko o ka Nūpepa
Kou lauoho ʻeleʻele o ka ʻaoʻao

ʻAe he ʻala nō hoʻi ko laila
He lei pili paʻa ia nou
ʻO wau kekahi e wehi like
E ka hoa e hele ana nō

Kéala

William (Pila) Wilson

The perfume of your lei maile lauliʻi
Invites me
Suggesting a kiss
Dearest who shared with me the beauty
of the lehua blossom filled mountain

"I will be going there" you told me
"Within a month's time"
"Well then you must go"

The way your hat sits on your head
reminds me of that picture
That was in the newspaper
Your black hair brushed to the side

Yes there is also a perfume there
And it's a lei you hold close to you
I'd like to share it as well
My friend who has decided to go

around them. The stems are easily harvested and then braided together, sometimes with maile, into neck and head leis.

Kahoʻolawe's flower is the hinahina, a perennial herb that grows profusely on the sandy beaches of the uninhabited island. It has small fragrant white and yellow flowers along with silvery green stems and leaves. Hawaiians sometimes call the plant "Pele's Hair," likening its leaves to the gray locks of the aging volcano goddess. Lei makers twist the leaves and flowers into an open-ended garland.

Niʻihau's symbol is a tiny seashell called the pupu. Their colors range from pearly white to a deep or reddish brown. These are strung into long strands by the residents of Niʻihau, most of whom continue to stick to a traditional rural Hawaiian lifestyle.

In addition to the above, a wide variety of flowers are used in making Hawaiian leis. Among the most popular are plumeria, orchids, and carnations. None of these is native to Hawaiʻi. Other favorite lei flowers are the pikake or jasmine, tuberose, violet, white and yellow ginger, gardenia, crownflower, and pua kenikeni. All of these flowers have been used, at one time or another, by the Brothers Cazimero in their Lei Day concerts.

Robert, like Roland and Jon, finds it hard to eat the day of the concert although he may try a bowl of saimin to calm down his stomach. Otherwise he relies on the group energy to keep him going.

"I'm usually backstage until right before showtime," he says. "There's so much going on that I've never been able to take a nap. If I run out of time to take a proper shower I've been known to just take my soap and shampoo and wash down behind the Shell with the gardener's hose."

One of the last things Robert does before each concert is to sit down backstage and make a lei for Roland and himself to wear during the show. It's now become a tradition as well as a good luck charm. "I just use whatever flowers and leaves are left over," Robert says. "They don't have to be fancy. We save the best of the leis for our guest performers."

Concert ticketholders begin lining up at the Waikiki Shell in the early afternoon. The gates open at 5:30 p.m. and soon the grassy lawn behind the reserved seats is covered with picnickers. Some spread out their sandy beachmats and break out beer and sandwiches. Others unravel a tablecloth beneath a gourmet dinner, complete with wine served in fine crystal and bouquets of colorful flowers.

By 7:30 p.m. the reserved seats are full and the excitement rises as the opening music builds to its climax. The crowd quiets and then, as the beautiful voices of Robert and Roland are heard, hearts stop and the clapping begins. The Brothers Cazimero greet their musical family and once again, May Day is Lei Day in Hawaiʻi. ■

Above left: May Day 1984 at the Waikiki Shell. Above right: yellow lei hulu manu (feather leis) can last forever and be washed with mild detergent. Right: a lei of roses and fern is worn as a sash by a hula dancer.

42

Islands Born Of Fire

Traveling to new lands
Finding what I can
Firing all these islands
Kamohoali'i
I've got to find me a home.

Still I search in vain
Through this island chain
Still it is the same
Kamohoali'i
I've got to find me a home.

I've Got To Find Me A Home

Roland Cazimero

I must fight to stay
There's no other way
NA IWI O PELE—
No, just bruised
Kamohoali'i
I've won me my home.

I sleep on this shore
Wake me, you live no more
But if your musts need me
Hi'iakaikapoliopele
She will bring my soul home.

H awaiian legend states that the Big Island volcanoes are home for a number of fire gods. The most important of these is the goddess Pele, the inspiration behind Roland Cazimero's highly acclaimed *Pele* (1979) album.

"Our original plan," Roland explains, "was to do a project which we called 'Genesis.' It was going to be an album that touched on all the gods and covered the entire subject range of Hawai'i's mythological beginnings.

"But the more research I did the more I came to realize that the story was just too big for me to tackle. I had to find a more manageable concept. Finally, during one of our frequent meetings, Jon and I decided to narrow the scope of the album down to just Pele."

Ideas, of course, seldom arrive out of thin air. The myth of Pele has long inspired island musicians, dancers, writers, artists and dramatists. Roland points out, for example, that a dramatic musical production entitled *Pele and Lohi'au* opened in 1925 at the Hawaii Theatre in Honolulu.

"Although," he says, "it was advertised as Hawai'i's first opera, this early production was probably

Above: a fern lei crowns a hula dancer. Before hula competition, many halau go to Kilauea and dance for Pele. At left: Pele's curtain of fire. At right: "Pele," a block print by Dietrich Varez.

more of a tableau. The cast included a dozen actors and actresses who took the roles of Pele and the other Hawaiian gods. Musical accompaniment was provided by a 60-voice chorus and Johnny Noble's Moana Hotel Orchestra."

Roland says his vision of Pele is a beautiful but highly temperamental woman. She is seductive yet dangerous and, when feeling either betrayed or jealous, can erupt into a fiery rage. One tradition places her high among the heavenly elite, a goddess born of a flame that escaped from the mouth of Haumea, the Earth Mother. Haumea and Wakea, the Sky Father, are the parents of all living things.

The myth of Pele, Roland continues, has long been associated with worship of the volcano deities and the origins of the hula. It begins with the migration of Pele and her younger sister, Hiʻiaka, from a mysterious and foreign land, believed to have been Tahiti.

"Hiʻiaka," says Roland, "was almost as lovely as Pele. During the long voyage to the Hawaiian Islands she took the form of an egg and was carried in the fold of Pele's gown. Hiʻiaka was the opposite in personality from her older sister. She was not fiery and emotional but, instead, calm and understanding. She was a composer of chants and a patroness of medicine and the dance."

The first island that Pele visited after her long ocean journey was Niʻihau. Finding it too small to make a home, she moved to Kauaʻi. She built a firepit here but was forced to flee when the ocean came crashing in to put out her flames. The pile of cinders she left behind is now called *Puʻu-ka-Pele*, the Hill of Pele.

Pele tried the island of Oʻahu next, stopping at Salt Lake and Waimanalo (*Ka-lua-o-Pele*, the Pit of Pele) and finally digging out a large burning crater that is today called Diamond Head. Ocean waves extinguished these fires, too.

As time went by, Pele also settled on the other islands, establishing volcanoes on Molokaʻi, Lanaʻi, Kahoʻolawe and Maui. On Maui she found refuge, living for many years far away from the ocean at Haleakala.

After the fires grew dark on Maui, Pele moved once more, to the Big Island of Hawaiʻi. Here she dug two connecting homes which she still inhabits today. The highest of the two is at the summit of Mauna Loa, while the second is in the Halema'uma'u fire pit at Kilauea. Both of these volcanoes are active today and in March 1984 they erupted simultaneously for the first time since 1868.

It is clear from the cycle of Pele legends that the ancient Hawaiians knew their environment well and recognized the relative ages of their home islands. Pele's wanderings generally correspond to the order in which today's scientists say the Hawaiian Islands rose from the ocean depths millions of years ago.

Before the 19th century, the Pele and Hi'iaka myths were passed by word of mouth and through the dancing of the hula. Later, they came to be written down and many of these stories appeared in the newspapers of the period.

A composite version of the legend was translated and compiled by Dr. Nathaniel B. Emerson for his book, *Pele and Hiiaka: A Myth from Hawaii*, first published by the *Honolulu Star-Bulletin* press in 1915, the same year as his death.

Emerson, a Honolulu surgeon and one-time president of the Territory's Board of Health, was also a noted collector of Hawaiian poetry. He was born at Waialua, O'ahu, in 1839 where his father was pastor of the native Hawaiian church. The Reverend and Mrs. John S. Emerson were members of the fifth company of New England missionaries.

Fluent in the Hawaiian language, he attended Oahu College and then continued his education at Williams College in Massachusetts. When not yet through with his studies, he enlisted for two years with the North in the Civil War and participated in the battles of Fredericksburg, Chancellorsville, and Gettysburg. He was wounded twice.

Returning to his studies at Williams College, he received his degree in 1865 and then began further courses in medicine at Harvard Medical School. He graduated from the College of Physicians and Surgeons in 1869.

Emerson practiced medicine in New York until 1878, then returned to Hawai'i at the invitation of Samuel Wilder, the Minister of the Interior. He accepted a government post and later established a private practice. Sarah Eliza Peirce, his wife, was Hawai'i's first woman doctor.

In 1909 the Bureau of American Ethnology published Emerson's first book, *Unwritten Literature of Hawaii: The Sacred Songs of the Hula.* He collected whatever printed sources he could collect but relied heavily on native Hawaiian informants who still practiced the hula.

Come love me now, come love me now
For I am yours, you are mine
Forever more.
But to command, but to command
For I am yours, you are mine
Forever more.

Then you came into my life
Life seemed like a dream
And then you departed,
Alone without you what could I do
I'm no good without you.

Those happy days beside the sea
You and me — Alone in our oneness

But cold and lifeless I hang
My heart no longer sang
Now I won't live without you.

But one day love awaits for me
This I see somewhere in my lifetime
But here in love now we are
There's no more to see
I feel you near me
Endeared to me forever.

So love we now
So love we now
For I am yours, you are mine
Forever more.

Come Love Me Now

Roland Cazimero

Above: bougainvillea on lava. Gin, leis, and sacred ohelo berries are cast into the volcano by Hawaiians for good luck or as offerings to Pele. At left: Mauna Loa erupts. Following pages: the island of Hawai'i grew from the glowing lava that Pele spewed.

Take a good look at me
Tell me what you see
Is it really me
Or some beauty you'd like to see.

E Pele
Roland Cazimero

I heard you beating on your pahu drum
Woke me up from my sleep . . . I had to come
Brought me here to Haena on Kaua'i
So look upon me now and enjoy me.

I'm not like any other woman you've known
I know about the many seeds you have sown
Enjoy me now, enjoy me now while I'm here
Care for yourself for I will soon disappear.

What is it you command of me
I who am from Hawaiki
Don't make me wait . . . I've waited too long
Before I go back to where I belong.

While Emerson included numerous references to the Pele legends in *Unwritten Literature of Hawaii,* and in his second book, *Pele and Hiiaka,* published in 1915, the latter book contains the most complete version of the legends in English.

"The story of Pele and her sister Hi'iaka," Emerson states in his preface, "stands at the fountain-head of Hawaiian myth and is the matrix from which the unwritten literature drew its life-blood. The material for the elaboration of this story has, in part, been found in serial contributions to Hawaiian newspapers during the last few decades; in part, gathered by interviews with the men and women of the older regime, in whose memory it has been stored and, again, in part, it has been solicited from intelligent Hawaiians. The information contained in the notes has been extracted by *viva voce* appeal to Hawaiian themselves."

Roland Cazimero based his music for *Pele* primarily on the material collected and published by Emerson. The three-year project entailed hours of library research, several visits to the Big Island volcanoes, and approval from *kupuna* such as 'Iolani Luahine, Vicky I'i Rodrigues, and Kamokila Campbell. Twenty years ago Campbell had portrayed Pele on an album produced by Jack de Mello.

"Listening to that album," Roland says, "can be a very moving experience. I can almost feel the heat coming off the turntable."

When first informed of the *Pele* project, Robert was against his brother doing the album. He felt that Roland was stepping into a controversial area that would eventually hurt the reputation that had already been established by the Brothers Cazimero.

"No matter how beautiful the music and words," Robert says, "any commercial version of the Pele myths is bound to upset some of the purists. To them this is sacred territory."

Roland finally solved part of the problem by traveling to Kailua on the Big Island and talking to the 'Iolani Luahine, one of Hawai'i's great hula dancers and an authority on Hawaiian legends and religion. She felt a special link to Pele and visited Kilauea to make an offering whenever the volcano erupted.

Aunty 'Io listened to some of Roland's songs and then gave him her blessing to go ahead with the *Pele* album project. She also discussed with him her interpretation of the ancient Hawaiian myths and their relevance to contemporary times.

"After Roland got all the approval he wanted," Robert now says with a laugh, "my reaction went from outright discouragement to jealousy. Why did people like his project? Why wasn't I doing something just as exciting?"

"Then I got upset because Roland didn't ask me to be on his album. When he did I told him I was busy. Then he asked 'Ala and she said 'yes.' I didn't turn him down again." When the album was finally released Robert was shocked at how well he liked it. "Today I love the album and wish I'd been more cooperative."

In a perceptive review for the *Honolulu Advertiser*, entertainment editor Wayne Harada termed *Pele* both "entertaining and innovative, and likely to be fodder for hours of intelligent discussion. The kupunas logically will be a bit astonished at what (Roland) Cazimero . . . has done to the legend of the volcano goddess.

"Simply, Cazimero has embraced—via music and verse—a bit of folklore that both fascinates and frightens, a subject that has concerned the historian, the anthropologist, the ethnomusicologist, and the educator for years. He has taken central figures in the legend of Pele—some with godly qualities—and has created what ultimately is a rock opera on the relationships of Pele, and her sisters Namakaokaha'i and Hi'iakaikapoliopele, her mother Haumea, and her eventual suitor, Lohi'au."

Harada continued writing that "in Hawaiiana circles, one does not rock the boat—or, in this case, the Richter scale—in dealing with Pele. But then, Cazimero is no ordinary artist in the Hawaiiana genre. What he has done is to bring sensitivity, invention, melody, and creativity to a sacred cow.

Rebirth Of Lohiau
Roland Cazimero

I must prepare myself for the duty at hand
To bring life again to this man
Gather me herbs and fragrances of this land
Then dance and play while I do what I can.

Hold fast his feet, the feet of Lohiau
As I force the essence of breath
into his empty shell
Into his eyes—down deep
into his chest Auwe—
I see once more, life giving breath.

I pray for the life—the life of this man
With the help of our Gods—
he will once more stand
The prayer must be faultless
Not too quick, not to slow
For if not right, "we live no more."

Attend 'o Uli a prayer for this life
Give it wings to fly to the heavens high
To Laka's mountain apples—
so rich—oh so ripe
To the clouds of Ku—the many-
colored clouds of the sky.

Hele mai la au 'o Hi'iaka e'e
I ke aloha a ka hanau e'e
Hanau ke ola—A ola, a ola, e'e
Na ke Aloha i kone e hele e'e.

Life in its fullness—life in every detail
This life is yours again—once more you can feel
Feel the spray of the surf
as you ride on the waves
Life to you, Lohiau
Life to Pele's new slave.

At left: panorama of an eruption. Hawaiians believe Pele can be seen somewhere in any photograph of an eruption. Above: the remains of Pele's anger.

Aluna au a Pohakea
Ku au, nana ia Puna
Po Puna i ka ua awaawa
Pohina Puna i ka ua noenoe
Hele ke a i kai o ka Lahiki o aʻu lehua,
O aʻu lehua i aina ka manu
I lahui ai a kapu
Aia la, ke hukiʻa la i kai o Nanahuki, e.
Hula leʻa wale i kai o Nanahuki, e.

Malama Pono

Roland Cazimero

On the heights of Pohakea
I stand and look forth on Puna.
Puna pelted with bitter rain
Veiled with a downpour black as night.
Gone, gone are my forests, lehuas
Whose bloom once gave the birds nectar.
Yet they were insured with a promise.
Look now the fire-fiends flit to and fro.
A merry dance for them to the sea
Down to the sea at Nanahuki.

"His visions are grand, his results are gorgeous. In *Pele*, Cazimero has not only simplified the legendary figures, but made them a living entity; his melodies breathe the essence of life, and his lyrics—largely picaresque, since the songs tell a story, in operatic fashion—are rich in history and culture."

Roland's lyrics for *Pele* follow the general story line of Emerson's *Pele and Hiiaka*. But to help listeners unfamiliar with the Pele legend, the album includes a pull-out sheet containing a fine narrative written by Brian Blevins. Each song is given its place within the story.

"Every line of the lyrics," explains Roland, "relates to an incident in the book. Sometimes a song covers a single chapter, at other times two or three chapters. Vickie Iʻi Rodrigues helped me trim the fat off the lyrics and define the story even further."

The lyrics to *Pele* are primarily in English, a decision Roland made to reach a wider audience. Still, he says, the lyrics alone don't tell it all. He advises listeners to check the album's pull-out sheet for the background story or, even better yet, to read Emerson's book.

Pele begins with the song, "I've Got To Find Me A Home," a cry from the fire goddess that she is tired of traveling and hopes to find a place to rest within the Hawaiian chain. On Maui she stops at Haleakala with her brother, Kamohoaliʻi, but is soon challenged to do battle by her elder sister, the powerful NamakaoKahaʻi.

The fight is fierce on both sides but in the end NamakaoKahaʻi appears victorious. Pele is killed and her body dismembered. The phrase "Na Iwi o Pele" is translated as "The Bones of Pele" and today this name is attached to a hill near Hana where some Hawaiians still point out the spot where they believe her bones remain.

It is only the body of Pele, however, that is dead. The gods free her spirit and she becomes immortal, rising high above the peaks of Mauna Loa and Mauna Kea. Sighting the fiery crater at Kilauea she descends to investigate. This is the place she's been looking for and declares "I've won me my home."

Pele acquires a beautiful new body and, a short while later, takes Hiʻiaka and Kamohoaliʻi to the seashore where they spend the whole day playing and dancing on the beach. Pele grows tired and decides to take a nap in a nearby cave. She asks only to be awakened in the event of an emergency.

While she is sleeping, Pele hears drums and follows their rhythmic sound to Haʻena on the island of Kauaʻi. Here she finds a handsome young prince named

Lohi'au who is doing the drumming. Lohi'au sees Pele and, not knowing it is the volcano goddess, falls in love with her.

The album's second song "E Pele" is sung by Pele to Lohi'au. "So look upon me now," she says to him, "and enjoy me." Lohi'au is cautious, however. Where, he wonders, did this beautiful woman come from?

Pele smiles at the young man's shyness but she also grows anxious and more seductive. "Don't make me wait," she sings. "I've waited too long. Before I go back to where I belong."

Lohi'au's heart is captured. In the song "Come Love Me Now" he embraces the woman and grows increasingly passionate. Now it is Pele's time to hesitate because she suddenly realizes that the mating of a goddess and a mortal man may lead to tragedy. She stays three days but grants him only her kisses. Finally, she tells the young man that she is not ready to make love and must return to her home on the Big Island.

After Pele leaves, Lohi'au falls to the ground, heartbroken. He gives up food, his love of dancing the hula, his responsibilities in the village, and even the consolations of other women. Believing that Pele will never return to him he takes off his *malo* and hangs himself from a rafter.

Meanwhile, Pele is growing lonely on the Big Island and asks her youngest sister, Hi'iaka, to make a trip to Kaua'i and return with Lohi'au. The goddess also gives Hi'iaka some of her heavenly powers to protect her on the journey. Pele warns her sister, however, that she should not to try and seduce Lohi'au. She wants him alone for a minimum of five days. After he will be free to make love to Hi'iaka as well.

Roland's song "Hi'iaka's Pledge" is a promise to Pele that the younger sister will not betray her sacred mission. She will find the man her sister wants as a lover and return with him safely to Kilauea. "Obstacles and trials may befall me," Hi'iaka says, "But I will endure."

Hi'iaka sets out on her journey accompanied by a newly found friend, Wahine'oma'o. Several times they are attacked or detained by monsters—Emerson devotes over a dozen chapters in his book to their adventures—but manage to survive, primarily because of Hi'iaka's good intentions and pure heart. When they arrive at Ha'ena, however, Hi'iaka learns that Lohi'au has committed suicide.

Pele's sister searches for Lohi'au's spirit and finds it wandering in sadness along the Na Pali Coast of Kaua'i. She catches the spirit and returns it to Lohi'au's body which is being preserved in a cave guarded by the priests. Hi'iaka now performs the song "Rebirth of Lohi'au" in an attempt to awaken Lohi'au from his deadly sleep. "I pray for life," she sings, "the life of this man. With the help of our gods he will once more stand."

Why Are We Apart
Roland Cazimero

You alone remain to me now
Your love if that is yet mine
If your heart remains with me still.

Through grassy meads tossed by the breeze
Thou art enshrined in my heart
Tho apart, thou art impressed within me.

I love you, why are we apart
I love you, let us make a start
Say you love me, say you do, love me too . . .

At left: the scars of a lava flow through Hawai'i Volcanoes National Park and into the sea, where a new island, Lo'ihi, is now growing underwater off the Big Island. At right: Kilauea erupts. In 1929, volcanologists used Army Air Corps planes to try and stop an eruption with bombs. Pele won.

I'm The One

Roland Cazimero

I'm the one, I'm the one
Yes, I'm the one you want
I'm the one, I'm the one
Yes, I'm the one you want
Because I'm full up on loving
And I'm full up with joy
'Cause when I love you, woman
All my loving you will enjoy
'Cause I'm the one.

I'm the one, I'm the one
Yes, I'm the one you want
I'm the one, I'm the one
Because I see two rivers
Chafing their banks as
They rush to enter the sea
A yearning for passions plunge
For the sea you enter in me
'Cause I'm the Master Lunge.

I'm the one, I'm the one
Yes, I'm the one you want
I'm the one, I'm the one
Yes, I'm the one you want, 'cause I
Care not for this woman
Who is like a mother to me
I care for you, Hi'iakaikapoliopele
Come, love, love, love, love, love me
We're the one, we're the one
We're the one.

Hi'iaka's prayer is answered and Lohi'au is reborn. A celebration is held and food is offered to the gods. Lohi'au tells his people that he will return with Hi'iaka to the Big Island and a canoe is readied for the voyage.

The travelers stop first at Mokule'ia Beach on the island of O'ahu. Hi'iaka goes to the top of Poha-kea in the Wai'anae Mountains and looks across to the Big Island. She sees smoke and realizes that Pele's erupting volcano is sending lava down the mountain to burn her beloved 'ohi'a lehua trees. 'Ohi'a trees were sacred in ancient Hawai'i because of their beautiful red flowers, a color reserved only for the gods and the highest chiefs. Hi'iaka composes the song "Malama Pono" with tears falling from her eyes.

"Gone are my forests, lehuas," she sings, "whose bloom once gave the birds nectar." She now feels betrayed by Pele but feels committed to finishing her mission. Even when hurt and angry Hi'iaka refuses to think badly of her sister. She and Lohi'au then visit a village located near what is today downtown Honolulu. Here lives Pele'ula, yet another sister of Pele and Hi'iaka.

At this point in the *Pele* album, a narrator (the voice of Wayne Chang) breaks into the story and explains that Pele'ula has invited Hi'iaka and Lohi'au to take part in a game of love called *kilu.* The game is played by a row of men and a row of women seated across the hall from each other. Each of the participants slides a piece of coconut shell toward short pyramidal blocks of wood which are placed before each person. The person whose block is hit becomes his or her partner after the game is over.

Lohi'au was an expert at playing *kilu* and tried to hit the block in front of Pele'ula. Hi'iaka, however, prevents their union. She uses her superior powers to win the game. Afterwards Lohi'au reveals in the song "Why Are We Apart?" that he loves Hi'iaka and was just trying to make her jealous of Pele'ula. "I love you," he confesses, "why are we apart? I love you, let us make a start. Say you love me, say you do, love me too."

Hi'iaka admits to Lohi'au that she does, indeed, return his love but her obligation to Pele must overrule her heart. They continue their travels by canoe and arrive finally on the Big Island. On their way overland to Kilauea, Hi'iaka observes at close range the burnt forests of her lehua trees and the anger begins to build inside her. When she learns that Pele's bad temper has also led to the death of Wahine'oma'o she is furious.

Upon arriving at Kilauea, Hi'iaka openly defies Pele in the song "A Promise Forgotten." She takes Lohi'au into her arms and tells Pele he will never be her lover. "I didn't ever touch your man," Hi'iaka sings, "till I saw my burnt homelands."

Pele is enraged and kills him with a bolt of molten lava. Hi'iaka flees the Big Island and takes refuge back in Kaua'i. When Pele learns later that Hi'iaka had remained loyal to her, even when tempted by Lohi'au, she is filled with remorse. She sings the song "Jealousy" to Hi'iaka. "This jealousy," Pele

admits, "made me blind. This jealousy too late made me see. Just how much I loved you."

True love, however, wins out in the end. A *kahuna* hears of the tragedy and brings Lohi'au back to life for a second time. The young prince of Kaua'i finds Hi'iaka at his old home in Ha'ena and they are reunited. Hi'iaka sings the lovely song "Destiny" to her lover. "Was it love or was it destiny," she wonders. "That brought you home again for me?"

Roland ends his *Pele* album with "I Am, I Am," a dramatic finale in which the volcano goddess again expresses sorrow for her actions but states proudly that she has a destiny as well. Here, in the Halema'uma'u firepit of Kilauea, she declares her identity and demands the respect of all those who fear her fiery fury. She sings:

> *I am, I am, I am the woman of the pit*
> *I am, I am, I make no qualms about this*
> *I am, I am, I am the ruler of this land*
> *I am, I am, I rule with a strong hand*
> *I am Pele, I am Pele, I am Pele, Pele e.*

Many admirers of Roland's *Pele* album do not realize that there is yet another Brothers Cazimero song that neatly fits into the Pele cycle. This is their beautiful hit single, "One Small Favor," which appears on the album *Hawaii, In The Middle of the Sea* (1980).

After *Pele* was released a friend of Roland's scripted out a stage musical based on the story and songs in the album. Because more songs were needed

A Promise Forgotten
Roland Cazimero

I loved you so
I did everything you asked and more
Yet I remembered my vow to you
Why was your promise forgotten so soon.

I did my duty to you
I thought that you'd see me through.

I didn't ever touch your man
Till I saw my burnt homelands
I remembered my vow to you
Is this the way I pay my dues to you?

My lands were wasted by you
You didn't stop at that you took Hopoe
and Lohiau, too.
Still remembered my vow to you
Seems you forgot—forgot about me, too.

And now my task is done
Still my heart longs for you
Too late I dream of
So many things for us to do
Now my heart yearns,
Yearns for all of you.

Panorama of Kilauea Caldera with Mauna Loa in the background.
On the edge of the caldera, scientists study eruptions year-round at the
Hawaiian Volcano Observatory.

Jealousy
Roland Cazimero

This jealousy made me blind
This jealousy too late made me see
Just how much I loved you
Now that you're not with me
To feel your arms no more
To feel your warmth no more
No more to love you
Now, now that you are gone
Away from me.

Just couldn't think, just had to do
Just didn't know that I would hurt you
But hurt you I did, but hurt you no more
To kiss your lips no more
To feel your heartbeat no more
No more to love you
Now, now that you are gone
Away from me.

Just couldn't think, just had to do
Just didn't know that I would hurt you
But hurt you I did, but I'll hurt you no more
The hurt that I feel I alone will endure
To feel your touch no more
To hear your singing no more
No more to love you
Now, now that you are gone
Away from me.

Roland wrote "One Small Favor" to fill a gap between the songs "Hi'iaka's Pledge" and "Rebirth of Lohiau." In this addition to the story, Hi'iaka asks Pele for a companion to accompany her on the hazardous journey to bring back Lohi'au.

Pele grants Hi'iaka this "one small favor" and introduces her to Wahine'oma'o. "You can have this favor that you ask of me," sings Pele. "You can have a friend to see you through just to walk beside you, some-one to talk to. You have a friend to see you through." On the song Roland takes the part of Pele and Sky Perkins is the voice of Hi'iaka. Kanoe Cazimero is Wahine'oma'o, the "one small favor" of the title.

"Roland taught Sky and I that song in Waimea, on the Brown Sugar Ranch," explains Kanoe. "I flew over there to be with Roland on his birthday while he and Robert were finishing up the *Hawaii, In The Middle of The Sea* album.

"Sky and I sung it first at the birthday party but Jon liked our voices so much that he asked us to sing on the record. We've performed the song a few times together in live concert and it's always been a hit with the audience."

For as long as history has been recorded the Hawaiian people have considered the Kilauea area sacred to Pele. In ancient times two temples were built on the side of the caldera to placate the fire goddess. One of the these was on the western side, at Uwekahuna, "The Place of Wailing Priests," and the other on the steamy eastern rim, near Kilauea Iki. Sacrifices of animals and plants were regularly thrown into the crater. The delectable 'ohelo berries which grow wild in the area were never eaten without throwing the first part of the harvest into the smoldering firepit.

With the arrival of Captain James Cook in 1778 the old Hawaiian ways began to unravel. Worship of Pele continued through the early years of outside contact but the introduction of Christianity hastened

Destiny
Roland Cazimero

Was it love or was it destiny
That brought you home again to me
Dreaming so long for a love long gone
Without you.

Waiting for you so impatiently
To hear your voice, singing in the breeze
Waiting so long for a love long gone
Without you.

Now I feel you close to me
I hear your voice answering my plea
For a love long gone
That has waited so long
Without you, without you
Now I'm no longer without you.

the decline of the Hawaiian religion. The *kapu* system, and worship in the main temples, was officially abolished in 1819.

Pele's priests, however, continued to defy the new laws and they had many supporters. In 1823 the missionaries William Ellis and Asa Thurston became the first foreigners to visit Kilauea. Their native guides were loyal followers of Pele and recited chants to her as they approached the volcano. After picking a handful of 'ohelo berries they tossed the fruit toward the largest steam vent.

The priests of Pele held a strong influence over the people until 1824 when the 250-pound high chiefess Kapi'olani, a newly converted Christian, visited the Kilauea Caldera and defied Pele at the volcano's edge. She returned unharmed, proclaiming the power of Christianity.

Pele may have shown religious tolerance in 1824 but her fiery temper has never been fully brought under control. During the years that followed Kapi'olani's actions, volcanic eruptions were almost commonplace. A particularly violent eruption at Mauna Loa in 1880-1881 sent a river of lava flowing towards Hilo in 1881. The townspeople, fearing Hilo was about to be destroyed, asked help from Princess Ruth, a half-sister of Kamehameha V.

Princess Ruth boarded an inter-island steamer the next day. She went ashore at Kailua and from there was put aboard a covered horse-drawn wagon for the ride to Hilo. Unfortunately, the first wagon broke an axle under the weight of the 375-pound princess. The second wagon was designed for only one horse, however, and had trouble pulling the weight. Princess Ruth then commanded her 25 retainers to take turns pulling and pushing the wagon toward the volcano.

When she finally arrived, the people took her up into the hills near Rainbow Falls. As the lava advanced one account says she climbed to the top of a wooden platform and ordered the killing of several chickens and pigs. These were then thrown into the burning lava. She also threw in red silk handkerchiefs and a bottle of gin. The lava flow suddenly stopped and Hilo was saved.

Around 1905 the Kilauea firepit of Halema'uma'u began to fill with lava and for the next two decades a lake of molten rock swirled within its walls. The area became a popular tourist attraction and was advertised on the Mainland. In 1912, the Hawaiian Volcano Observatory was built on the crater's rim by its first director, Dr. Thomas A. Jagger. Four years

Above: an ohi'a-lehua tree grows in Hawaii Volcanoes National Park.
The gentle movements of the tree's red blossom inspired
the graceful hula gestures. Following pages: an eruption ignites
the sky and a palm tree.

later President Woodrow Wilson signed the papers designating the immediate area surrounding Kilauea as Hawaii Volcanoes National Park.

Ray Jerome Baker, a Honolulu photographer, went over to the Big Island in 1918 and took the first motion pictures of the Kilauea eruptions. Later he hand-colored each black-and-white frame to produce a "color" movie that was shown to much acclaim on the Mainland. During 1924, a century after Kapi'olani had challenged Pele's authority, Halema'uma'u collapsed in on itself, forming a hole 1600 meters wide and 400 meters deep. Since then the firepit has become even shallower due to subsequent eruptions.

Today the Hawaii Volcanoes National Park attracts thousands of visitors a year, a number which increased considerably during 1984 when Mauna Loa and Kilauea erupted together. Hilo residents were once again put on alert but the lava flow, which did destroy several homes, stopped short of the town. During the month-long eruption a new generation of Hawaiians made their pilgrimage to the volcanoes and threw in sacrifices of gin, fish, taro, and 'ohelo berries.

It is clear from their actions that Pele not only still lives in the songs of Roland Cazimero, but in the hearts of all people who cherish the traditions of old Hawai'i. For them the fire has never gone out.
I am ruler of this land . . . I am Pele. ∎

I am, I am, I am the woman of the pit
I am, I am, I make no qualms about this
I am, I am, I am ruler of this land
I am, I am, I rule with a strong hand
I am Pele, I am Pele, I am Pele, Pele e.

I am, I am, I am here to stay
I am, I am, I'm your nows and yesterdays
I am, I am, I am everything you see
I am, I am, All the lands down to the sea
I am Pele, I am Pele, I am Pele, Pele e.

I am, I am

Roland Cazimero

I am, I am, Consuming more and more each day
I am, I am, Giving more in every way
I am, I am, Full of love and energy and jealousy
I am, I am, The queen of Hawaiki
I am Pele, I am Pele, I am Pele, Pele e.

I am Pele Of these islands called Hawaii
I am Pele The third planet in this galaxy
I am Pele Come sail this ocean,
the stars are your seas
I am Pele Come, come with me
I am Pele, I am Pele, I am Pele, Pele e.

Coming Of The Hawaiians

Na wa'a kaulua
noho malie
ma Honolua Mo'olele
me Hokule'a

Le'i nei o Maui
ma ke kahakai
hau'oli na po'e
i ka la e holo ai

Ho'onani Ia Hokule'a

Keli'i Tau'a/Roland Cazimero

Hulo mau na keiki
a ho'oili na holoholona
a ho'omaikai ke Kahu
i na lala o ka wa'a

Mele pu na lahui
me ka malua
haina kapuana
he inoa no na wa'a kaulua

Two double hulled canoes
sitting peacefully
at Honolua Mo'olele
me Hokule'a

Maui is crowded
at the shores
joyful are the people
on this day of sailing

The children shout and play
as the animals are put on board
as the priest begins to bless
The paddlers of Oka wa'a kaulua

The multitude sang
As the breeze filled the sails
Tell the story of the name
na wa'a kaulua

Prehistoric artists have left their marks in rock carvings throughout the world. Their simple drawings, called petroglyphs, share similarities but each culture developed a distinctive style of its own. Hawaiians were the most prolific petroglyph makers in Polynesia and the largest concentration of their work can be found on the Big Island.

The majority of Hawaiian petroglyphs are human figures, some of which are canoe paddlers. There are also numerous representations of canoes and sails, either alone or in combinations with each other. It is obvious from these petroglyphs that the canoe belonged at the very heart of ancient Polynesian culture.

Scientists now tell us that long before Captain James Cook first set eyes on Hawai'i, dark-skinned seafarers from both the Marquesas and Society Islands had sailed here in their large, double-hulled canoes. Evidence also indicates that these early voyages were not accidental. Once a new land was discovered, navigators could work out sailing directions for it. Guidance was provided by a compass derived from the rising places of stars on the eastern

Above: a petroglyph of a family at 'Anae Ho'omalu, North Kona, the Big Island. At left: the double-hulled sailing canoe, Hokule'a, rides at anchor. At right: Richard "Babe" Bell blows a conch shell.

horizon, their setting places on the western horizon, and the constant direction of dominant ocean swells.

It was about 1500 years ago that the first South Pacific islanders discovered Hawai'i and made it their home. Legends, however, do not exist for this early period and the names of the first settlers have been lost. It was not until a few centuries later, when the second wave of sailors arrived from the Society Islands (Tahiti), that Hawaiian voyaging stories begin.

One famous voyager who later made the trip from Havaiki (then the center of Tahitian culture, now known as Ra'iatea) to Hawai'i was Pa'ao. He looked around the Islands and found that the people did not have rulers with a pure enough lineage to serve as conduits of *mana* from the gods to their people. At the end of his reconnaissance mission, Pa'ao sailed back

to Havaiki again and returned with Pili, a prince of the highest pedigree. It was Pili who finally conquered the archipelago ("Hawai'i" is derived from "Havaiki") and founded the powerful dynasty from which eventually emerged Kamehameha the Great.

Since the time of Captain Cook there has been a controversy over whether contacts between Hawai'i and Tahiti were the result of accidental canoe "drift" or planned navigation. In 1976, during the U.S. Bicentennial Year, the Hokule'a, a 60-foot-long, double-hulled ocean canoe sailed to Tahiti and back to prove the possibility of two-way canoe trips.

The voyage of the Hokule'a ("Star of Gladness") became an unprecedented cultural event. It was covered extensively by Pacific area newspapers, magazines and television. *National Geographic* published several articles on the controversial project and then released a television documentary film.

Nani Kualoa
hemolele i ka malie
ilaila wau la 'ike
i ka wa'a kaulana

Hele mai la ho'i
na lahui e 'ike
i ka hana ho'olana
Ka Mo'i o ke Kai

Pau 'ole ko'u ho'ohihi
i ka wa'a kaulua
ka nani ho'okahi o ka moana
e'olino nei i ke kai

E ho'ano ia ka Hokule'a
ua nui kona mau la
haina mai kapuana
no ka wa'a kaulana
no ka wa'a kaulana

La Ho'olana

Keli'i Tau'a/Roland Cazimero

Beautiful is Kualoa
sublime in the calm
there I saw
the famous canoe

The multitude came
to see
the launching ceremony
Of the King of the Sea

My never ending fascination
in the double-hulled canoe
most beautiful on the ocean
brilliant on the sea

We honor the Star of Gladness
many are his days
Tell the refrain
for the famous canoe
for the famous canoe

Previous pages: "Hokule'a," a painting by Herb Kawainui Kane. In 1976, this canoe sailed to Tahiti and back to Hawai'i, proving that the Islands' first settlers directed their migration with stellar navigation.

Wa'a kaulua e o	*Double-hulled canoe*
wa'a kaulua e	*Paddling on by the sea*
paddling on by the sea	*Star of Gladness*
Hokule'a e	
Wa'a kaulua e o	*Double-hulled canoe*
wa'a kaulua e	*double-hulled canoe*
sailing on by the sea	*Sailing on by the sea*
Hokule'a e	*Star of Gladness*
Wa'a Kaulua e o	*Double-hulled canoe*
wa'a kaulua e	*double-hulled canoe*
steering on by the sea	*Steering on by the Sea*
Hokule'a e	*Star of Gladness*
Wa'a kaulua e o	*Double-hulled canoe*
wa'a kaulua e	*double-hulled canoe*
returning safely by the sea	*Returning safely by the Sea*
Hokule'a	*Star of Gladness*

In early 1977, Roland Cazimero as composer and Keli'i Tau'a as lyricist, fused their talents in the studio to create an album which they named *Hokule'a* in honor of the canoe. With some of their friends (Michael Ka'awa, Dwight Hanohano, Kalani Whitford, Hinano, and Friday Fellez) helping out on guitars and vocals, the *Hokule'a* songs capture the spirit of the legendary Pacific voyages of centuries past.

The cover of the album features a contemporary artistic interpretation by Edward Stasack of the canoe petroglyphs left behind in stone by Hawai'i's prehistoric artists. A few years before, Stasack and J. Halley Cox, colleagues at the University of Hawai'i, had collaborated on an excellent book, *Hawaiian Petroglyphs*, published by the Bishop Museum Press. *Hokule'a* was Roland's first serious attempt to interpret "history" through music and his first album project apart from Robert and the Brothers Cazimero.

The songs are sung in Hawaiian with an occasional English lyric added. *Hokule'a* follows the general story of the 1976 canoe voyage and its individual tunes capture perfectly the nautical flavor of long days at sea.

During the months that Roland was working on *Hokule'a* his professional relationship with Robert was probably at its lowest point. Robert, in fact, was barely aware that Roland was involved with the project.

"This was a dangerous period for the Brothers Cazimero," Robert says. "It wouldn't have taken much for us to call it quits. Mostly it was my fault. I wasn't giving enough time to our own thing. At the time I was into organizing my *halau* and dancing at the Merrie Monarch Festival.

"Now it's obvious to me that the Hokule'a group was Roland's chance to have his own *halau*. He was having fun while at the same time getting back at me for my growing interest in hula. If Jon hadn't been around to keep us together I'm not sure where we'd be today."

The *Hokule'a* album begins its narrative with the song, "Ho'onani Ia Hokule'a," or "Praise for the Hokule'a." It was at Honolua Bay, on Maui's rocky northwestern shore, that the canoe underwent its final preparations for the 6,000-mile voyage to Tahiti. The actual day of launching was May 1, 1976. "Maui is crowded at the shores," the song

At far left: the manu or end piece of a fishing canoe is full and blunt. For racing, the bow is narrower and sharper. At left: canoe sail and male petroglyphs at Olowalu, Maui, one of many places in the Islands where ancient Hawaiians chiseled pictures of daily life.

Huki mai ke kaula
huki mai ka lau
pa mai ka makani
popoho na pe'a

Pull the ropes
pull the sheets
the wind blows
filling the sails

Nā Pe'a O Hokule'a

Keli'i Tau'a/Roland Cazimero

Pohai na 'A'a
la i ka wa'a
ho'okele pololei
ia Hokule'a

The Redfooted-Booby
surrounds the canoe
steer straight
The Hokule'a

Imi no na pe'a lua
e 'ike ala pono no
ku aku i ka 'aina
me ka lanakila

Look at the two sails
see straight ahead
reaching the destination
victoriously

Lele i ka po'ele
Malolo o ka lewa
ho'ili i ka papahele
maunu i ke kai

'A'ai ka Mano i'a
i ka Malolo nui
malunu a'e ka Mano
mauna i ke kai

Na Aku o Piko o Wakea
mau na Aku punahele
ho'omo'a i ka imu
ka i'a stew o Hokule'a

Ua pakele mua ka Ono
alaila ho'ohe'e ke Ahi
eia ka mo'olelo pokole
o na i'a o Hokule'a

The I'a Stew
Keli'i Tau'a/Roland Cazimero

Fly in the dark
Malolo of the heavens
landing on deck
bait to the sea

The shark bites
the large flying fish
up came the shark
bait to the sea

There are Aku at the Equator
caught the favorite fish
cooked in the imu
the fish stew of the Hokule'a

The Ono escaped
then the Ahi slipped away
here is the short story
of the fishes of Hokule'a

says. "Joyful are the people on this day of sailing."

Roland says that "Ho'onani Ia Hokule'a" is his favorite song on the album. Whenever he hears Keli'i's lyrics he can practically "see the canoe moving through the water." Altogether the *Hokule'a* collaboration took Roland and Keli'i six months to write and another nine months to record.

Next on the album is "La Ho'olana" or "Day of Launching." As crowds lined the cliffs above the bay, the canoe's sails unfurled and the Hokule'a met the full force of the tradewinds. The canoe was tacked north around Maui and the Big Island before it was turned southward in the direction of Tahiti. "The multitude," this song says, "came to see the launching ceremony of the King of the Sea . . . we honor the Star of Gladness."

"Na Pe'O Hokule'a" or "The Sails of the Hokule'a" gives the first glimpse of what life aboard the canoe is like out at sea. The most important

order of business is to keep the canoe shipshape and moving. "Pull the ropes," the song commands, "pull the sheets. The wind blows filling the sails."

Roland and Keli'i provide a whimsical interlude on the *Hokule'a* album with the song that follows, "Maxwell Namunamu" or "Complaining Maxwell." The song relates how Maxwell, a white-haired *haole* pig brought aboard the canoe at the last minute, manages to provide minutes of humor on the long, lonely voyage. "Oink oink," says Maxwell. "I'm the rascal of the canoe."

"Oni Wa'a Kaulua" or "The Moving Double-Hulled Canoe" is the last song on side one. Much of the time aboard the canoe is monotonous. Hours are spent watching the clouds overhead or listening to the waves slap against the hull. This rhythmical song captures the monotony of the voyage, changing only a single word in each of the four verses. "Double-hulled canoe, double-hulled canoe," the fourth verse repeats,

At left: ocean racing in outrigger canoes is a popular sport in Hawai'i,
where paddlers race offshore and between the Islands. Above: the ama that
extends from the hull stabilizes the canoe as it glides through
the water. Each part of the canoe, including lashings (nananana),
has a Hawaiian name.

"returning safely by the sea, Star of Gladness."

The song "Hokuli'ili'i" or "Little Star, The Dog" begins side two. One of the companions that the Hokule'a crew took with them on the voyage to Tahiti was Hoku, a dog that the Honolulu Zoo had supplied for the trip. Zoo officials had been trying to breed back to the type of poi dog that had accompanied early voyagers on their trips to Hawai'i. This song tells about the bonds of affection that develop between human beings and their pets. "Tell the story for the Little Star," the singer says. "My friend to play with, my lively dog."

"The I'a Stew" or "The Fish Song" presents another amusing vignette aboard the canoe. This song talks about fishing, a favorite subject among the sailors. Everybody takes their turn with line and baited hook sometime during the day. But not everyone is lucky. "The Ono escaped," the singer reveals, "then the Aku slipped away. Here is the short story of the fishes of Hokule'a."

"Dreams" or "Moemoea" is a backward glance in which the sailor begins to think about the cultural significance of the Hokule'a voyage and how his ancestors once sailed these same seas. "I could not sleep after (the dreams) for the joy within my heart," explains the singer. "The thought of seeing my ancestors tore my heart apart."

In perhaps the *Hokule'a* album's strongest song, "Doldrum Blues," a sailor reflects on the world he's left and tries to look ahead toward the future of his people: "Here I am a Hawaiian, sailing on distant seas. Searching for my birth land, looking for my identity."

"Ho'okele" or "Steering" picks up the canoe after a month at sea. Tahiti is sighted and the Hokule'a sails toward land. "The Gods protect," the singer says. "Be careful of driftwood. Look for the birds. There is the land, Tahiti."

The final song on the album is "E O E Hokule'a" or "Announcing Hokule'a." It is a chant by Keli'i Tau'a to welcome the arrival of the canoe and its crew. "Here are the Heroes of the Sea, famous heroes of the Pacific who have returned. Rejoice Hawai'i. Let it grow, let it live forever, all the works of Hokule'a."

Despite the popular success of their *Hokule'a* album, released in February 1977, the group remained together for only a few more months. Roland and Robert were soon back to playing music at the Ala Moana Hotel and Keli'i Tau'a and the rest of the Hokule'a band decided to go on to their own personal projects.

I te maurora'a ote anatau
A tere atu ai to'u mau
tupuna na te ara
ua moemoea hia vau e
e ho'i fa'ahou mai a ratou

I to'u arara'a mai ite ho'po
hi'o atura vau i nia ute ra'i
i te atura vau ia Hokule'a
i te anapa noara'a mai

Aore atura to'u ta'oto
i topa fa'ahou
Inaha ua oto to'u mafatu
Ite ha'a mana'o ra'a
i to'u mau tupuna
Aue atura te oaoa
Aue atura te oaoa

Chorus:
ite ho'i fa'ahou ra'a mai ratou
I to ratou fenua tamu
na ni'a i toratou va'a
tau'ati o Hokule'a

Dreams

Keli'i Tau'a/Roland Cazimero

Many years past

Since my ancestors left
I dream someday
the offspring will return

I awoke one evening
and looked into the skies
There was Hokule'a
Shining upon my eyes

I could not sleep after
for the joy within my heart
the thought of seeing my ancestors
tore my heart apart
Happy is this day
Happy is this day

Chorus:
They will return
on to their homeland

with their double hulled canoe

A second voyage to Tahiti was made in 1980 by the Hokule'a and, since then, it has also completed a number of Neighbor Island trips. It is now being exhibited by the Hawai'i Maritime Center at Pier 7 in the Honolulu Harbor waterfront area. The *Falls of Clyde,* the world's only full-rigged, four-masted sailing ship, is also anchored nearby.

Roland says he gets concerned whenever he hears talk of taking the Hokule'a on another voyage. He feels that the canoe represents the pride that all Hawaiians now have for their culture and that it should remain in a museum environment.

"I think they should take it out of the water immediately, clean it up, and keep it in a museum for future generations to visit and enjoy. If we continue to fool around with the Hokule'a it's only a matter of time before the boat is lost at sea. Let's build a second canoe to play with and put the Hokule'a away for safekeeping. It's now a part of history."

The Polynesian Voyaging Society, which gave birth to the Hokule'a project, was founded in 1973 by anthropologist Ben R. Finney, artist-historian Herb Kawainui Kane, and expert waterman Tommy Holmes. From their idea the concept grew into a movement that involved thousands of people, the actual building of the canoe, and the historic Bicentennial year voyage.

Finney's interest in the early Polynesians began in the 1950s when he began studying cultural anthropology at the University of Hawai'i with Dr. Kenneth Emory, perhaps the foremost authority on Hawai'i before European contact. While working with Emory, Finney became intrigued with the traditional sailing methods used by Pacific islanders. He kept this concern through Ph.D. graduate work at Harvard and later during his first teaching assignment at the University of California in Santa Barbara.

In 1966, Finney and a group of his students built a replica of an 18th Century double-hulled inter-island sailing canoe and took it to Hawai'i for testing. Despite its rounded bottom, and small sprit sail, it possessed the ability to sail windward. This is an important factor since it allows sailors to go where they want. In the context of Pacific voyaging theory, this discovery meant that perhaps the Polynesians had been more in control of their settlement destiny than once had been believed.

Paddling home after practice for a weekend regatta. Canoes—once used for traveling, in warfare, or for fishing—are mostly pleasure crafts today.

Kane's interest in the Polynesian voyagers and their canoes began in 1967 while he was in Chicago working as a painter, illustrator, and graphic designer. Returning to his native Hawai'i in 1971 he began working on a series of 14 oil paintings and 13 architectural drawings that were grouped under the title "Canoes of Polynesia" and eventually acquired by the State Foundation on Culture and the Arts.

These artworks and the first draft of Kane's illustrated book, *Voyage: The Discovery of Hawaii (1976),* sparked widespread interest in the Hawaiian community and subsequently inspired Finney and Holmes to join him in chartering the Polynesian Voyaging Society.

"Polynesian canoes," Kane writes in the Prologue to *Voyage,* "were instruments of purpose and fulfillment, the embodiment of the elan of a seafaring people. Each canoe was named, and was regarded as a living member of the community. The building of an important canoe was a community project. Entire villages would turn out to haul rough-carved hulls and lumber down from the mountains to the canoe yards. Children would gather the long pandanus leaves and cure them, and their mothers would plait them into sails. Old men braided miles of the sennit rope which became the muscles of the canoe. High chiefs slept in the hulls in order that their personal *mana* might flow into the vessel. The launching ceremony was the occasion of a community-wide feast and celebration.

"These canoes probably exerted a shaping influence on their makers and crews to an extent unparalleled by any other artifact of man. Favored for selection for a voyage, and for survival on a long exploration, were persons with powerful muscle, stamina, and ample fat to sustain the body through times of hunger and insulate it against deadly exposure to wind and spray. The survivors of a voyage, once settled on a newly discovered island, would form an ancestor-pool for future generations of explorers. Such rigorous, oft-repeated selective pressures on small groups who lived for many centuries in the awesome isolation of the Pacific must have influenced the physical evolution of the race. Thus, by their large musculature and size, the Polynesians may be identified as the Children of the Long Canoes."

Our best available evidence today—acquired by such methods as radio carbon dating, linguistic studies, pottery comparisons, and genealogical accounts—indicates that groups of people from southeast Asia first sailed their canoes into Western Polynesia around 1300 B.C.

These pioneering travelers settled in Tonga, Samoa, and Fiji. Later, sometime about the first century A.D., a new stream of migrating groups arrived in the Marquesas Islands and from there progressed to Tahiti and the Society Islands.

Easter Island was settled about 500 A.D. and the Marquesan canoes probably reached the Hawaiian

Aloha wale 'oe
ku'u hanai a huhu
ho'okahi wale no
ku'u 'ilio 'akeu

My love to you
my pet
I am lonely
for my lively dog

Ua hele 'oia
i ka holo ana
ma ka huaka'i
i Kahiki Nui

Hokuli'ili'i
Keli'i Tau'a/Roland Cazimero

He went
sailing
on a voyage
to Tahiti Nui

Ha'ina ka puana
no Hokuli'ili'i
hoa pa'ani
ku'u 'ilio 'eu'eu
Hui:
E hele me ka poina 'ole
E huli 'e ke alo i hope nei

Tell the story
for the Little Star
my friend to play with
my lively dog
Hui:
go and do not forget
to return again

Islands between this date and 750 A.D. New Zealand is believed to have been settled slightly later.

A second wave of voyagers, from the Society Islands, arrived in Hawai'i between 1000 and 1250 A.D. Until archaeologists found evidence of the earlier Polynesian settlements it was assumed that these Tahitians were the first outsiders to reach Hawai'i.

Local legends refer to sea voyages between Tahiti and Hawai'i from the 10th to the 13th centuries. One story tells of a departure from Kaho'olawe and the southwestern point of this island is still called *Ke-ala-i-Kahiki,* "The Route to Tahiti." Hawai'i's name, too, is Tahitian in origin. It is derived from Havaiki, the ancient name for Ra'iatea, second largest of the Society Islands. Ra'iatea, as mentioned earlier, was the cultural center of the Society group during the period of the great Tahiti-Hawai'i voyages.

For over 20 years Dr. Yoshihiko H. Sinoto of the Bishop Museum has played a major part in unraveling the origins and history of the first Polynesians to settle in Hawai'i. Since 1973 he has been excavating a large area on Huahine in the Society Islands.

Tests have revealed that a village existed there as far back as 850 A.D. (the oldest human date known in the Society Islands) and the findings make it possibly the most significant site ever found in Central Polynesia. Sinoto's theory, confirmed by geologists, is that a giant tsunami demolished a village on this site about 1,100 years ago. The remnants indicate that the inhabitants were an advanced seafaring people.

Among the over 500 artifacts found beneath five layers of earth were a stone adze—still intact after 1,000 years—and the planks and mast of a large canoe, from 60 to 80 feet in length. This is the first physical evidence (previous knowledge came from reports of Capt. James Cook and other early European explorers) that such ocean-traveling canoes actually existed.

Despite the tradition of exchange between Hawai'i and Tahiti there have always been critics who dismissed these stories as total fabrications. Thor Heyerdahl argued in his book, *American Indians in the Pacific* (1953), that the first Polynesians probably arrived by raft from South America. Heyerdahl ignored the Polynesian canoes by stating that early Pacific navigators could not have sailed against the winds and currents to Hawai'i. He reasoned that they must have drifted here by accident.

Then, in 1956, Andrew Sharp came out in support of Heyerdahl's theories with the publication of his book, *Ancient Voyagers in the Pacific.* A New Zealander, Sharp wrote that the islands of Polynesia were colonized through a long series of accidental landings. He maintained that these early Pacific navigators, sailing inferior canoes, could not fix their position at sea or steer an accurate course. Planned voyages, he wrote, were impossible.

Finney came back to the University of Hawai'i as an assistant professor in 1970. One of his primary

Above: Pu'uhonua-o-Honaunau National Historical Park, Kona, the Big Island—a place of refuge in ancient times, when Hawaiians were protected by priests if they could reach the sanctuary. Following pages: a paddler strokes his canoe.

Doldrum Blues

Keli'i Tau'a/Roland Cazimero

My Doldrum Blues
Hele au a hapa lua like i Kahiki
ho'ohali'ali'a mai ana ia'u
he mea nui keia ia'u
no keia au o makou

Heaha ko'u makemake
heaha la keia halia ana
ho'omana'o i na wa i hala
wa na i ka wa mahope

Eia au la he Hawai'i
e au ana i ke kai loa
e imi ana i ko'u 'aina hanau
e ike ho'i i ko'u kumu

Hui-My Doldrum Blues
My Doldrum Blues
kani le'a ka makani
ho mai ka pane

My Doldrum Blues
I've traveled halfway to Tahiti
as I sit and ponder
this is a turning point for me
in my present generation

What is my desire
what is my premonition
to recall the past
or look to the future

Here I am a Hawaiian
sailing on distant seas
searching for my birth land
looking for my identity

My Doldrum Blues
My Doldrum Blues
sing cheerfully the winds
bring forth the answer

goals was to prove that Heyerdahl and Sharp were wrong. He was convinced that the early Polynesians did possess the skill and knowledge necessary to colonize the Pacific Islands.

Kane's research and designs pushed Finney's dreams into reality. When the artist put his brushes down and said "let's build a canoe," the anthropologist was only a few steps behind. They called their canoe Hokule'a or "Star of Gladness," the Hawaiian name for Arcturus the zenith star of Hawai'i. This star passes over Hawai'i and would lead the Hokule'a and its crew on the long, 6,000-mile voyage.

With Kane supplying his visual research, a catamaran designer drew out the lines of the twin hulls. They had a rounded "V" shape that contrasted strongly with the "U" shaped hulls commonly used for inland sailing and the straight "V" shapes usually designed for the open ocean. Overall it would be built 60 feet long, with a beam 15 feet wide. Each of the two hulls measured

three and a half feet wide by five feet deep.

Due to time limitations, and the fact that giant trees were no longer plentiful, the hull skeletons were made of plywood frames and long wood stringers. Over this came three layers of narrow laminated plywood strips applied diagonally, in opposite directions, for strength. Over this went a veil of fiberglass.

Prow and stern pieces were fashioned in like manner and ten cross beams that connected the two hulls were fabricated of oak. Later came the decking, masts, booms, and steering paddles. When finished, the Hokule'a weighed approximately four and half tons. Later, traditional sails, similar to those depicted in the ancient petroglyphs, were added. Their claw-shaped contours minimized stress by displacing excess wind.

Pa mai ka makani Pu'ulena
hiki mai ka la ha'aheo
a hiki pu me na 'A'a

eia na Me'e o ke Kai
na Me'e Kaulana o ka Pakipika
ua ho'i mai
e lohe kakou ka nuhou
ua ho'i mai na kama
ku aku i ka home me ka lanakila
oli e oli e o Hawai'i
e ulu, e oli mau na hana apau
o Hokule'a

EOE Hokule'a

Keli'i Tau'a/Roland Cazimero

A cold wind Pu'ulena blows
The great day arrives
It arrives with the Red Footed Boobies

here are the Heroes of the Sea
famous Heroes of the Pacific
who have returned
listen all to the news
the children have returned
arrived home victoriously
rejoice rejoice Hawai'i
Let it grow, let it live forever,
all the works of Hokule'a

The Hokule'a was first put into the water in March 1975 from the North Shore of O'ahu. Kane captained the vessel during its initial testing period but then handed over the leadership of the canoe to Kawaika Kapahulehua, an experienced ocean-sailor, as the launch day approached.

Because an important part of the Hokule'a voyage required sailing without modern instruments, a traditional navigator was required. David Lewis, the author of *We The Navigators* and other books, informed the Society's members that none would be found in Polynesia because modern transport systems had too-effectively replaced inter-island sailing canoes.

Pius (Mau) Piailug, a Micronesian sailor from Satawal, eventually joined the Hawai'i crew as both navigator and teacher. Mau was not only a skilled non-instrument sailor but sophisticated enough to cross the needed cultural boundaries. Upon joining the Hokule'a team, Mau infused the project with a sense of dedication and craft. Here was a person who regularly sailed between small islands with only the stars and sun to guide him. He could walk into the woods and pick the right tree limbs for booms, use the adze to split planks, and make rope out of coconut sennit. Mau's workshop on the beach was a popular gathering spot for the young Hawaiian crewmen.

In addition to testing navigational theories, the Hokule'a project provided a foundation for other experiments. One of the most important of these concerned the food to be taken on the voyage. What foods did the early voyagers take with them on their oceanic journeys? How was it prepared?

June Gutmanis, a research consultant for the Polynesian Voyaging Society, was given the task of preparing an authentic menu for the crew. In charge of the actual provisioning was Paige Kawelo Barber and Alice Moku Froisetch. According to Gutmanis the Polynesian canoes probably carried little, if any, fresh food. The diet probably was built around sun-dried items.

"After studying the old chants and legends," she says, "we got a fairly good idea of what was taken along on the old canoes. High on the list was coconut, breadfruit, sweet potatoes, bananas, taro, pa'i'ai (hard taro poi), sugar cane, pandanus fruit, and limu. Drinking water was carried in bamboo tubes and hollow gourds."

Following a ritual meal on May 1, 1976, two wooden images were lashed to the port and starboard hulls of the canoe. A conch shell was blown and the Hokule'a set sail for Tahiti. The story of the trip is told by Lewis in a *National Geographic* article, "Hokule'a Follows The Stars To Tahiti" (October 1976) and by Finney in his book *Hokule'a: The Way to Tahiti* (1979). Kane's *Voyage* and Holmes' *The Hawaiian Canoe* (1981) are also good sources of information.

On June 4, the canoe was met at Papeete Harbor by 15,000 well-wishers, and estimated one out of every five Tahitians on the island. That evening the mayor of Papeete threw the grandest reception in recent years. A month later the Hokule'a, and a new crew that included two women, departed Tahiti. After three weeks at sea the canoe sailed around Diamond Head, past the beach at Waikiki and then into the Ala Wai Yacht Harbor.

Roland Cazimero was waiting on shore when the great canoe returned to Honolulu. For him the voyage not only symbolized a cultural revival but, on a smaller scale, provided inspiration for his own music. Although not technically a Brothers Cazimero album, *Hokule'a* remains as important to him as the Hokule'a, itself, has become to the entire Hawaiian community. ∎

E hoʻokele pololei, la ea *ma ke ʻAlenuihaha, ea ea*		**Steer straight through the** **Channel ʻAlenuihaha**
E hoʻopaʻa ka hoe uli, la ea *o ka waʻa kaulua, ea ea*		**Hold the steer of the double** **hulled canoe**
ʻElua kiʻi e malama ai, la ea *akahele i ka papa, ea ea*	*Hoʻokele* Keliʻi Tauʻa/Roland Cazimero	**The Gods protect** **Be careful of driftwood**
ʻIkea na manu, la ea *aia ka ʻaina Kahiki, ea ea*		**Look for the birds** **There is the land, Tahiti**
Haʻina ia mai ka puana, la ea *ka hoʻokele Hokuleʻa, ea ea*		**Tell the refrain,** **steering the Star of Gladness**

Men in replicas of feather cloaks and helmets and the
fiberglass-hulled Hokuleʻa off the Ala Wai Yacht Harbor: contemporary
reminders of Hawaiʻi's past.

Let The Dancing Begin

Hawaiian hula eyes
When you dance you hypnotize
Though I can't believe it's true

Hawaiian hula eyes
It's you I'm dreaming of
With a haunting dream of love

Hawaiian Hula Eyes
William Harbottle
Randy Oness

On the sands of Lunga bay
Where the sighing zephyrs play
I'm reminded of the one I love
'neath the swaying palms
I held you in my arms
My Hawaiian hula eyes

Hula has always been an important part of the Brothers Cazimero experience. Robert has his own all-male hula *halau*, Na Kamalei, and Roland has recorded a solo album, *Pele,* about the mythological volcano goddess long associated with Hawaiian dance. Their 1982 album, *Hawaiian Hula Eyes,* contains both traditional and contemporary tributes to the hula.

Leina'ala Kalama Heine, like Robert, was a student of Ma'iki Aiu Lake. Today she is also a *kumu hula* for Na Pualei o Likolehua, a highly respected women's dance troupe that started out at Kamehameha Schools. Her *halau* performs regularly around the state and during the Brothers' frequent stage shows and concerts.

"Without the hula," Robert explains, "the music of the Brothers Cazimero would not be the same. It is an essential ingredient, both in terms of support of our live concert performances and as an inspiration for the way we approach the songs themselves. Through hula we have established a cultural link to our past."

The origin of hula remains buried in Hawaiian mythology. One story tells of two gods, male and female, who arrived from Tahiti in a canoe and danced for the people. Both went by the name of Laka.

Above: a 1920s historic photo of a hula girl and her 'ukulele, a popular instrument brought to Hawai'i by Portuguese immigrants. At left: fern leis and yellow pa'u costume this dancer. At right: the dancer's face expresses her love for hula. Following pages: a dancer's hand illustrates the words of the hula song.

Kapilimehana
C. Manu Boyd

'O Kapilimehana, 'auhea wale 'oe
E maliu i ka heahea 'ana mai
he 'eu ka 'ano'i wela i ka piko
Hō'olu mai ho'i ē

E ka pā aheahe 'inikiniki mālie
Kai lawe mai ia'u ka ho'ohihi
E mai ana e ka ahe me he ipo ala
He pono ho'i kaua

Maika'i ke anu i ka Nu'uanu
Noenoe i ke kapa 'ohu o luna
Uhiuhi ke ahu welo a'o Hina
Lawe mālie i ka pō

Nani wale ka 'ikena o ka lā pi'i
Ka wena lamalama 'olu i ka poli
Ua ala ke aloha ma ka hikina
A e pi'o mau i nā lani

Eia ka puana o ka mele wehi
No Kapilimehana e ō mai
I laila i kahi hele 'ole 'ia
E nanea hou i ka la'i

Where are you Kapilimehana
Heed my beckon
Alive and burning is the desire within
Lend comfort to me

Oh gentle breeze lightly pinching the skin
You who have brought this infatuation
Come to me as a lover
As we should be together

So pleasant is the cool air at Nu'uanu
With a hazy blanket of mist above
Hina has unfurled her starry cloak
So serene upon this still night

How beautiful the sight of the climbing sun
A radiant glow so soothing within
For love has risen in the east
And will forever arch the vast skies

Here is the conclusion of this adoration
For you Kapilimehana, answer
And some day in a distant untraveled place
We will once again delight in the calm

In the female form, Laka is the sister and wife of Lono, one of Hawai'i's major gods.

The male Laka continued on his journey and left the female, Lakawahine, to dance by herself. The Hawaiians learned the dance from her and eventually took the hula as their own.

Another tale says that the hula was sacred to the men and was ruled over by a single male god, Laka. Hi'iaka, the youngest sister of Pele, learned the dance from Laka and playfully danced it before her friend, the poet Hopoe, by the crashing sea at Nanahuki.

Sometime later, Pele was passing by and saw Hopoe teaching Ha'ena the hula at Nanahuki. She asked her sisters if they knew how to dance and Hi'iaka revealed her secret. She then began to hula and chanted a song about Hopoe and Ha'ena that brought back her own memories of dancing on the beach with Hopoe. This was the first of the known hula chants to be recorded.

Ke ha'a la Puna i ka makani
   (Puna dances in the breeze)
Ha'a ka ulu hala i Kea'au
   (While the pandanus trees shake in Kea'au)
Ha'a Ha'ena me Hopoe

(Ha'ena and Hopoe dance)
Ha'a ka wahine
   (The woman dances)
'Ami i kai o Nanahuki, la-
   (Swaying close by the sea at Nanahuki)
Hula le'a wale
   (The dancing is most pleasing)
I kai o Nanahuki, e-e!
   (Close by the sea at Nanahuki)

'O Puna kai kowa i ka hala
   (Puna's voice echoes in the pandanus trees)
Pa'e ka leo o ke kai
   (Sounding like the distant sea)
Ke lu la i na pua lehua
   (The lehua blooms are blown away)
Nana i kai o Hopoe
   (Hopoe is dancing near the sea)
Ka wahine 'ami i kai
   (The woman is swaying)
'O Nanahuki la,
   (By the sea at Nanahuki)
Hula le'a wale
   (The dancing is most pleasing)
I kai o Nanahuki e-e!
   (Close by the sea at Nanahuki)

P ele was happy with Hi'iaka's performance and from that day on it was common for women, as well as men, to dance the hula. As time went on individual teachers or *kumu hula* attracted groups of dancers and they banded together to form a *halau* or dance school. There was always strong competition to see which group could please the gods more.

Hula, from whatever its legendary beginnings, gradually became a central part of everyday life and was performed for secular as well as religious occasions. Dancing and its accompanying chants were never isolated from the mainstream of Hawaiian culture.

Hawai'i's prehistory ended with the visit of Captain James Cook and his ships, the *Resolution* and *Discovery* at Kaua'i and Ni'ihau in January 1778. Cook and his men bridged the ancient and historic worlds of the Hawaiians by witnessing and recording their lifestyles, daily events, and rituals.

The first described Hawaiian hula performance was observed by Cook on Kaua'i soon after his arrival. Not knowing the religious background of the dance, however, he thought of it as simply a show of musical entertainment.

"... We had no opportunity to see any of their amusements," Cook wrote in his journal, "and the only musical instrument that was seen among them was a hollow vessel of wood like a platter and two sticks, on these one of our gentlemen saw a man play: One of the sticks he held as we do a fiddle and struck it with the other, which was smaller and something like a drum stick and at the same time beat with his foot upon the hollow vessel and produced a tune that was by no means disagreeable ..."

Today, we recognize this dance as the *hula kala'au.* It was performed with sticks and the *papa hehi,* or treadle board.

This is a flat stone or piece of wood placed upon a crossbar and tapped by the player's foot.

"This Musick," he continued, "was accompanied with a song, sung by some women and had a pleasing and tender effect. Another instrument was seen among them, but it can scarcely be called an instrument of music; this was a small gourd with some pebblestones in it, which they shake in the hand like a child's rattle and are used, as they told us, at their dances . . ."

When the *Discovery* returned to the Big Island a year later, its surgeon, David Samwell, observed another dance that took place somewhere along the Kona Coast. His journal description suggests that the female performers were members of an organized *halau* or hula school.

"The ships continue far from shore," he wrote, "two or three canoes came up to us, many girls on board. In the afternoon they all assembled upon deck and formed a dance; they strike their hands on the pit of their stomach smartly and jump up all together, at the same time repeating the words of a song in responses . . ."

It is clear from the various accounts that hula played several roles in the early culture of the Hawaiians: it was used to commemorate, to entertain, and to entice. Many of the dances undoubtedly fell into the latter category and for these British sailors, far from home, the sexually-themed dances had an obvious popularity.

On its last day before leaving the Hawaiian Islands, the *Discovery* lay anchored at Waimea Bay on Oʻahu to take on water. A group of women came aboard and Samwell again described their dancing.

". . . it was performed two at a time. They did not jump up as in the common dance but used a kind of regular step and moved their legs something like our sailors dancing a Hornpipe, they moved their arms up and down, repeated a song together, changed their places often, wiggled their backsides and used many lascivious gestures. Upon the whole we thought it much more agreeable than their common dance."

During the early 19th century, valuable historical descriptions of hula were provided by Archibald Campbell, an English seaman who lived on Oʻahu in 1809; Peter Corney, another temporary resident during the same period, and Adelbert von Chamisso, a naturalist aboard the visiting Russian ship *Rurick* in 1816. Two performances were given for the Russians while their ship was anchored in Honolulu Harbor.

All of these accounts, however, emphasize the hula as popular entertainment. Outsiders were either uninterested in the religious side of the dance or did not have the opportunity to witness more sacred performances.

Kūwiliwili iho au	I churn with thoughts of emotion
A he māpu maoli nō	As the air is filled with sweet scent
'O ka hanu 'a'ala ku'u ipo lā	This being the fragrance of my lover
Kūwili o ka pili aumoe	Which stirs us to embrace in the late night hour

Kūwiliwili Iho Au

Henri Berger

'O ka waimaka pū me 'oe	Tears are for you
Ka ma'u pū aku me ka ihu	Dampening too your nose
Good bye pū kāua lā	Let's say our goodbye Though we
'Oiai ka pilina ua la'i	feel contentment in being together

Ahi wela mai nei loko	My emotions burn with heat
Lauwili i ka iwi hilo	Arousing the very core of my being
'O ka hanu ia a ke aloha lā	Oh to breathe love's sweet scent
'O ka hu'e pau i ka waimaka	Releases feeling from the depths

Ho'oniponipo iho au e moe	I felt drowsy with sleep
'O'e 'o'e ana ko ia ala kuli	But his knees kept prodding
Kuhi au lā 'o sa li'a lā	I should know it's that feelings of yearning
Ku'u hoa ho'onipo o ka pō	From my lover of the night

80

Previous pages: the dancer extends the ancient hula rhythm with an uli'uli or gourd rattle. Some purists believe hula tradition is lost as more kumu hula incorporate ballet and jazz steps into their dances.

'Auhea wale 'oe e ku'u ipo
Kahi mea ho'ohenoheno
'O 'oe no ka'u i aloha
A loko e hana a'e nei

Listen to me my sweetheart
The one I cherish so
You are the one I love
The one that arouses my heart

Ho'okahi nō wau i aloha
'O ka leo lā a ke aloha
I ka ne'e mai ia'u
E nanea kāua i 'ane'i

Mai Lohilohi Mai 'Oe

Lena Machado

There's just one thing I love
The voice of my love
murmuring to me Come to me
for some relaxation and enjoyment

'A'ohe o'u moe pono i ka pō
I ka hana nui a loko
Kahi a ka mana'o
E lauwiliwili nei

I could not sleep well last night
Because of all these crazy feelings inside of me
Where my emotions
Toss and turn to no end

Hā'ina 'ia mai ka puana
Kahi mea ho'ohenoheno
'O 'oe nō ka'u i aloha
A loko e hana a'e nei

Tell now the refrain
Of the one I cherish so
You are the one I love
The one that arouses my heart

At left: hula bodies in motion. Above: performers at the Prince Lot Festival
at Moanalua, one of the major hula events held annually in the Islands.

In 1820, with the arrival of the Protestant missionaries from New England, hula began to suffer a decline. For a while the native religion was able to co-exist with the newly introduced Christianity but gradually the hula was abandoned by both the monarchy and ruling chiefs. Only in isolated areas did the "licentious" dancing continue.

Hiram Bingham, the stern leader of the first missionary company, apparently enjoyed the dance as an art form but objected to its often suggestive movements and the fact that "much of the person is uncovered." His book, *A Residence of Twenty-One Years in the Sandwich Islands* (1847), mentions one performance in which he counted 270 dancers.

"All parts of the hula," Bingham wrote in his book, "are laborious, and under a tropical sun, make the perspiration roll freely from the performers. Sometimes both musicians and dancers cantilate their heathen songs together. Occasionally a single female voice carries on the song, while the rest are silent, and sometimes hundreds of voices are heard together. Melody and harmony are scarcely known to them, with all their skill and art. The whole arrangement and process of their old hulas were designed to promote lasciviousness, and of course the practice of them could not flourish in modest communities."

Despite frowning glances by the missionaries, however, the hula did not die. The dancers simply stayed out of sight. Laws were passed prohibiting the public display of hula in the early 1850s but the ban, despite its damage, lasted only a couple of decades. The laws were lifted in the early 1870s and by the time David Kalakaua was elected king in 1874 traditional dance was undergoing something of a revival.

"If ever a prince had dreams, some impossible to fulfill," columnist Samuel Crowningburg-Amalu has written for the *Honolulu Advertiser,* "it was David Kalakaua. His dreams stretched far beyond his own little kingdom.

"He dreamed of a pelagic empire under his single crown, of a united Polynesia, of a new oceanic Rome set in the Pacific. He dreamed of uniting by marriage his own royal house to the royal and imperial families of the world. He dreamed of his little Hawai'i becoming a great naval power in Oceania. He robed his ladies in gowns of precious silks from Paris, hung diamonds on their necks and tiaras to crown their brows. He put shoes upon their feet.

"Kalakaua," Amalu continued, "dreamed of elegance in his little court at 'Iolani and to house that court, he erected a new palace, bought crowns to grace his head, created new medallions to begem his breast, and a new protocol to enhance his throne.

"King Kalakaua turned the eyes of his people away from their own provincial and insular past. He gave them the world. He brought the Hawaiian people out of a simple yesterday and promised them a bright and sophisticated tomorrow. Almost single-handedly he created the romance that somehow to this very day has never quite departed from the Hawaiian Islands. At exactly the right time that he was most needed, this prince of dreams was there."

David Kalakaua was a fun-loving king and justly earned his nickname of the "Merrie Monarch." Music and the hula were important to his own life and his personal enthusiasms caught the imagination of his people. Kalakaua invited many chanters and dancers to perform for him at 'Iolani Palace.

One of hula's finest moments occurred in 1883 when Kalakaua called a special coronation day on February 12 for himself and Queen Kapi'olani. For the afternoon and evening of February 24 he invited seven of Hawai'i's foremost *kumu hula* to perform for him along with members of their *halau*. Over 260 chants and dances were performed during this special occasion.

A similar program was held in 1886 for the king's 50th birthday. This time several *halau hula* performances were accompanied by musicians playing the 'ukulele, an instrument highly favored by the king. Kalakaua died in 1891 but his encouragement of traditional Hawaiian dance and the other ancient Hawaiian arts set an example that was continued into the 20th century. With the publication of N. B. Emerson's classic *Unwritten Literature of Hawaii* in 1909, the hula entered the modern period.

Much of the credit for hula's "rediscovery" goes to the entertainment business, although many of the hula dances that were performed for Hawai'i's growing tourist trade during the early decades of this century could hardly be traced to their legendary origins. Gesture and movement overpowered the poetry of the words and, in many instances, the original chants were forgotten in the search for pretty melodies.

Hollywood was especially taken by the visual possibilities of the hula. A large number of movie actresses—from sexy Delores Del Rio to wholesomely pint-sized Shirley Temple—gave their hips a sway on the silver screen. Clara Bow, Jeanette MacDonald, Eleanor Powell, Dorothy Lamour, and Betty Grable all made their marks dancing the "Hollywood Hula." The best known local hula dancer to score in the movies was bouncy Clarissa Haili who gained fame around the world for her comic dancing under the name of Hilo Hattie. Seriousness was thrown out the window when Hilo Hattie did the "Hilo Hop."

While this commercialized dancing style proved popular with both local and tourist audiences the traditional hula was kept alive by various *kumu hula* who sometimes gave public performances but generally kept a lower public profile. Among the most visible was 'Iolani Luahine, who, before she died in 1978, had become Hawai'i's foremost solo performer of the classical hula. Another was the dynamic Tom Hiona who, during the 1930s, led the only all-male dancing troupe in the Islands.

Aloha e ka u'i ē
Maka hō'eu'eu ē
'Alawa mai 'oe me ka mālie
Ma ka poli e nanea ē

Pehea e ka u'i ē
E honihoni mai ē
A laila kāua moe i ka 'olu
O ke ano ahiahi ē

E ala e ka u'i ē
Ke kani nei ka moa ē
Mahalo a'e ana i ka le'ale'a
He mana'o ho'oheno ē

Hā'ina ka puana ē
No ka maka 'eu'eu ē
Me a'u iho nei e pili ke aloha
Goodbye e ka u'i ē

Ka U'i Ē

E. Kaipo Hale

Greetings, you beautiful thing
With your flirty eyes
Glance my way carefully
And rest in my arms

And so, you beautiful thing
How about a kiss
Then you and I can lie in the cool
Of the evening's calm

Awake, you beautiful thing
The rooster crows
Thanks for the gratification
For which I will always cherish

The refrain is told
For my flirty-eyed friend
Whose compassion will remain close to me
Farewell, you beautiful thing

At left: ancient hula was drawn by Louis Choris during an 1816 expedition to the Sandwich Isles. The explorers thought the "wriggling backsides" was lascivious entertainment. Above: Hawaiian kupuna or elders will tell you hula is life—good, bad, and the smile on this woman's face.

‘Auhea wale ‘oe
Mahina ‘o Hoku
Hō‘ike a‘e ‘oe
A i kou nani

Ua la‘i nā kai
Mehameha nā pali
‘O ‘oe a ‘o wau
E ho‘oipoipo nei

Hā‘ina kou inoa
Mahina ‘o Hoku
Ke noho nani maila
Ma nā lani ki‘eki‘e

Lillian Awa

Where are you
Moon of Hoku
Show yourself
And all your beauty

Seas are calm
The cliffs so lonely
As you and I
Make love

This is dedicated to you
Moon of Hoku
Reposing so splendidly
In the heavens so high

The hula survived the bombs of Pearl Harbor, the coming of statehood and even the frenzied excitement of rock & roll. Today hula, in all of its various forms, is alive and well in Hawai‘i. Some visitors may get no further than the free Kodak Hula Show in Kapi‘olani Park or a revue in their Waikiki hotel but sophisticated audiences can take their pick from dozens of traditional performances throughout the years. There are also several popular annual events, including the Prince Lot Festival at Moanalua Gardens, the Kamehameha Day hula and chant competition at La‘ie, and the Merrie Monarch Festival which is held each April in Hilo.

The Merrie Monarch is certainly the best known of all the state's annual hula events. It is often called the "World Series" or "Olympics" of Hawaiian dance. The first Merrie Monarch Festival, named to honor King Kalakaua, was held in 1963. It was the brainstorm of George Naope and Gene Wilhelm who were then cabinet members in the Big Island's county administration. Their original idea was to create a carnival-like tourist event that would promote Hilo as a visitor destination.

In the beginning the festival accomplished its aim. Tourists began discovering that Hilo had an unassuming small-town charm and a friendliness towards visitors that was hard to match anywhere in the islands. But after five years the festival seemed to have run its course. Enthusiasm had waned and funding became harder to find.

Dottie Thompson, who became chairman of the Merrie Monarch in 1968, decided to fight back. She raised the money to continue and brought back Naope, who had since left the county government, to coordinate the festival. Three years later, in 1971, Naope added a hula competition to the Merrie Monarch and this first contest included nine participating *halau.*

It was not until 1976, however, that the Merrie Monarch and the hula became almost synonymous in Hawai‘i. This was the year that a *kane* or men's competition was added to the festival to balance out the already existing *wahine* or women's events. It was the primitive and robust dancing of the men that

Above: without leis, hula dancers would look naked. Wrists, ankles, necks, and heads are sometimes adorned with a flower mentioned in the hula's song. At right: full moon over Koko Head, an extinct volcanic crater on the east end of O‘ahu.

finally ignited the sleepy crowds and put Hilo's Merrie Monarch on the road to becoming the most exciting dance competition in the Pacific.

Robert Cazimero and his former hula partner, Wayne Chang, brought their Na Kamalei *halau* to the Merrie Monarch during that important transitional year of 1976. They returned in 1977, winning the men's modern hula division, and again in 1978 when they were closely defeated in the hotly-contested finals by Waimapuna, of Oʻahu.

That was the last year that Robert took Na Kamalei to Hilo. He says that the festival's "intense competition" is not only physically exhausting but puts a strain on friendships. The timing is also bad. In 1984, for example, the contest events were held the same weekend that he and Roland were doing the final blocking for their May 1 Lei Day Concert at the Waikiki Shell.

For many years the Merrie Monarch Festival's hula competition had been held in the Hilo Civic Auditorium. With its growing popularity, however, a change of location was necessary and in 1979 the festival moved to the tennis stadium. Today the Merrie Monarch has even outgrown the stadium. It can accommodate 7,000 spectators but many more are turned away.

At the Merrie Monarch there are two major group divisions. These are the *kahiko,* or ancient hula, and the *ʻauwana* or modern hula categories. One evening of the three-day festival is devoted to each division. Another evening focuses on the graceful individual dancing for the coveted title of Miss Aloha Hula.

Each year the Merrie Monarch Festival committee selects contest chants for the *hula kahiko* in the *kane* and *wahine* divisions. In 1984 the committee turned to Hawaiian language authority Theodore Kelsey, 92, of Waiʻanae, Oʻahu. Kelsey, one of the state's "living treasures," has provided material for many ethnographers who have studied the Hawaiian language and culture during the past fifty years.

Kelsey, who grew up in Hilo, was unable to attend the 1984 festival in person but sent over two Hawaiian transcriptions and his English translations of chants he had recorded in the early 1930s from Kuluwaimaka, the last living chanter from the royal court of King Kalakaua. The *kane* division chant, which appears at right, was composed by Kuluwaimaka for the original Merrie Monarch.

A dancer at a Hauʻula, Oʻahu, festival. He wears a malo around his loins, Kupeʻe lei around his wrists and ankles, and a neck lei of maile— a plant sacred to Laka, goddess of hula.

'Ōpae ē, 'Ōpae ho'i
Ua hele mai au
Ua hele mai au, na Kuahine
'Ai ā wai
'Ai ā Puhi
Nui 'o Puhi, a li'ili'i au, 'a'ole loa

Pūpū ē, Pūpū ho'i
Ua hele mai au
Ua hele mai au, na Kuahine
'Ai ā wai
'Ai ā puhi
Nui' o Puhi, a li'ili'i au, 'a'ole loa

Kūpe'e ē, Kūpe'e ho'i
Ua hele mai au
Ua hele mai au, na Kuahine
'Ai a wai
'Ai a puhi
Nui 'o Puhi, a li'ili'i au, 'a'ole loa

'Ōpihi ē Opihi ho'i
Ua hele mai au
Ua hele mai au na Kuahine
Mai maka'u, na'u e pani
I ka maka a 'ike 'ole kēlā puhi

'Ōpae Ē
Traditional

O 'Ōpae (the shrimp) hear me I have come
I have come to seek help for my sister
She'll be eaten— "Eaten by who?"
She'll be eaten by Puhi (the eel)
"But Puhi is so big and I am so small,
It's impossible for me to help."

O Pūpū (the seashell) hear me I have come
I have come to seek help for my sister
She'll be eaten— "Eaten by who?"
She'll be eaten by Puhi (the eel)
"But Puhi is so big and I am so small,
It's impossible for me to help."

O Kūpe'e (a kind of shell fish) hear me
I have come
I have come to seek help for my sister
She'll be eaten— "Eaten by who?"
She'll be eaten by Puhi (the eel)
"But Puhi is so big and I am so small,
It's impossible for me to help."

O 'Opihi (a kind of shell fish) hear me
I have come
I have come to seek help for my sister
"Don't be afraid. I will cover the eyes
and make that puhi sightless"

He Mele Hula No Ka Mo'i Kalakaua
(A Hula Chant for King Kalakaua)

Ke'owe mai nei e ka ua Lihau i ka welelau pali
Ka hikina 'ana mai a ke aloha
Ho'opumehana i ku'u poli
Nani wale au 'e 'ike nei i ke ki'owai kapu a ha'i
E moani lehua i Hi'ilawe
I hanua mai e ke Kehau
Kaua i ka wai o Kapu'a
Wai ho'onanea a na manu
Kolonahe mai ana ke 'ala
O ku'u pua o ka wekiu
Ua kini ua lau ke aloha
Ku'u kino kahiko i ka 'ohu
I ka noe hali mai uka
Eia la e hoho'i mai 'oe
Ne'ene'e pono mai i ke alo
Puana 'ia a'e kou inoa
No ka hiku kapu o ka lani

The cool and gentle Lihau rain sighs on top of the cliffs
The arrival of the loved one from the east
Warming my breast
Beautiful is the sight of the forbidden pool belonging to someone else
The lehua waft to Hi'ilawe
Breathed upon the Kehau
You and I at the water of Kapu'a
Water where the birds pass the time away
Pleasantly blowing hither is the fragrance
Of my flower of the summit
Multitudinous is the love
Four thousand is the count within the body
My body beautifully adorned by the fog
In the spreading mist from upland
Here it is, return again and again
Move right up to the front of my body
Tell the refrain that puts forth your name
For the seventh sacred one of the heavens.

The "seventh sacred one" mentioned in the last line refers to King Kalakaua, the seventh of the Hawaiian monarchs. The lehua mentioned in this chant, and the *wahine* division chant as well, is a red flower especially common to Big Island trees and shrubs. It was sacred to the goddess Pele and even today lehua leis are often thrown into the crater at Kilauea as an offering.

During the late 1970s, hula was a part of the cultural revival in the arts that George Kanahele, founder of the Hawaii Music Foundation, termed the "Hawaiian Renaissance." Suddenly students began paying attention in their Hawaiian language classes and there was renewed popularity in local music, dance, crafts, the visual arts, and literature. The Merrie Monarch Festival helped to force hula back in the spotlight.

"Thanks to Kalakaua," Kanahele wrote in the November 1977, issue of *Honolulu* magazine, "the hula has maintained a steady number of devotees over the years, but the number and level of activity seem to have exploded in recent years. There are more hula classes and teachers to accommodate the growing lines of students. Many of these are studying ancient hula, along with the chants. Indeed, interest in *hula kahiko* (ancient hula) is greater now than it has been in decades."

Kanahele wrote that "the most exciting aspect of the hula revival is the return of the male dancer to his rightful place. There are far more young male hula dancers nowadays than at any other time in recent memory . . . Male dancers," he stated, "have become the favorites of local audiences."

Robert and Roland Cazimero spearheaded the contemporary hula revival by integrating Hawaiian dance into their live musical performances. Na Kamalei, the *halau* which Robert helped start in 1974, has been especially influential in the growing popularity of male dancing.

Above: plumeria leis and ti leaf skirts decorate these 'auwana or modern hula dancers at Hilo's Merrie Monarch Festival, the state's most competitive and best known hula contest held annually in April. At right: more than 7,000 people crowd into the Edith Kanaka'ole Multi-purpose Stadium in Hilo to watch three nights of Merrie Monarch competition.

Ka Hikina (a) ka wahine āiwāiwa lā
Me he 'iwa kākele i ka moana uli
Huli mai ka 'ale kū (o) ka moana lā
Ke māpu nei i ka hulu (o) Hōnaunau

Ho'oniau 'ia ka wahine mai Ka'iwa lā
No kona kikaha (i) ka lani Ulupō
Pō puni ana ke 'ala i ka pua hala
Ka mōhala pono i ka Haleokeawe

Kiawe hāweo (ka) wahine o Ka'iwa la
Kona 'uhane kihei pua i ke Konalani
Nauane la, e ki'i i ka hulu hiwa
No Ka'iwakalemeha kani nā hālau

Niau kololani ke helena a ka manu lā
Ka 'iwa hulu 'ena ki'i Makalei
Hā'ina e ka ulu o ka wahine lā
Me he manu 'iwa kia'i (i) nā 'auwa'a

Ka'Iwa Hulu 'Ena Ki'i Makalei

Kihei de Silva

The coming of the mysterious woman
(is) Like an 'iwa soaring freely over the dark sea
A wave rises in the ocean, and breaks,
Spraying the feathered one of Honaunau

The woman of Ka'iwa is imitated
For her soaring in the skies of Ulupō
The fragrance of the hala flower
spreads everywhere
Blooming profusely at Haleokeawe

Gold-streaked and glowing
is the woman of Ka'iwa
Her spirit of inspiration (emerges)
in the Konalani wind
Move along, fetch the precious feather
For Ka'iwakalameha who sings out over halau

Silent and swift is the going of the bird
Like the fiery feathered 'iwa
who carried Makalei
Tell of the woman's inspiration
She is the one who guides the (hālau)
canoe fleets

Some critics have charged that Robert and his dancers are too modern, that they have strayed too far away from traditional styles. His response is that the evolution of Hawaiian dance did not stop with the death of Kalakaua in 1891. "Today," he says, "the hula is not frozen in time but very much alive."

It is likely, too, that during the Kalakaua years there were hula teachers who didn't fit in with the rest of the crowd. After mastering the acceptable movements they probably composed new chants and added some fancy footwork of their own.

Robert Cazimero, had he been around a century ago, would no doubt have found himself among the rebels. Using the traditional hula as the foundation for his own teaching, he adds unusual costumes and innovative body movements. The latter are often quite erotic in nature.

When Robert first started mixing the elements of ballet and modern dance with hula, the "purists" made lots of noise. In fact, several times his *halau* was disqualified in contests due to its controversial style.

Today, of course, the situation has gotten somewhat looser. A number of the *halau* that frequently win the big contests do so with the help of contemporary movements.

"Sure, my boys will still get criticized for their hip motion," he says. "But I don't agree with those who say it's too feminine. Ask the women in our audiences. They know. They'll tell you it's sexy."

Hawaiian Spirits Live Again

Jon Osorio

Cast your eyes down the mountainside
Out from the surf in to the valley wide
Breathlessly waiting through the years
Solemn and silent
Souls have gathered here
Hawai'i
Where the old ways like the sea
Seem to flow unceasingly
And a thousand voices sing to me
Where the wave rushes on
And the mist rolls in
And Hawaiian spirits live again

Far from the surge of the city we stand
Hearing the pulse of our people in this land
Daughters of life and sons of the sea
Cling to the earth and live in harmony
Hawai'i
Where the old ways like the wind
Seem to breathe and stir within
And a thousand voices sing again
Where the wave rushes on
And the mist rolls in
And Hawaiian spirits live again

I f asked to describe the overall style of his *halau,* however, Cazimero backs away from the word "sexy." He prefers to call it "manly grace." Indeed, the name he picked several years ago for his Halau Na Kamalei is "The Gentlemen of Na Kamalei."

"When you get right down to it," Robert continues, "only style separates any *halau* from the other. Every good group has a certain level of energy and a love of the dance.

"Hula is a great expression of the Polynesian people and I'm happy that it's so popular now. It would be nice to some day have this kind of dance recognized on a level with ballet. But we've got a long way to go."

Robert studied hula from Ma'iki Aiu Lake and in 1973 graduated from her Halau Hula o Ma'iki. He and the others in the graduating class were thus given the right to become teachers themselves.

He was at Kamehameha Schools at the time, instructing a boy's concert glee club and trying to teach them to dance on the side. From the original 40 he whittled the number down to six—the first nucleus of his *halau.* As the group grew he was aided by a co-teacher, Wayne Chang, who also taught at Kamehameha Schools.

"A lot of changes have taken place in the last few years," Robert says. "Wayne is no longer with me and neither are any of the original six boys. But what has happened is that a lot of talented dancers have come and gone. They have, in turn, been replaced by others and now there are 18 in the performing group and 10 helpers who support the group from off-stage."

Robert says that his *halau* may not have been the first post World War II group to spotlight male hula dancing. But he knows of no other "completely all-male" *halau* during this period that pre-dated Na Kamalei.

"The whole purpose of the *halau*," Robert explains, "was that I wanted to show people that men could dance hula and do so without being thought of as effeminate. Our popularity proves that we've succeeded in doing so."

Every summer, usually in May, Robert opens his *halau* to new members who go through a difficult five months of basic hula instruction. During the month of September he picks those "who have promise" and drops the rest. The survivors are immediately put into the *halau* core group from which the dancers who perform at the Brothers Cazimero concerts, and other occasions, are drawn.

"In the early years," Robert says, "working with my *halau* was so exciting for me that I failed to put in enough time working with Roland. He used to get really upset at me for that. Once it got to the point that he was ready to quit the Brothers Cazimero and just go off by himself—and I was ready to say go-ahead."

Luckily the "verbal blows" were stopped short of breaking up the group. Robert says that today he sees the difference between work and play and that the Brothers Cazimero is the vehicle that allows him the experience of running a *halau*. If work interferes with play, he chooses to work.

"We keep the same *halau* rehearsal schedule before concerts, working out whatever we can. Sometimes I'll just tell Roland what dances we're doing at the moment and at other times the *halau* will build something around a song the Brothers Cazimero have already recorded.

"Sometimes it's difficult to explain exactly what happens but one thing is certain. Like those Hawaiians during the visit of Captain Cook or later during the time of Kalakaua, we find that it's practically impossible to separate the music from the dance." ■

At left: fern leis decorate a Hawaiian musician, her pahu, drum, and ipu heke, a double gourd—the instruments that hold the beat during a kahiko or ancient hula. Above: arms extended, heads bowed: the end of this hula performance.

Hawaiʻi, The Big Island

Mahalo aʻe nei iā Hilo
I ka hoʻokipa ʻana mai
Me ka ua Kanilehua
A me ka maile aʻo Panaʻewa

Aia ma ka hale kamaʻāina
I noho a luana aku ai
Kilohi aʻe ana i ka nani
A me ka uluwehiwehi o ka ʻāina

Aia lā ʻo Halemaʻumaʻu
Ka home o Pele mai Kahiki
I laila au i ʻike iho ai
I nā hana nui a ka wahine

Nani Waimea i ka ʻolu
A me ke aheahe a ka makani
Ia uka ka home hoʻokipa
I ka laʻi o ke kula māhie

Puana ʻia me ke aloha
No ka mokupuni nui o Hawaiʻi
Hoʻohihi ka manaʻo i ka nani
A me ka hoʻokipa ʻana mai

Hoʻokipa Hawaiʻi
Kaipo Hale

Many thanks to Hilo
With the Kanilehua rain
For welcoming me
And the sweet maile
of Panaʻewa

There at the hosting home
I stayed and relaxed
Gazing out at the beauty
And verdant surroundings

There's Halemaʻumaʻu
The home of Pele
There I saw
The things she had done

Beautiful is Waimea in the cool
And in the gentle breeze
In the uplands is the welcoming home
Amidst the calm and pleasant pasture

With love the refrain is sung
For the island of Hawaiʻi
The beauty is cherished in thought
Along with its welcome

When the subject of the Big Island comes up in conversation, both Robert and Roland Cazimero often talk about it in terms of "roots." Their father, Bill, and their mother, Betty, were born and raised in Kohala and many members of the family still live there. The Brothers may think of Oʻahu as their "home island" but it is the Big Island that now occupies their dreams.

"For many years," Robert explains, "neither Roland nor I cared much for the Big Island. After all, we grew up in Honolulu and got used to living in the city. The Big Island was beautiful to look at but its beauty somehow escaped us. The pace was much too slow.

"Then, during our time at Kamehameha Schools, we changed our attitudes about a lot of things. Our 'family' ties took on a new meaning and our visits to Kohala became more frequent. Now that we lead such busy lives the Big Island has turned into our secret hideaway. This is where we rest when the weight of the world gets a little too heavy around our necks."

Outside of the family, the Big Island holds still other meanings for the Brothers. Robert associates it with the mysticism of the volcano, hula's legendary past, and his own participation at the Merrie Monarch

Above: the late kumu hula Edith Kanakaʻole (center) and her daughters, Nalani Kanakaʻole and Pualani Kanakaʻole Kanahele, at the Kilauea Caldera. At left: waterfalls among Hamakua coast cane fields.

93

Festival in Hilo. Roland has done two solo theme albums which relate directly to the Big Island: *Pele* (1979), discussed previously, and *Warrior* (1983), his tribute to Kamehameha the Great.

Together, in December 1980, the Brothers Cazimero released a third album loosely tied to the Big Island. Entitled *Hawaii, In The Middle Of The Sea,* side one begins with the popular song "Home in the Islands," written by fellow recording artist, Henry Kapono Ka'aihue. The lyrics say a lot about how Robert and Roland view themselves as entertainers: "We're two happy guys, beneath tropic skies; living the life of the gypsy musician."

Also included on the album are two songs that hold special meaning for them because of the place they celebrate. The first is "Pu'u 'Ohu (Waimea Fantasy)" and the second is "Waimea Lullaby." The album, itself, was recorded during an 11-day period at Waimea's Brown Sugar Ranch.

If there is a particular spot on the Big Island the Brothers find most inspiring, it is certainly the misty cattle country of Waimea and its town of Kamuela. Roland says that Waimea, with its crisp, cool climate, is "my definition of the perfect Hawai'i. I wish that more places in the Islands were like this."

The Big Island, on a higher level, also holds special meaning to the Hawaiian people. It is the dwelling place of the "spirit" of Pele, the volcano goddess, a favored home of the early Polynesian settlers, and an important place in the history of the hula.

Kamehameha, or Tamehameha, whose name means "the lonely one," was born during the 1750s on the Big Island and it is from these shores that he launched his war canoes to unite all of the Hawaiian Islands. In his *Warrior* album Roland uses English lyrics and an electrified background sound to illuminate the young Kamehameha's rise from soldier to future king. The song cycle brings to light the human frailties of love, hate, and the fear of failure that even kings must experience. All that keeps him going during these difficult times is his overwhelming certainty of a royal destiny.

An interesting note about *Warrior* is that the name "Kamehameha" is not mentioned once in the lyrics themselves. Nor is there any reference to Hawai'i. Roland was inspired by the legend of Kamehameha but kept true to his imagination. He decided to tell the story of a man born to destiny in universal terms.

During ancient times, Hawai'i had a system of individual chiefs who ruled various islands or sections of islands. Kamehameha, who was born in Kohala, was the nephew of Kalaniopu'u, ruler of the Big Island. In late 1778, the future king met Captain Cook on his second visit to the islands with his two ships, *Resolution* and *Discovery.* When Kalaniopu'u called upon the British explorer off the coast of Maui, Kamehameha joined his uncle's party aboard the *Resolution.* The Hawaiians spent the night aboard

Waimea
Lullaby
Patrick Downes

As early evening rains come down
I hold you in my arms
I try to smile away your tears
And rock away all harm
Please close your eyes again for me
Hush now don't you cry
The showers sing a sweet, sweet,
sweet Waimea lullaby.

Dans la soiree il pleur douchment
Je te tien dans mes bras
C'est toi le larm le chanson trise
Mon amour ne pleur pas
J'adore les yeux qui son si beau
Hush now don't you cry
Les nuage chantant une sweet, sweet,
sweet Waimea lullaby.

My darling I'm in love with you
And times like these are very few
If I had my way right here I'd stay
And hold you forever.
Please dream a pleasant dream for me
Hush now don't you cry
I'll sing for you a sweet, sweet,
sweet Waimea Lullaby

As early evening winds blow soft
I hold you to my breast
I run my fingers through your hair
To put your mind at rest
Please dream a pleasant dream for me,
Hush now don't you cry
The breezes sing a sweet, sweet,
sweet Waimea Lullaby

the ship as the expedition sailed south to the Big Island.

The young warrior's exposure to Cook's visit made him realize that Hawai'i was changing. As an upstart chief, without a political base, Kamehameha also saw that by adopting the superior firepower displayed by the foreign visitors he could put his rival chiefs on the defensive.

By 1790, a number of Hawaiians had come back home to the Islands after long voyages aboard fur-trading ships. They told tales of continents teeming with masses of people, material wealth, and technology. Kamehameha knew that if the Islands were not put under one rule they would eventually fall piecemeal to the foreigners. This monarchy had to be aligned, too, with a friendly, strong Western nation in order to preserve its sovereignty.

I have a deep respect for Kamehameha," Roland says. "He's someone I admire a lot. If I could go back in time it would be to the early years of Kamehameha when he was building his power base on the Big Island. I would like to have been standing at his right side when he unified the islands."

Roland opens his *Warrior* album with the title song. "Warrior" introduces the future king as he asserts his authority and begins to put together a loyal band of followers. Today we usually think of Kamehameha as a wise old man who led his people to glory but Kamehameha was also the product of an age full of bloodshed. "He became king,"

Roland says, "because he was as tough as he was intelligent. He fought and killed his way to the top."

"I'm coming your way," Kamehameha sings, "I'm here to purge and slay. Get out of my way, I'm a Warrior." The song ends with the future king giving a pep talk to his men. "Be Number One, Be a Warrior, Be Number One."

Roland has been criticized for showing the savage side of Kamehameha's early life but he says those critics fail to see a simple truth. "There's a bit of Kamehameha in all of us," he explains. "At times we all lose our tempers, display prejudices, and act cruel. We shouldn't forget that Kamehameha was a man before he became a king."

The album's second song, "A New Way of Life," provides a clue to Kamehameha's success. He was cautious in dealing with foreigners but was not afraid

Left: Waimea—misty cattle country with a crisp, cool climate and velvet hills. At right: Paniolo at Parker Ranch, Waimea, which began with a king's gift of 642 acres, eventually growing to 250,000, one of the largest, privately owned ranches in the United States.

TAMEHAMEHA

I'm coming your way
I'm here to purge and slay
Get out of my way
I'm a Warrior

Here to do a job
Here to kill and rob
Get out of my way
I'm a Warrior

I'm Number One
Take all that you possess
Take your life and leave the rest
Get out of my way
I'm a Warrior

Ready for the kill
Your life can fill my bill
Get out of the way
I'm a Warrior

I'm Number One
I'm Number One

Well let me tell you something boys
Something you might already know
If you don't fight, fight for your life
I'll be standing here all alone
Be a Warrior
You better be Number One
Be Number One

Warrior

Roland Cazimero

He said, "kill everyone here"
Kill the king and all his peers
You make me real proud
You're my Warriors

We do whatever he says
Better you than me dead
We will make him real proud
We're his Warriors
We're Number One

He said, "kill everyone here"
Kill the kings and all his peers
You make me real proud
You're my Warriors

We do whatever he says
We will always, always obey
We will make him real proud
We're his warriors
We're Number One
We're Number One

Well let me tell you something boys
Something you might already know
If you don't fight, fight for your life
I'll be standing here all alone
You better be a Warrior
Be Number One
Be a Warrior
Be Number One

to try Western ways if they helped him achieve his goals. "I leave myself open to new experience," he says, "I leave myself open to all life's circumstance. I do the right things that will make me strong. I'm still learning the difference between right and wrong."

One of the most famous stories in Kamehameha's life occurred in 1783 when he led his warriors in a raid against a village along the Puna coast. He had just leapt ashore from his canoe to attack a group of fishermen loyal to the enemy when he tripped and caught one of his feet in a crack in the rocks.

Seeing an opportunity, one of the fishermen turned and struck Kamehameha on the head with a paddle. It broke into several pieces. Kamehameha was rescued but not before the fishermen escaped down the beach. Years later, as king, he remembered this incident when he established *Kanawai Mamalahoe*,

The Law of the Splintered Paddle. He decreed that under his rule any conscious attack on a defenseless person would be punishable by death.

Kanawai Mamalahoe also removed the threat of death that chiefs formerly held over commoners who disobeyed their orders. On the surface this law showed Kamehameha's regret over attacking the defenseless fishermen. Politically, however, this action reduced the parochial powers of the chiefs. It made it more difficult for them to raise an army against Kamehameha.

On the third song in *Warrior*, "Time and Again," Kamehameha begins to trust in himself. But although he now has a confidence to match his abilities he begins to question his motives. "Time and again," he says, "I wonder why I am here. Time and again I seek to find the answers to quell me. Time and again I find it is all up to me."

"Tamehameha," by Herb Kawainui Kane. The king was ruthless in his battles to unite the Hawaiian Islands, but he was charitable and peaceful in victory. His name became "Kamehameha" when the missionaries established the written Hawaiian language.

I'm home
I'm home, by the sea
Now my weary spirit
Flys so high and free

I'm home
This is where I want to be
Where my soul
My soul believes

I leave what I did behind
I look at what now is mine
I live for only today
Yesterday was yesterday
Now there is peace here for me
Now I can breathe, I can see
I see the road up ahead

Don't look back
Just move instead

Home has been my dream
Now it is a reality
I've dreamed the same old dream
Now I know it's here for me

I leave what I did behind
I look at what now is mine
I live for only today
Yesterday was yesterday
Now there is peace here for me
Now I can breathe, I can see
I see the road up ahead
Don't look back
Just move instead

I'm Home
Roland Cazimero

The great love of Kamehameha's life was Ka'ahumanu, a princess from Maui. She became the favorite of his wives and was probably the second most powerful person in the kingdom. In the fourth song on *Warrior,* "Now I Know You," the young Kamehameha reveals the depth of his feelings for this woman who would eventually run the kingdom after his death. "Now I know you," he says. "You came into my life. Love will never be the same. Now I know you."

In 1780, Kalaniopu'u, named his son, Kiwala'o, as his heir. At the same time Kamehameha was made guardian of the family war god, Ku-ka'ili-moku. This god was represented by wooden or feather-covered images that were carried into battle. "War," the next song on the album becomes Kamehameha's battle cry. "Kill everybody so we can unite this land . . . War is the God who wakes me . . . War is a necessity."

Kalaniopu'u died in 1782 and soon afterwards Kiwala'o was killed on the battlefield. After ten more years of civil war, Kamehameha emerged, at age 33, as ruler of the Big Island. "It's Not Easy," the last song on side one of *Warrior,* reflects on these years. "It's not easy," Kamehameha says, "trying to move men's minds. It's not easy, even though you try and try. It's not easy being number one. But you've got to stay on top."

Maui fell to Kamehameha in 1790 and all of the major islands, except Kaua'i, were conquered one at a time. One contemporary estimate reports that Kamehameha's warriors numbered over 16,000.

"Follow Me," the first song on side two of Roland's album, represents Kamehameha urging his men forward to fight the last battles. Victory is now within reach. "I know that in the past I've called you to fight," he tells his men. "Fight with me. I call on you again now to rally beside me.

"For a new day to come. A new way for some. But a better way for all. We will all stand tall, one and for all, or we all will fail." But in the end there was no failure. In 1810 the ruler of Kaua'i, King Kaumuali'i, finally surrendered and was allowed to remain on the island as governor for the rest of his lifetime.

The success of Kamehameha's campaign owed much to John Young and Isaac Davis, two English sailors who instructed his men in the use of guns and cannons. Young later married Kaona'eha, one of Kamehameha's nieces. In the next song, "I'm Home," Kamehameha finally has time to reflect back on the past and to think about what he will do in the future. "Yesterday was yesterday," he says, "Now there is

peace here for me. Now I can breathe, I can see. I see the road up ahead. Don't look back. Just move instead."

But still there are second thoughts. Not everything goes according to plan. In the song that follows, "Struggle," Kamehameha asks himself a number of questions: "Was it worth all the struggle? Was it worth all the pain? Was it worth ever starting? Would I change anything?" He thinks not. "I would have still done it this way. I know no other way."

In the next song, "Sit and Ponder," the first of Hawai'i's monarchs begins to realize that he has the hardest job in the kingdom. Besides setting up a new central government and protecting his people, Kamehameha knows he must accommodate the cultural changes that the Westerners are introducing to his Islands. "Love, Peace and Joy," he says, "for all to feel and to be. This is the way I hope it will be. But I sit here and ponder and wonder what the future will bring."

Cattle were first brought to the Big Island in 1793 by British Captain George Vancouver as a gift to Kamehameha. The king immediately put a 10-year *kapu* or taboo on them. Death was the punishment for anyone who slaughtered them. The purpose of the *kapu* was to give the cattle a chance to multiply. It succeeded well and by the end of the period there were thousands of the animals roaming widely across the island. Horses were introduced later and they, too, were soon running free.

The capital of the Hawaiian Kingdom was located at Kailua, on the Kona Coast, until 1804. At that time Kamehameha moved his court to Honolulu in order

Above left: Kona, once the capital of the Hawaiian Kingdom and final residence of Kamehameha the Great, is now a destination resort for tourists. At right: Kamehameha put a 10-year kapu or taboo on cattle when they first arrived in 1793. They multiplied quickly and most of the native koa forests were turned into pasture lands.

to take better economic advantage of the increased foreign trade. After 1812, however, he returned to the Big Island and retired to a home along Kailua Bay. Nearby was the old Ahu'ena temple, or *heiau,* which he had restored and re-dedicated to the god Lono.

The last song on Roland Cazimero's *Warrior* album is "Move On." Kamehameha is now able to concentrate his full energies on improving the social and economic welfare of his people. "Better move on while you can," he sings at the end, "to a land of peace, a land of joy. A land worth living for . . . the promised land."

Archibald Campbell, a 22-year-old Scottish sailor, met Kamehameha in 1809 and left his impressions in his fine book, *A Voyage Round the World.* The king was, Campbell wrote, "a stout, well-made man, rather darker in the complexion than the natives usually are, and wants two of his front teeth.

The expression of his countenance is agreeable, and he is mild and affable in manners, and possesses great warmth of feeling; for I have seen him shed tears upon the departure of those to whom he was attached, and has the art of attaching others to himself. Although a conqueror, he is extremely popular among his subjects; and not without reason, for since he attained the supreme power, they have enjoyed repose and prosperity."

In 1815, another visiting merchant sailor, John Palmer Parker, was hired by Kamehameha to hunt the wild cattle that were now multiplying rapidly over the Big Island. From the captured stock Palmer began raising his own herd. He married a member of the king's family and was thereafter welcomed in the island's highest social circles.

Samuel Crowningburg-Amalu, writing for the *Honolulu Advertiser,* wrote that "the glory of Kamehameha lies in the truth that although he was utterly ruthless in battle, he became charitable in victory . . . He became a gentle and loving father to all his people and not merely to the aristocracy as did many of the ruling Hawaiian chiefs prior to him. He left behind him a race that was united, and he singlehandedly created the Hawaiian nation.

"Today, one can say I am a Hawaiian and at the same time not understand really what he is saying. Prior to 1810 and the submission of King Kaumuali'i of Kaua'i to Kamehameha, there was no such thing as a Hawaiian. They were people (kanaka) from Hawai'i or Maui, from O'ahu or Kaua'i—but no Hawaiians. Then in 1810, Kamehameha created the Hawaiian Kingdom, and the Hawaiian people as a nation and a single people were born. This may be the greatest gift that

Kamehameha gave to his people—that single identifying factor that made them and still makes them a separate people in the eyes of the world."

Kamehameha the Great, warrior and statesman, died in 1819 at Kailua. The body of the late king was taken to the Ahu'ena *heiau* and wrapped in banana and taro leaves. It was then placed in a trench and covered with a thin layer of earth. A fire, to help decomposition, was started above.

After ten days the flesh was removed and discarded at sea. The king's bones, which were important relics, were cleaned and wrapped in fine *kapa* cloth. This preparation was done within the mortuary, a house that sat on a large rock platform next to the *heiau* platform. A casket of sennit rope was wound around the bones and covered with red

This woman plucks anthuriums, part of the Big Island's agricultural industry. Cattle and paniolo—the art of cowboying was brought to Hawai'i by Spanish-Americans, imported as tutors.

feathers. Two round shells were affixed to the bundle in place of the eyes.

Kamehameha's casket was then positioned above ground on a wooden platform in the *heiau.* Later it was hidden in a secret cave by trusted friends. The actual location of the burial cave is still a secret today and, according to a popular saying, "only the stars in the heavens know the resting place of Kamehameha."

Roland Cazimero never intended for *Warrior* to be a history lesson but, for many listeners, especially visitors, the album has sparked their interest in the life of Kamehameha and the world in which he lived. Over the years a number of good biographies have been published about the first monarch, with the most recent being *Kamehameha* (1976) by Walter F. Judd. The November 1983 issue of *National Geographic* magazine also contains a lengthy story entitled "Kamehameha: Hawaii's Warrior King."

L iholiho, a 22 year-old son of Kamehameha, was named successor after his father died. Because of his youth, however, he was forced to share power with Kamehameha's widow, Ka'ahumanu, who was named *kuhina nui.* Soon after Liholiho's inauguration, Ka'ahumanu invited him to her house and revealed her intention to break the *kapu* that prevented women from eating forbidden foods and from dining together with men at the same table. She did both, knowing that the only way she could rule the kingdom was to elevate the position of women. She was reluctantly joined in her defiance of the Hawaiian gods by the Queen Mother, Keopuolani.

News of this action of the two women spread quickly throughout the kingdom. Others followed their example and soon the nation was in turmoil. Liholiho's

advisors sought punishment for Ka'ahumanu but her influence spread quickly throughout the Islands. During these agonizing days it was largely the administrative abilities of Prime Minister Kelanimoko and royal counselor John Young that kept the government from falling apart.

The young king had no choice but to give in and eat with the women himself. From that moment forward the old Hawaiian religious system was doomed. The breaking of the eating *kapu* led also to the public destruction of god-images and temples. A few months later, in March of 1820, the brig *Thaddeus* arrived at the Big Island with the pioneer company of New England missionaries. It didn't take long for Christianity to find a ready-made path into the hearts of the Hawaiian people.

Liholiho (Kamehameha II) never had a chance to become a strong leader. In 1824 he and Queen

Kamamalu, traveled to England in order to find out how this monarchy ruled its people. Unfortunately, both died of the measles in London. Kauikeaouli, a younger brother of Liholiho, became Kamehameha III at the age of 10.

During his youth, Ka'ahumanu was appointed to serve with him as regent. Kamehameha III became the kingdom's sole leader in 1833 and his rule lasted until 1854 when he died at the age of 41. His reign was the longest of the seven Hawaiian monarchs.

In 1847 John Parker received from Kamehameha III a two-acre home site near Waimea. An additional 640 acres was given to Parker's wife, Kipikane, in recognition of her royal ancestry. This was the beginning of Parker Ranch, gradually expanded by six generations of the family and today sprawling across

Isle keikis are usually a mixture of the races that have immigrated to Hawai'i. Hawai'i's kupuna (elderly) give information to young people on quilting, dancing, chanting, and other arts that might be lost without their sharing.

101

Our friends and we have often roamed
The trails of Mauna Kea
And in the evening we'd come home
And see her standing there

The moon moves around her
when she sleeps
The clouds stand beside her
when she weeps
And I could be forgotten And a thousand
miles away And still I would recall,
The Beauty of Mauna Kea

Down to any land you go,
She will be with you If you love her
as I do, Mauna Kea

Now we live in the city and we see
different things
In the night when I'm alone
She is in my dreams

The wind spins around her when she wakes
The sun spreads it's warmth across her face
And we could be forgotten And a thousand
miles away And still I would recall,
The Beauty of Mauna Kea

The Beauty Of Mauna Kea

Keola Beamer

250,000 acres of the Waimea countryside. The first cowboys here were imported Spanish and Mexican range riders who taught the local Hawaiians how to ride horses and herd the cattle. The Hawaiian word for cowboy is *paniolo,* the local pronunciation of *Espanol.*

The Parker Ranch could only fit comfortably on an island the size of Hawai'i. It is the largest of the Hawaiian Islands and gives the entire chain its name. With an area of 4,035 square miles the "Big Island" is twice the size of all the other islands combined. It is also a young island in terms of geology. Few coral reefs have built up yet and wide sand beaches are relatively scarce.

Volcanoes, of course, dominate the Big Island landscape and have provided a source of artistic inspiration since ancient times. Two of the five, Mauna Loa and Kilauea, are still active and a third, Mauna Kea, is the highest summit in the state at 13,796 feet. Several astronomical observatories are located on the summit where the thin, clear air makes for excellent star gazing. It is fairly cold at this height and during the winter months Mauna Kea's peaks are blanketed with snow. Skiing is popular along its long, gently-curving slopes.

Kailua, the final residence of Kamehameha the Great, is south from Waimea along the Queen Ka'ahumanu Highway. The town is often called Kailua-Kona to avoid confusion with the community of Kailua on O'ahu. Today this is the Big Island's major resort center. It is an attractive coastal area clustered around Ali'i Drive, a five-mile long avenue of hotels, restaurants, bars, and tourist shops. At the south end is the Keauhou Resort and hotel, at the north end, Kailua Village and the King Kamehameha Hotel. Among the other large hotels in Kailua are the Kona Surf, Kona Hilton, and the Kona Lagoon. Between Waimea and Kailua are located some of the Big Island's finest resort hotels, the Mauna Kea Beach Hotel, the Mauna Lani Bay Hotel, the Sheraton Royal Waikoloa, and the Kona Village. The Naniloa Surf and the Hilo Hawaiian are but two popular hotels in Hilo. The Volcano House, run by Sheraton, is perched on the edge of Kilauea Crater in Hawaii Volcanoes National Park.

The King Kamehameha Hotel was built along Kamakahonu Bay and Cove, on the spot where Kamehameha had his personal compound of grass houses. Inside the lobby is a large mural by Herb Kawainui Kane that Roland Cazimero used as one of his visual sources for the *Warrior* album. The

Above: the Kona Surf resort, one of several that attracts visitors
to the Big Island's sunny west coast. At left: snow-capped Mauna Kea
—the highest summit in the state (13,796 feet)—
and Mauna Loa beyond.

beautiful painting depicts Kamehameha, dressed in a simple wrap of *kapa,* talking on the beach with his son, Liholiho. At the left sits his favorite wife. Ka'ahumanu.

Near the hotel is located the restored Ahu'ena *heiau* and the mortuary platform where the bones of Kamehameha the Great were prepared for burial. An "oracle tower" also rests on the stone platform. Just past the pier is the Victorian-era Hulihe'e Palace, a summer home for the royal family from its construction in 1838 to 1916. Before the seawall was built on the oceanside of the property canoes could be dragged ashore. The two-story palace is now a museum operated by the Daughters of Hawaii. Next door is

Moku'aikaua Congregational Chruch, the first Christian church in the Islands. The original building was destroyed by fire and the present building, of coral, lava, and 'ohi'a lehua wood, dates from 1837.

Three other important historical sites linked with the life and times of Kamehameha the Great are found outside of Kailua-Kona. These are Kealakekua Bay, Pu'uhonua-o-Honaunau (Place of Refuge), and the Pu'u Kohola *heiau.*

Kealakekua Bay was where Captain Cook and four of his marines were killed the morning of February 14, 1779. Cook was killed as he attempted to take King Kalanioupu'u (the island's high chief and Kamehameha's uncle) hostage against the return of a stolen boat. He did not realize that he was going up against the king's personal guards who were ready at any time to give up their lives in their duty. When Cook fired his musket, and ordered the marines to fire, the bodyguards charged instead of fleeing. Cook is believed to have been hit behind with a club and then stabbed to death with several daggers. Kamehameha, who participated in the charge, was awarded Cook's hair as a relic of an important, sacred chief.

Lord Byron, captain of the *HMS Blonde,* erected the first monument to Captain Cook at Kealakekua Bay in 1825. His ship was returning the

Mauna Kea Beach Hotel, a luxury resort on the Kona coast.

bodies of King Kamehameha II and Queen Kamamalu who had died while visiting London. The present concrete obelisk dates from 1877 and is built upon land deeded that year to the British Government by Princess Likelike, a sister of King Kalakaua. A nearby commemorative plaque, dedicated in 1928 and now submerged because the shoreline has been subsiding, marks the approximate spot where Cook stumbled his way into immortality.

A dozen miles south of Kailua is the ancient sanctuary of Pu'uhonua-o-Honaunau. Lawbreakers and enemy warriors sought asylum within its walls and were protected by its priests. Each of the Hawaiian Islands had at least one such refuge. The Big Island had six, one for each of its major districts, but the most famous was Honaunau. Located on a six-acre shelf of black lava extending into Honaunau Bay, the refuge is bounded on two sides by the ocean and on the other two sides by a stone wall that is 10 feet wide and 17 feet wide. It is believed to have been built around 1550. Wooden *ki'i* images guard the reconstructed temple, Hale-o-Keawe. The temple once housed the bones of Chief Keawe, a one-time ruler of the Kona areas and an ancestor of Kamehameha the Great.

One legend tells of the time Kamehameha and his wife, Ka'ahumanu, got into a violent lover's quarrel while living in Kailua. She fled for safety to Honaunau and hid near a large rock. Her dog, which followed her trail, was recognized by some of the king's followers and Kamehameha was notified where his wife was hiding. He went to the refuge and they mended their disagreement, living happily ever after. The Ka'ahumanu Stone remains in the sanctuary today. The Pu'uhonua-o-Honaunau National Historical Park was established in 1961 and covers 180 acres.

North from Kailua-Kona, and just a few miles from Waimea, is the *heiau* of Pu'u Kohola. The original *heiau* like the large wall at Honaunau was built overlooking Kawaihae Bay around 1550. It was rebuilt in 1791 by Kamehameha the Great to honor his war god, Ku-ka'ili-moku. A *kahuna* from Kaua'i instructed Kamehameha to build the temple if he wanted to fulfill his dream of conquering all the Hawaiian Islands. The completed *heiau,* measuring 224 by 100 feet, is built of waterworn rocks set without mortar. Grass houses and wooden images of the ancient gods once sat on the platform. Pu'u Kohola means "Hill of the Whale" and, when viewed from the beach below, does resemble the hump of a giant whale.

Kamehameha dedicated the *heiau* by inviting a cousin, the enemy chief, Keoua Ku'ahu'ula, to the ceremony. Tragedy struck, however, as soon as Keoua stepped ashore. Ke'eaumoku, a temperamental chief, threw a spear and set off a skirmish. Keoua was killed before Kamehameha could stop the fighting. Keoua's body was then sacrificed to the gods. Today Pu'u Kohola is a National Historic Site managed by the National Park Service. Also located on the property is the house site of John Young, Kamehameha's trusted *ha'ole* or foreign adviser. He served as governor of the Big Island from 1802 to 1812 and then retired, living here until his death in 1835 at the age of 90.

On the northern coast of the Big Island is Waipi'o Valley, a spectacular slash in the rugged windward side of the Kohala Mountains. The stream through the center is fed by the twin Hi'ilawe waterfalls, the highest in Hawai'i, which drop over the 1,000-foot cliffs. Some myths say that first settlers to reach the island of Hawai'i landed at Waipi'o Valley and that the valley was home for the ancestors of Kamehameha. Artist-historian Herb Kawainui Kane, whose early childhood was spent in Waipi'o, used the beautiful valley as the landing place for the fictional canoe voyagers in his book, *Voyage: The Discovery of Hawaii.*

In 1791, soon after completing Pu'u Kohola *heiau,* Kamehameha fought an important naval battle off the shores of Waipi'o. The attackers were allies of the slain chief, Keoua. Kamehameha's war canoe fleet was led by the *Fair American,* a captured 54-foot schooner with artillery commanded by John Young and Isaac Davis. Kamehameha proved victorious although there were heavy casualties on both sides.

Once there were thousands of Hawaiians living in Waipi'o. But the labor demands of World War II, the increased importation of Mainland rice, and the

The Hi'ilawe Falls in Waipi'o Valley. Once home for thousands of Hawaiians, the valley now supports a dozen or so taro farmers.

We belong in the land of the Pueo
Yes, everyday me and Tara
We would watch it dance across
the land
From the mountain slopes it glided
to the Kona Coast
Then led up to Waimea

Pueo, The Pueo

Then Tara B woke me up and said
Where did it go
It went Home
Please sing for Tara The Pueo and Me
Forever free

Pueo, The Pueo

Pueo, Tara And Me

Noland Conjugacion

Yes, Mother I say the Pueo
Everyday we watch it spread
its wings so free
As it floated into the sunset
I thought of my City home
Waiting for me

Pueo, The Pueo

Then Tara B woke me up and said
Where did it go
It went Home
Please sing for Tara The Pueo and Me

Pueo, The Pueo

Yes, Father I saw the Pueo
It reminded me of how it must have been long ago
To have lived in a village
forested by Sandalwood

Then Tara B woke me up and said
Where did it go
It went home
Please sing for Tara The Pueo and Me

Pueo, The Pueo

When the sun goes down in Kona (captured in this multi exposure photograph), you can watch for the "Green Flash"—an elusive phenomenon that happens just as the sun drops below the horizon and the sky turns green.

107

devastating 1946 tsunami, dwindled the population down to only few hundred. Today this isolated valley is a popular destination for backpackers and campers but less than a dozen full-time farmers remain.

Hilo, the largest city on the Big Island, has one of the major historical relics of the Kamehameha story. This is the Naha Stone, a 4,500 pound lava obelisk that lays in front of the Hawai'i County Library. According to legend, the large stone (four-sided and about 12 feet long) originally rested by the Wailuku River on Kaua'i. Centuries ago it was brought by outrigger canoe to the Big Island and placed in front of the Pinao *heiau.* Over the years the stone acquired special properties and it was prophecied that the young warrior who could overturn it would eventually be king of all Hawai'i. Kamehameha is thought to have accomplished this test of strength around 1775 in front of the island's assembled high chiefs.

For many years the Naha Stone lay forgotten in the back garden of a house in Hilo. In 1915 it was placed on the grounds of the old Hilo Library and in 1962 moved to the new county library. Beside it sits a smaller stone also from the Pinao *heiau.*

It is fascinating to note the similarities between the Hawaiian legend of the Naha Stone and the British legend of the young King Arthur who pulled the sword, Excalibur, from his stone. There used to be skeptics that said no man could turn a 4,500 pound stone. In 1973, however, a professional strongman from Missouri, Bill Bangert, conducted an interesting experiment. He duplicated the shape and weight of the Naha Stone in a Waimea concrete yard and then trucked it to Hilo.

Bangert was convinced that Kamehameha the Great could have moved the Naha Stone if he'd thought out the problem carefully. Bangert chose to wear a special shoulder and waist harness while lifting with his legs. He said that Kamehameha could have used a rope hung over his shoulders. In any case, Bangert managed to move his duplicate stone with relative ease.

Northwest of Waipi'o, in the town of Kapa'au, an eight-foot tall statue of Kamehameha stands in front of the Kohala Court House. The romantic figure was fashioned by Boston-based sculptor Thomas R. Gould in 1880 and cast in a Paris foundry. This is a twin of the more famous Kamehameha statue that's located in front of Ali'iolani Hale in downtown Honolulu.

Hiking is a popular sport and above Pololu Valley near Kohala, you must dodge the waterfall.

*Koʻiʻi ka lehua i ke anu
Kīpuʻupuʻu aʻo Waimea*

*Hanohano ia hale o ka manu
ulu e aʻo mealani*

*A he manu i pu lia i ka nuʻu
Ka ʻōʻō hae a ke kia manu*

*Welo lua e ka hulu nani i ka laʻi
I ke ani mālie hea ka moaʻe*

*Hoʻoipo i ka hoa o ka lehua
ʻAʻohe lua ke ʻike aku*

*Puana ke aliʻi hulu mamo
ʻO Kalanipō ʻoe e ō mai*

Ke Aliʻi Hulu Mamo

Helen Desha Beamer

*Ever so fresh is the lehua bloom in the chill
O the Kīpuʻupuʻu rain of Waimea*

*So prestigious is the home of the bird
Where the heavenly one flourishes*

*The flock of birds is trembling
In the nest on high
enraged is the ʻōʻō and the birdcatcher*

*Flutter again your
beautiful feathers in the calm
As the gentle breeze of the moaʻe
beckons quietly*

*My beloved companion is the lehua
Beyond compare*

*Tell the refrain of the mamo
feather cape of the aliʻi
You are Kalanipō, answer*

The sculptor posed Kamehameha the Great in a classical mold, complete with his left hand holding a spear and outstretched right arm. Some Hawaiians believe that Kamehameha is taunting his enemies and throwing up a challenge to meet them on the field of battle. At the installation of the statue in 1883, however, the official government explanation was that the gesture portrayed "the successful warrior inviting the people to accept the peace and order that he had secured." War and peace, peace and war. Once again it is Kamehameha's conflicting character that makes this first Hawaiian king, and the subject of Roland Cazimero's *Warrior* album, one of history's most fascinating heroes. ◼

Wooden kiʻi images stand guard at Puʻuhonua-o-Honaunau National Historical Park, a place of refuge for ancient Hawaiians.

109

Maui, The Valley Isle

When all is calm and nothing moves
When things go wrong
and nothing soothes
I feel so lonely deep inside
'Cause I've got Maui on my mind

From scenic points on distant shores
My sad eyes search the sky for you
I may have lost you once before
But I will lose you never more

Sloping Haleakalā
You burn a fire in my soul

Maui On My Mind
Kenneth Makuakane

Haleakalā
Someday I'll be with you again

When first your mountain's peak I saw
A happy feeling filled my soul
For many hours I sat and stared
And dreamt the dreams we both
had shared

I long to be with you my love
Upon your velvet mountainside
Wherever I may roam I pray
My heart will find you there some day

Over the past few years the Brothers Cazimero have made frequent nightclub and concert appearances on the island of Maui. One popular engagement, at the Sheraton-Maui in the Ka'anapali Beach Resort, was called "Maui, Moonlight, Magic," a phrase that neatly sums up their general feelings about the Valley Island.

"Maui *is* magic," Robert says. "The beaches are perfect and the mountains have the power to take your breath away. In whatever direction you look, from Hana to Lahaina, you'll find somebody's idea of paradise. But, of course, the island is not just beautiful. It has a fascinating history, especially during the whaling decades, and a wide variety of lifestyles geared both to work and pleasure."

The slower pace of Maui provides a welcome break from the flash of Waikiki. Their recordings of songs such as "Haleakala" and "Maui Waltz" are also favorites with audiences on the Valley Isle. Their 1983 album, *Proud Family,* begins with a medley, "Hana Chant/Pu'a Ana Ka Makani," and includes another Haleakala-inspired song, "Maui on My Mind." The Brothers also wrote a song themselves for the album, "Maui's Not the Same Anymore."

"In a broader sense," Roland explains, "this song is not just about Maui but about all those places in Hawai'i that have changed. We have nothing against

change for the better but often we don't realize how precious something is until it's gone. Slabs of cement take away not only our grass and trees but the very character of the Islands themselves."

When visiting or performing on Maui both Robert and Roland have their favorite island spots. Robert finds inspiration in isolated Hana, cozy Pa'ia or the scenic Upcountry. Roland, because of his strong interest in Hawai'i's earlier days, prefers to explore the legendary 'Iao Valley or the historic streets of sunny Lahaina.

At left: Haleakala National Park, home of Maui the demigod,
who lassoed the sun and held it in place until it agreed to lengthen the day.
Above: Front Street of Lahaina, once capital for the Hawaiian
Kingdom, then home for whalers and missionaries, and
now a popular tourist town.

One of the main reasons for Roland's fondness for Lahaina, of course, is its association with Kamehameha the Great. Hawai'i's first king lived here for a single year—1802—and afterwards this area, like Kailua on the Big Island, became a favorite hideaway for the *ali'i* or members of the noble class.

Lele is the earliest known name for the Lahaina district. In the old days the area was known for the large, shady breadfruit trees which provided shelter from the hot sun. The present name, Lahaina, is, in fact, usually translated as "cruel sun."

Prior to the coming of the European explorers, the entire district of Lahaina was a residence of the Maui chiefs. A number of famous battles were fought here, including a particularly fierce 1783 encounter between the forces of Peleioholani, a chief from O'ahu, and Alapa'inui, a chief from the Big Island.

The chiefs had taken different sides in a local dispute and soon found themselves facing each other on a Lahaina battlefield. When the fighting was over the winner really didn't matter. The land however was a clear-cut loser. By the time Captain George Vancouver arrived on the scene in 1793 he reported the village was in tatters and the countryside blackened by conflict. Human bones dating from this bloody period are still being unearthed today.

During the king's short residence in Lahaina the most striking building in town was the so-called "Brick Palace." It had been built between 1798 and 1802 by two ex-convicts from the British penal colony at Botany Bay, the Australian men had joined Kamehameha's army after the Battle of Nu'uanu on O'ahu. Kamehameha used the brick building, the first Western-styled structure in the Islands, for his headquarters.

The two-story house had two rooms on each front of Ali'iolani Hale in downtown Honolulu.

After Kamehameha moved his court to Honolulu the masonry building was used as a warehouse until it finally fell into ruin and was torn down. In front of the present-day Lahaina Library is a rectangular clearing that indicates the approximate position of the "Brick Palace."

By the time of Kamehameha's death in 1819, Lahaina had grown from a village encampment into a small dusty town stuck between the beach and the West Maui mountains a mile in from the sea. In addition to the brick building, now a warehouse, there were now dozens of grass houses lining the main road. One of the finest of these houses belonged to Princess Nahi'ena'ena, the only daughter of Kamehameha the Great. It was high-roofed and about 30 feet by 40 feet in size. A seawall separated it from the beach and her yard was planted with decorative trees and plants. Dry banana stalks lined the inside walls and woven mats covered the hard dirt floor.

A few months after Liholiho had assumed the throne as Kamehameha II, a French ship, the *Uranie,* arrived at Lahaina under the command of Captain Louis de Freycinet. The crew included a number of scientists who set up an observatory close to the warehouse and made a complete survey of the West Maui seaport. Their mapping was the earliest made of the island.

Above: Lahaina town in 1866, when sin and salvation competed for Hawai'i's hearts. At right: an aerial view of West Maui and Lahaina, with crops growing in the mountain valleys.

The year 1819 also marked the arrival of the first American whaleships to Hawai'i. During the reign of Kamehameha the Great sporadic trading vessels had stopped at Lahaina but the *Balena,* from New Bedford, and the *Equator,* from Nantucket, represented a more permanent economic gain for the town.

Lahaina got its first Protestant Christian missionaries in 1823 and they were welcomed to the island by Keopuolani, the highest born widow of Kamehameha the Great. An interesting description of Lahaina during this time was made by Rev. Charles S. Stewart, one of the new arrivals. In his diary he wrote that "the number of inhabitants is about 2,500. Their houses are generally not more than eight or ten feet long, six or eight broad, and from four to six high, having one small hole for a door, which cannot be entered but by creeping, and is the only opening for the admission of light and air. They make little use of these dwellings except to protect their food and clothing, and to sleep in during wet and cool weather and most generally eat, sleep, and live in the open air under the shade of a kou or breadfruit tree.

"The land begins to rise abruptly about three-fourths of a mile from the sea, and towers into lofty mountains, three rude elevations of which, immediately east of Lahaina, are judged to be 4,500 or 5,000 feet above the level of the ocean. From the first swell of rising ground, almost to the summits of these mountains, there is nothing to be seen but the most

drear sterility and sunburnt vegetation, intersected by gloomy ravines and frightful precipices."

While the missionaries may have found a sterile environment, foreign sailors found Lahaina an attractive place to kick up their heels. The climate was bearable, the chiefs friendly, and the women willing. Shops along Front Street catered to their every pleasure. Lahaina's anchorage was an open roadstead and the ships could approach in almost any wind and without the need for a local pilot.

Herman Melville, a novelist greatly admired by Roland Cazimero, was still in his 20s when he arrived in Lahaina by whaleship in 1843. He spent a couple weeks here, sampling the seaport's pleasures and exploring the surrounding countryside. One of Melville's seafaring cousins, Pierre Malvill, died in Lahaina and is buried in the Seamen's Cemetery on Waine'e Street. Melville couldn't find work in Lahaina so he took a schooner to Honolulu where he found employment as a pin setter in a bowling alley and then as a store clerk. Three months later, when the warship *United States* docked at Honolulu he signed aboard as an ordinary seaman and spent another 14 months at sea before returning home to New England. Seven years later he would publish *Moby Dick,* the greatest of all whaling novels and one of the masterpieces of world literature.

When the whaling waters east of Japan were discovered an increasing number of New England whalers followed their prey into the Pacific. Since Japan was still closed to foreign vessels, Hawai'i became the principle forward base for provisioning and repair.

In response to the increase in foreign business, Kauikeouli (Kamehameha III) decided to move his court to Lahaina and the capital of the kingdom remained here until the mid 1850s. In the peak year of 1846, a total of 429 whaleships visited Lahaina.

Above: Lahaina and the red-roofed Pioneer Inn. To the hotel's right is the largest and oldest banyan tree in Hawai'i, planted in 1873.

The decline of the Pacific Islands whale fishery began in the late 1850s with the discovery of petroleum. Kerosene eventually replaced whale oil in lamps and wax did the same for the whale spermaceti used in candles. During the American Civil War a large number of New England whaleships were destroyed in the fighting. Most of those that survived the war turned to fish the richer Arctic waters.

Lahaina, now designated a National Historic Landmark, still retains its nautical flavor. Today, however, the salty 18th century atmosphere is aimed at tourists instead of sailors. Hundreds of shops, bars, restaurants, and art galleries serve the thousands of visitors who pour into the town by bus, car, and bicycle each day.

Whaling is the commercial gimmick that keeps this trendy town alive and shaking. Take, for instance, the names of the businesses themselves. The Whale's Tale is a popular restaurant, the Super Whale sells clothes for children, and the Whaler's Realty office will find you a condominium for the summer. Over at The Whaler, a gift shop, the glass cases are full of scrimshaw, the delicate ivory artwork once carved by lonely sailors aboard the whaleships.

Outside of downtown Honolulu there is no place else in the Islands with such a wealth of historic spots to visit. One of these is Maui's unique Lahainaluna School, which is located two miles above Lahaina.

When classes started in 1831 it was not only the first secondary school in Hawai'i but also the first free public high school west of the Rocky Mountains. Lahainaluna was run by the Protestant missionaries and provided advanced training for native Hawaiian teachers. Most of the original students were adult married men and their instruction was given in the Hawaiian language.

On the campus of Lahainaluna, which continues today as the only public boarding school in Hawai'i, is the newly restored Hale Pa'i, or "House of Printing." The first Hawaiian language newspaper in the Islands, *Ka Lama Hawaii* (The Light of Hawaii), was printed on the school's second-hand Ramage press in 1834, the first Hawaiian dictionary in 1837, and the first Hawaiian history in 1843. Students were also taught how to make intaglio engravings on copper sheets that were bought from visiting ship's stores. The bottoms of the whaleships were covered with the copper sheets to protect their wooden hulls from worms and other marine organisms.

Down near the Lahaina waterfront spreads the largest banyan tree in the islands, now 60-feet tall and covering two-thirds of an acre in front of the courthouse. It was planted in 1873 to commemorate the fiftieth anniversary of the first Christian mission in Lahaina. Nearby is the red-roofed Pioneer Inn, a wooden hotel built in 1901. It has been used as a setting for a number of Hollywood films.

Lahaina's small boat harbor is crowded with fishing and pleasure craft. Many are used in the tourist industry or are individually available for hire. The harbor's centerpiece is the 93-foot Carthaginian II (#1 sank), a 1920s schooner that's been restored to resemble the type of whaling ships that once called at Lahaina. Below deck there is an exhibit of photographs and miniature models depicting the whaling era. Also shown are two documentary films, one on the life of the adult humpback whales which spawn off Maui each winter; the other about the birth of a baby whale.

An estimated 250 to 600 humpback whales come to breed in Hawaiian waters each winter. Whale watching from the shoreline is a popular pastime.

At left: the all-wood Pioneer Inn was built in 1901 and remains a Lahaina favorite for locals and visitors. Across the street is the Carthaginian II (at right), a steel-hulled square rigger that houses a whaling exhibit.

From historic Lahaina it is only a short drive to Ka'anapali, a three-mile long stretch of sandy beachfront that was once the ancient homesite for several villages of Hawaiian fishermen. Today this slice of Maui's leeward coast has been developed by American Factors (Amfac) into the Ka'anapali Beach Resort. The most prominent geological feature in the area is Pu'u Keka'a, the remains of a volcanic cinder cone at the water's edge. Pu'u Keka'a, commonly called Black Point, was sacred to the old Hawaiians who built a *heiau* on its summit.

The Royal Lahaina, dating from 1963, was the first resort hotel opened for business. It's since been joined by the Sheraton-Maui, the Ka'anapali Beach, the Maui Surf, the Maui Marriott, and the Hyatt Regency Maui. The Ka'anapali Beach Resort's shopping center is the Whalers Village which, in addition to its shops, features an outdoor whaling museum.

A few miles north of Ka'anapali is the smaller resort area of Kapalua, developed by the Maui Land & Pineapple Co. The jagged coastline embraces quiet bays and short stretches of white sand beach. Its shoreline is dotted with 18th century pine trees which were planted by British sailors as a future supply of masts for their ships. The resort includes the Kapalua Bay Hotel, two golf courses, and a few hundred low-rise condominiums.

Maui's third seaside residential resort area is Wailea, situated along East Maui's leeward shore. It is a joint development of Alexander & Baldwin and The Northwestern Mutual Life Insurance Company. These two large companies have transformed 1,500 acres of arid and rocky land into a luxurious self-contained community. Located here are Stouffer's, Wailea Beach Resort and the Hotel Inter-Continental Maui. Nearby, in a sheltered ravine, is the Wailea Tennis Club, one of Hawai'i's finest tennis centers.

Above: the Ka'anapali coast was mostly sugar cane in the 1960s.
It became one of the state's popular resort areas constructed along a
three-mile beach. Following pages: the trees rise high
at Wai'anapanapa State Park in Hana, a peaceful agricultural
town and hideaway home for millionaires.

Maui's Not The Same Any More

Time's gone by
The days they come and go
Living here
Isn't quite as slow
Room to breathe
Open spaces, country stores
But Maui's not the same any more

I wish I could leave
More of me behind
The part of me
That makes this island mine
Stories, places, friends
at my front door
But Maui's not the same any more

Robert Cazimero
Roland Cazimero

We love these islands and all that they share
Warmth, love, happiness and time to care
Untold tales of times long pass
Of kings and queens Of this and that
Trust in us and you'll know no cares
Throw back your arms and take to the air

These hidden valleys
have a story to tell us
Of secret wishes magic people and kingdoms
Gaze into the sea to know what life brings you
Power, majesty and strength
can you see through
The barrier of years and the passing of ages
Know the meaning of what was is now
Ours to give and ours to show

These
Hidden
Valleys

Robert Cazimero
Roland Cazimero

Give from the heart for the body and soul
Trust in us and you'll know no cares
Throw back your arms and take to the air

Fly until you know no boundaries
Laugh a melody of joy and illusion
Grab a sunbeam shining into the canyon
Coloring the mountains over and over
If you ever, if you ever,
ever want to believe in
The mysteries of glory that we speak of to you.
Look into the mirror of this life as we know it
Come my friends we'll take
the best and we'll share it
Trust in us and you'll know no cares
Throw back your arms and take to the air!

Above: 'Iao Valley State Park was once a sacred burial site for Hawaiian
royalty. Today it's a state park, where visitors go see the 'Iao Needle
(upper right photo), a 2,250-foot cinder cone. At right: illustration of a protea,
an exotic South African flower grown on and exported from Maui.

Robert and Roland Cazimero may not have written their song, "These Hidden Valleys," about a specific place but for many listeners on Maui it reminds them of their visits to 'Iao Valley, the mysterious cloud-covered canyon that penetrates the West Maui Mountains. Its most spectacular landmark is 'Iao Needle, a sharply pointed pinnacle that rises 1,200 above the valley floor.

Ancient tradition says that 'Iao Valley was the burial place for Maui's royalty. Their bones were laid to rest in caves far into the gorge. In 1790 the valley was the site of a battle between Maui's king, Kalanikupule, and Kamehameha the Great. The younger Kamehameha won the battle using the superior cannon fire provided by his British comrades, Isaac Davis and John Young. Kalanikupule escaped over the mountains to the west but both armies suffered heavy casualties. The dead bodies so clogged 'Iao Stream that the area is still called Kepaniwai, the "damming of the waters."

Kepaniwai Park and its Heritage Gardens are also located in 'Iao Valley. The park takes its name from the famous battle but there is no trace of past violence in its peaceful setting. It was conceived as a memorial to the various ethnic groups which have settled on Maui. The house is used as a symbol of these peoples and the park includes several representative dwellings, including a Hawaiian stone-walled grass house. 'Iao Stream is now dammed to provide visitors with a pool for swimming or wading.

Upcountry Maui is a cool, green carpeted landscape on the western slopes of Haleakala. This district is full of cowboys and cattle, ranchers, farmers and fertile fields of flowers, fruits, and vegetables. Its primary towns are Pukalani and Makawao, the later well-known for its annual July 4th Makawao Rodeo. The first rodeo was held in 1955 and today it attracts over 10,000 spectators who cheer their favorites in the calf roping, bull riding, and bronco busting competition.

Robert and Roland Cazimero never pass through Makawao without stopping at the Komoda Store and Bakery to buy fresh bread and cakes for friends and family. Once or twice in the past they've also passed out samples to their concert audiences. "Komoda is my favorite bakery in the Islands," Robert says with a smile. "I can resist almost anything except their cream puffs."

Kula is not officially a town but rather an area famous for its large cabbages, sweet onions, colorful carnations, and rainbow-hued proteas. The protea is really in a class by itself. There are over a thousand species of this flower, named after the Greek sea god Proteus. Like Proteus, a god who could assume many forms, the protea grows into a wide variety of shapes, sizes, textures, and colors. Proteas were introduced to Hawai'i in the 1960s from their native Australia and South Africa. The king protea, with its spectacular 9- to 12-inch blooms, is South Africa's national flower.

Kilakila ʻo Haleakalā
Kuahiwi nani o Maui
Haʻaheo wale ʻoe Hawaiʻi
Hanohano ʻo Maui nō ka ʻoi

Kau ana lā kau ana
Kau ana ko ia ala maka
ʻO ua lio holopeki
Mea ʻole ko ia ala holo

Majestic is Haleakalā
Beautiful mountain of Maui
Hawaiʻi is proud
Grand Maui, the best

Riding along, Riding
Her eyes glancing over
Oh that pacing pony
Her moving along doesn't bother me

Kilakila ʻO Haleakalā
Traditional

*A*short drive out of Kula is the 'Ulupalakua Ranch, the legendary "Rose Ranch" that Captain James Makee, a former Massachusetts whaler, built in the 1850s on the lee side of Haleakala. Makee's vast plantation, which had its own steam mill, was turned over principally to sugar cane. Enclosed by over 40 miles of stone walls and wire fence 'Ulupalakua Ranch was also planted with an estimated 150,000 evergreen and eucalyptus trees. Makee's wife, Catherine, grew flowers in her own garden. Her favorites were the roses which the Hawaiians collectively called lokelani. Together they became Maui's official flower.

Makee knew five of Hawai'i's kings but was closest to King Kalakaua and Queen Kapi'olani. In 1874, shortly after the king's election to the throne, the monarch decided to come to Maui for a rest. After being welcomed at the Makena landing the royal party was escorted to 'Ulupalakua Ranch by 80 torch bearers. The king and queen stayed for three days in a roomy cottage which still stands on the grounds.

Today the 22,000-acre 'Ulupalakua Ranch is operated by Pardee Erdman, who bought the ranch in 1963. About 20 acres are leased to Emil Tedeschi, a young Italian winemaker from the Napa Valley in California. Erdman and Tedeschi began their partnership by collecting 120 varieties of grapes that could survive in the ranch's climate. These grapes were planted on seven acres above the Wailea Resort, on the slopes of Haleakala. By 1977 a grape had been chosen. This was the Carnelian, a strong hybrid of the Cabernet Sauvignon, Grenache and Carignane grapes. At the present time the vineyard produces a Hawaiian Champagne and Maui Blanc, a unique wine made from pineapple juice. It will take several more years before Erdman and Tedeschi will be able to produce their ultimate goal, a premium red table wine.

The town of Pa'ia, at the intersection of Baldwin Avenue and the Hana Highway, is Robert Cazimero's favorite place to prowl on Maui. He enjoys walking from store to store shopping for bargains that he can take back to O'ahu for family and friends. During the 1920s and 1930s when the Pa'ia Sugar Mill was in full operation, the town supported dozens of shops which dealt in everything from dry goods to groceries to clothing. These small stores extended credit to mill workers who were paid once a month.

A fire in 1930 destroyed 15 businesses in lower Pa'ia, along the Hana Highway. The buildings that were rebuilt, with their wooden false fronts and balconies, are those that can be seen in the town today. Since there have been no modern improvements since this 1930s rebuilding, Pa'ia remains the most authentic plantation town on Maui.

*C*ontrasted to the hustle and frenzy of Lahaina the town of Hana, on the opposite side of the island, seems practically asleep. Kamehameha the Great was apparently conceived here about 1758 and, although born on the Big Island, he returned to beautiful Hana a quarter-century later as a muscular young warrior.

It was at Hana that Kamehameha's enemies took to calling him Pai'ea (hard-shelled crab) because of his fierce abilities as a fighter. He also fell in love with the 17-year old High Chiefess Ka'ahumanu, who subsequently became the most favored of his wives. Ka'ahumanu had been born in a cave at the base of Ka'uiki Head, a hill guarding the southern end of Hana Bay.

Preceding pages: the red hills of Haleakala National Park.
The crater rises 10,023 feet above the sea, making it the best and coldest
place on the Valley Isle to watch a sunrise. At left: the West Maui mountains
and an angry sea. Above: the mountains behind Lahaina.

Maui Waltz
Bob Nelson

I hear the Maui waltz
It brings back memories
I hear the Maui waltz
And you are haunting me
The night you told me that
You loved me so
But no one told me
That when the dance was through
I'd be losing you

I hear the Maui waltz
My arms are empty now
I hear the Maui waltz
It doesn't hurt some how
You're here with me
When the music starts to play
Play on,
play on Maui waltz
Play on, play on Maui Waltz

In ancient days, rainbows ('anuenue) symbolized the presence of chiefs and gods. Today, some say its spectrum represents the different races that live together in Hawai'i.

Because of its isolation, Hana grew slower than other parts of the island. The New England missionaries, who came to Hawai'i in 1820, took another two decades to reach Hana and in 1846. While Lahaina was overflowing with foreign sailors, the farmers in Hana were putting their economic faith in sugar cane.

Hana's first hotel was built in 1900, a year before the Pioneer Inn at Lahaina. The Hasegawa General Store was opened in 1912 but it was not until 1927 that the road was finished linking the town with Pa'ia. Today the winding stretch of Hana Highway between Pa'ia and Hana is considered one of the most scenic drives in the Pacific. Fragrant flowers grow everywhere and giant trees hang over the road like a tropical canopy. Waterfalls reveal themselves at nearly every turn. Speed is of little concern on the road to Hana because cars and buses must cross 56 one-lane bridges and negotiate over 600 curves.

Paul I. Fagan, a wealthy San Francisco-based businessman, came to Hana soon after the road was built. He bought a sugar plantation in 1930 and operated it at a profit through World War II. By the time the war ended, he had 15,000 acres to worry about as sugar sales began to drop. In 1945 workers cut the last sugar crop and planted grazing grass for cattle. Fagan shipped hundreds of Herefords from a successful ranch he owned in Moloka'i and soon the new Hana Ranch was thriving, too.

In an effort to encourage tourist development, Fagan built his own hotel, now the Hotel Hana-Maui, in 1946. His first guests were members of the famed San Francisco Seals of the Pacific Coast League. The owner of the now-defunct team was Fagan himself and one of his star players was a young power-hitter by the name of Joe DiMaggio. During the 1950s, Fagan built the Hana Ranch Center and new buildings to house a U.S. Post Office, a branch of the Bank of Hawaii and a barber shop. He constructed an activity center down at the harbor and donated it to the community. Fagan died in 1960 and was buried in San Francisco. A giant lava stone cross was later erected, in his memory, on Lyon's Hill, a rolling mound of grazing grass above the Hotel Hana-Maui.

Beyond Hana the road continues winding around the eastern end of Maui toward the Seven Pools area and Kipahulu. The pools, a popular stopping point for sightseers as well as residents, are fed by streams flowing out of the 'Ohe'o Gulch. In 1969 the seven pools and all of Kipahulu Valley became a part of Haleakala National Park.

Scenes of Hana (left to right): paniolo stop at Hasegawa General Store; a gazebo for horses and cattle at the Hotel Hana-Maui; waterfalls splash beside the roads to Hana; the seven pools of Kipahulu; on the road to Hana; and "Hana Ranch," a painting by Robert Lee Eskridge in the Hotel Hana-Maui.

In the late 1960s the pioneer aviator and environmentalist Charles Lindbergh purchased five acres of oceanfront land in Kipahulu. He and his wife, writer Anne Morrow Lindbergh, built a cottage here close enough to hear the pounding surf. Lindbergh died in 1974. His body was put into a rough hewn casket of eucalyptus wood and buried in the cemetery of the Ho'omau Congregational Church in Kipahulu. The simple Hawaiian-style grave, visited by hundreds of travelers each year, is covered with smooth native stones. A granite block is cut with words Lindbergh chose from the 39th Psalm: ". . . if I take the wings of the morning and dwell in the uttermost parts of the sea . . ."

A number of Brothers Cazimero songs celebrate the legends and beauty of majestic Haleakala, a large dormant volcano that has overshadowed the lives of people on Maui from the time of the first Polynesian settlers. Haleakala, the "House of the Sun," was named by the ancient Hawaiians because of the volcano's association with their demigod folk hero, Maui, for whom the entire island is named.

Centuries ago, when gods still walked upon the earth with men, the days were extremely short. Nobody had time to finish their chores. Even Maui's mother, Hina, had trouble drying her *kapa* (tapa) because the sun passed overhead too fast. In the morning it would leap over the mountains in the east and race across the sky to the west. Then, just as quickly, it would plunge into the western sea.

Ha'aheo 'o Hāna eō
Ku'u pu'u Ka'uiki e ho'i
Ku'u lei lokelani he pua onaona
He ali'i eō
Ka'ahumanu no Kamehameha
He inoa no Ka'ahumanu nō Kamehameha

Ha'aheo 'o Hāna lā 'eā 'eā lā
Ku'u pu'u Ka'uiki he u'i lā
Ku'u lei lokelani la he pua onaona lā
He ali'i lā eō
Ka'ahumanu lā Kamehameha
He inoa no Ka'ahumanu no Kamehameha

Hana Chant
Traditional

Proud Hana calls
My Mountain Kauiki
My Rose Lei of Heaven,
so fragrant

Proud Hana Calling

A Chief Calls
Ka'ahumanu of Kamehameha
In the name of Ka'ahumanu
of Kamehameha

Pua Ana Ka Makani

E pua ana ka makani lā 'eā
I nā hala o Malelewa'a

Kui 'ia e Lūpua la 'ea
Hālua 'ala i ke poli

Maika'i pa pua hinano lā 'eā
Nā pua i Waialoha

'Upu a'e ana ka mana'o lā 'eā
E 'ike iā Halali'i

He ali'i na'u ke aloha lā 'eā
A he lei no ku'u lani

Ha'ina mai ka puana lā 'eā
No Ka'ahumanu he inoa

Above: the Hana coast; Charles Lindbergh's grave at the Ho'omau Congregational Church in Kipahulu; and the stone cross above Hana is dedicated to Paul Fagan, founder of Hana Ranch. Following pages: sunrise at Haleakala.

aui, a trickster who delighted in pitting his wit and superhuman strength against the gods, solved the problem by climbing to the summit of Haleakala and throwing a net over the sun as it passed by in the morning. He refused to let the sun continue until it promised to slow down its travels.

Haleakala, dormant since 1790, is massive in size. The crater is over seven miles long and over 21 miles in circumference. Red Hill, its highest point, is 10,023 feet above sea level. The volcano is particularly famous for a unique plant, the silversword. A member of the sunflower family, it has a round cluster of dagger-like silver-green leaves. The silversword blooms only once in its lifetime as it sends up a long stalk covered with yellow and reddish-purple blossoms. After flowering the plant simply dies.

Most of Haleakala's colorful cinder cones look like anthills when viewed from the summit but the largest is over 1,000 feet tall. From above can also be viewed Maui's neighbor islands of Hawai'i, Moloka'i, Lana'i, and small uninhabited Kaho'olawe. O'ahu, 130 miles away, is visible on very clear days.

The journalist Mark Twain, not yet the famous novelist, visited Maui in 1866 at the age of 31. He was then on assignment for the *Sacramento Union* newspaper in California. During his visit to Maui, Twain rode a horse up to the chilly summit of Haleakala and stood where the demigod had once snared the sun. He described the experience of looking down into the crater in *Roughing It*, a semi-autobiographical travel book published in 1872. "I felt like the Last Man," Twain wrote, "neglected of the judgment, and left pinnacled in mid-heaven, a forgotten relic of a vanished world . . . It was the sublimest spectacle I ever witnessed, and I think the memory of it will remain with me always."

The House of the Sun, as evidenced by the many songs that have been written about it, clearly has the ability to inspire and enchant. Roland Cazimero says that he seldom finds a song about Maui that does not mention the crater. "Robert and I first visited Haleakala while we were in elementary school," he says. "I can remember looking down from the edge of the crater and imagining that I was on the moon. Whenever I sing about Haleakala today I can close my eyes and be transported to another world. Haleakala is one of those few places in Hawai'i, perhaps in all the world, that is truly impossible to forget." ■

Haleakalā

Jay Kauka

Hele aʻe ana i Haleakalā
I luna o ka wēkiu
I laila e pā mai ka makani

We are going to Haleakalā
Up to the summit
The wind strikes us there

Holo aku ana i Kula
Aia lā e pōʻai ʻia
E ke ʻala anuhea o ka noe

Riding up to Kula
Where we are surrounded
By the cool fragrance of the mist

Piʻi ana ma ke alahele
I ka uka ʻiu ʻiu

Riding higher Up the slopes
Feeling love for the land,
Maui is the finest

Aloha ʻāina ʻo Maui nō ka ʻoi

Hāʻina mai ka puana
No ka holo aloha ʻana mai
I Haleakalā e kū kilakila nei

The story's told
About our memorable trip
To Haleakalā standing so majestically

Kaua'i, The Garden Isle

'O Hanalei e ku'u aloha
Ka nani a'o Hanalei
Ho'ohihi ana 'oe i ku'u aloha lā
Ē ē ē ē Hanalei nō e ka 'oi

Ho'ohihi ho'i ko'u mana'o
Ka nani a'o Hanalei
E Pakika e pāhe'e Ē ē ē
Ka limu o Manu'akepa

Hanohano Hanalei
I ka ua nui 'ana lā
A me ka wailele a'o Molokama Ē ē ē ē
Ka makani 'Āpa'apa'a

Hā'ina mai ka puana
Ka nani a'o Hanalei
Ho'ohihi ana 'oe i ku'u aloha lā Ē ē ē
Hanalei nō e ka 'oi

Nani Hanalei
Kai Davis

Hanalei is my love
And the beauty of Hanalei
How I admire the love you give
Hanalei is the best

My mind is attracted
To the beauty of Hanalei
And the smooth, slippery
Seaweed of Manu'akepa

Honored is Hanalei
For her heavy Rain
And the waterfall of Molokama
And the 'Āpa'apa'a wind

The story is told
Of the beauty of Hanalei
How I admire the love you give
Hanalei is the best

Robert and Roland Cazimero have fond memories of Kaua'i, an island celebrated for its scenery and lushness of vegetation. They have recorded a number of fine songs about the Garden Island and regularly perform several more during their concert and nightclub appearances.

Just as a majority of songs about Maui seem to mention Haleakala, a large number of Kaua'i songs refer to the north shore town of Hanalei. The Brothers Cazimero picked two of their favorites, "Nani Hanalei" and "The Breeze and I" to include on their 1978 album, *Ho'ala*.

Hanalei, one of the most beautiful places in Hawai'i, actually provided the backdrop for the entire album. The recording was done over nine days in a beach house that Jon de Mello rented from tennis star Billie Jean King. In addition to the instruments, all of the sound equipment was shipped over to Kaua'i from Honolulu. The only item de Mello borrowed locally was a piano from the Kauai Resort Hotel in Kapa'a.

"In the beginning," says Roland, "we had talked of recording the album in Carmel. The idea was to get away from Hawai'i and lay low in California while we were recording. After a couple of delays Jon flew over to Kaua'i and found that King's house was empty and available. I don't think we could have found anything better."

Robert and Roland picked out and rehearsed most of the songs for *Ho'ala* in Honolulu. One notable exception was "Na Menehune Ekolu," written by Keli'i Tau'a and Friday Fellez. The final lyrics weren't completed until a day before the Brothers left for Kaua'i. "That song almost didn't make it in time," Roland says. "We started to figure out our phrasing on the way to the airport."

The high-beamed house in Hanalei matched everybody's expectations. It had four bedrooms, a

Above: rain forest ferns grow thick on the slopes of Wai'ale'ale, the highest mountain on Kaua'i and the wettest spot in the Hawaiian Islands, shown at left.

spacious living room, an upstairs room that could be used for recording, and a large kitchen. Outside King had naturally built a tennis court. The biggest problem, according to Jon de Mello, was noise. The equipment was quite sensitive. It picked up everything from the sound of the surf outside to the hum of small fans and the kitchen refrigerator.

During the actual recording sessions all the windows were closed and the fans turned off. This made the room uncomfortable after a few minutes. By the end of each song Robert and Roland were drenched with sweat. Everybody rushed to open the windows again.

"The day's recording usually started at late morning," de Mello says, "and we'd go until the middle of the afternoon. Sometimes we'd record at night, too, but usually we'd just rehearse for the next day's session or overdub the background singing of the choir. The upstairs room was where the Brothers recorded but we found out that the kitchen was the best place for the choir. This was a smaller room with a tile floor. It gave us a tight, lively sound."

Robert compares the experience in Hanalei to a summer camp. "Everybody lived together, worked together and ate together. We played tennis in the morning and went swimming in the late afternoon. We got the album recorded but we also had a lot of fun doing it."

Ho'ala is the perfect musical introduction to the Valley Isle. Its opening song, "Nani Hanalei," pays tribute to the natural beauties of the island while the last, an instrumental entitled "Pierre's Song" was inspired by a helicopter flight over the dramatic Na Pali Coast.

This "bird's-eye-view" by helicopter can serve as a reminder that Kaua'i, with its fertile heartland of undisturbed wilderness, is one of the last remaining habitats for Hawai'i's endangered forest birds. The rarest of these is the beautiful Kaua'i *'o'o,* the sole surviving species of four related birds that once flew free across the Hawaiian Islands.

During ancient times the *'o'o* were collected for the bright tufts of yellow feathers under each wing. The feathers of the *'o'o* and other forest birds (such as the *'apapane, 'i'iwi* and *mamo*) were especially prized by the Hawaiians in the making of *'ahu'ula,* or feather cloaks, and *mahiole,* or helmets, for the highest ranking chiefs. The largest cloaks required some half-million feathers, representing 80,000 to 90,000 birds. Most birds were not killed for their feathers. They were caught during the moulting season, plucked for their

Above: "Kaua'i o'o," a painting by Martin Charlot. The o'o is the endangered surviving species of a bird that once flourished in ancient Hawai'i, when it provided feathers for royal cloaks. At right: helicopter tours are a popular way to see Kaua'i, whose rugged, inner beauty is often unreachable. Following pages: the Na Pali Coast, where Kaua'i's civilization stops.

feathers, and then set loose again. Undoubtedly the most famous of these garments is the golden cloak of Kamehameha the Great. Made of about 450,000 yellow *mamo* feathers, it was handed down throughout the monarchy period and is now in the collection of the Bishop Museum.

*I*t was at Waimea, on the southwestern shore of Kaua'i, that Captain James Cook first anchored his two ships off the Hawaiian Islands on January 20, 1778. O'ahu had been sighted first but the winds favored an approach to Kaua'i. There was a small sheltered cove here but no real harbor. Inland there was a wide valley and a river flowing out of it into the sea.

Cook found a village ashore and spent three days at Waimea, taking on food, water, and other supplies. He enjoyed his first experience with the native Hawaiians and found them to be a kind and fair people. He also respected their crafts and artistry. Later, he wrote admiringly of the feather cloaks he saw by comparing them "to the thickest and richest velvet."

After leaving Waimea, Cook and his men visited the small island of Ni'ihau and took aboard salt and yams. Cook suspected that more of the Hawaiian Islands lay to the east but he decided against a complete survey and ordered his two ships north to continue their search for a northwest passage between the Pacific and Atlantic Ocean.

Some legends say that long before the arrival of Captain Cook the island of Kaua'i was inhabited by a

E hele au ma ke kai
I ke kai hānupanupa
I ka pili ano ahiahi
E hele au ma ke kai

E hele au ma ke kai
I ke kai hānupanupa
Me ke aloha o Hawai'i nei
Kēia 'āina ho'i mai au

Kai Hānupanupa

Phil & Ken Emerson

I go to the sea
The surging sea
At the quiet evening time
I go to the sea

I go to the sea
The surging sea
With love for Hawai'i nei
To this land I have returned

race of leprechaun-like little people called *menehune*. They were a short, muscular, and fun loving people who slept during the day and worked only at night. On Kaua'i there are numerous ancient stone structures attributed to the *menehune*, including several *heiau*, the Alekoko Fishpond near Nawiliwili Harbor, and the Menehune Ditch. Each of these projects was finished in a single night by hundreds of *menehune* who formed long double rows of workers and passed the rocks hand-to-hand from the quarry to the construction site.

Alekoko Fishpond is a mullet-raising lagoon that was created by building a 900-foot stone wall to cut off a bend of the Hule'ia River. One story goes that a Kaua'i princess and her brother asked the *menehune* to construct the fishpond but were asked by them not to watch while they did it. They agreed but broke their promise. The *menehune* turned them to stone. Their bodies are now two pillars on a hill above the fishpond.

The Menehune Ditch is the most famous example of *menehune* handiwork on Kaua'i. It is the remains of an ancient watercourse that is walled with a stone causeway. The ditch formerly ran for many miles delivering irrigation water from a dam upstream of Waimea River. All that can be seen today, however, is a stone wall about 200 feet long that flanks the road along the Waimea River. According to the story, a band of helpful *menehune* built the ditch for a king who wanted to bring water to irrigate the taro fields near Waimea.

Near the mouth of the Waimea River, is also found the crumbling ruins of Fort Elizabeth, often just called the "Russian Fort." Fort Elizabeth was named for the consort of Emperor Alexander I, then the Russian czar. Russian ships, particularly on round-the-world cruises, began to visit Hawai'i around 1804. One of these, the schooner *Nikolai*, stopped at the Islands in 1807 and Kamehameha the Great gave the captain a feather cloak and helmet to take back as a gift to Alexander Baranov, then head of the Russian American Company, a fur trading operation.

The Russians, who had already set up outposts in Alaska to collect furs, told Kamehameha they were interested in obtaining supplies from the Hawaiian Islands. Kamehameha agreed to supply the Russians with provisions, including the valuable salt needed to preserve the animal pelts they collected. Trade was thus started on a regular basis.

In 1815, a Russian ship, the *Bering*, was wrecked off Waimea during a storm. Kaumuali'i, who had been allowed to continue governing the island of Kaua'i for Kamehameha, confiscated the ship's cargo of furs. The value was estimated to be about 100,000 rubles. Upon learning of the wreck, the Russians dispatched George Anton Scheffer, a German doctor, to check out the situation in Kaua'i and recover their property.

The doctor found an ally in Kaumuali'i. The Kaua'i ruler was still jealous of Kamehameha for taking control of the islands. He allowed Scheffer to build Fort Elizabeth and to raise the Russian flag over

The breeze and I at Hanalei
We're softly sighing so tenderly
The breeze went out to sea caressingly
Embraced the rolling surf
Then kissed the shore

Recalling the days we knew
The days I shared with you

The Breeze And I
Mokihana

Moments so precious and few
I'm lost without you

And though you're far away
The breeze is here to stay
Within this lonely bay
At Hanalei

*Protected by a narrow bridge, Hanalei hasn't changed much
in the past 50 years.*

Waimea. In return Scheffer promised Kaumuali'i the help of Russia if there was ever trouble in maintaining his rule over Kaua'i.

Scheffer was also given the Hanalei Valley area of Kaua'i. He built two more small outposts here, Fort Alexander and Fort Barclay, both of which have vanished without a trace. Fort Elizabeth, itself, was finally abandoned in 1817 when Baranov refused to support Scheffer's grand designs for imperial power. The Russians felt that Kaua'i was too remote for them to govern properly. They chose instead to make peace with the aging Kamehameha and the Americans who were already well established in the islands.

After the death of Kamehameha in 1819, his son and heir, Liholiho, brought Kaumuali'i to O'ahu and had him placed under house arrest. The Kaua'i high chief was forced to marry Ka'ahumanu, Kamehameha's ambitious widow, so that the monarchy could cement its ties with Kaua'i. Kaumuali'i died in 1824 and Kaua'i was thereafter an integral part of the Hawaiian Kingdom.

Fort Elizabeth itself was eventually taken over by the monarchy and used for a time to house a small complement of the king's soldiers. Salutes were fired by its cannon to celebrate holidays and welcome visiting ships. Once in a while it was also used as a prison. By the 1850s the old fort had completely fallen apart. The guns had been dismounted and a Hawaiian chief had moved into the magazine warehouse. According to one report he had planted the courtyard full of sweet potatoes.

Today the remains of Fort Elizabeth have been declared a National Historic Landmark but little has been done to preserve the structure or to interpret its past. Most visitors to the site stop only long enough to use the park's public restrooms before turning off Kaumuali'i Highway, and driving up the Waimea Canyon Road toward Koke'e.

Winding several miles from the mountains to the sea, the west wall of Waimea Canyon traces the west boundary of the Makaweli depression. This area is a down-faulted segment of the single massive shield volcano that formed Kaua'i. The caldera, the largest in the Islands, once measured a dozen miles across and stretched from the present canyon to Mount Wai'ale'ale. From the lookout on top the canyon drops 2,450 feet to the Waimea River below.

It was the collapse of the volcano caldera that led to the formation of Waimea Canyon. Little lava flowed in this area after the initial eruptions and erosion from wind and rain gradually shaped the irregularities of cliffs and gullies. In time the streams mixed up the volcanic soils and the rocks were splashed by a kaleidoscope of earthy greens, rusty reds, and sun-dripped oranges. Waterfalls sparkle in the clean air as they bounce from high ridges and cascade into the valley.

Koke'e State Park encompasses much of Waimea Canyon and continues to the edge of fabled Kalalau Valley. At the Kalalau Lookout visitors look toward the sea and Na Pali Coast State Park. The road through Koke'e ends at the park headquarters and Koke'e Lodge. Here a small museum features natural history exhibits and a restaurant serves a hearty lunch to guests.

Waimea Canyon is the eroded remains of the massive volcano that formed Kaua'i.

Aia i ke anuanu o Koke'e
Ho'opumehana i ka pili me 'oe

Mapu ana i ka la'i o ka uluwehi
'O ka mokihana,
a he pua ho'oheno

I ka lihi o ka pali loa o kalalau
I ho'oipo ai i ka holonihi o ka noe

Puana e ka wehi o Kaua'i malie
'O 'oe e Ka Hanu Pua Mokihana

Noenoe ka mana'o i ka hali'a ia 'oe
'O 'oe e Ka Hanu Pua Mokihana

Puana e ka wehi o Kaua'i Malie
Me ka pualei nani i aloha 'ia

Ka Hanu Pua Mokihana

C. Manu Boyd

There is the cold of Koke'e
I was warmed by your embrace
Perfuming the stilled grove
Is the mokihana, a cherished bloom
Upon Kalalau's distant cliff edge
Sweetly wooing the creeping mist
Tell of peaceful Kaua'i's beauty
You, the sweet breath of mokihana

The mile-high park is a popular attraction for campers on Kaua'i. Most escape the cold mountain nights in tents but there are also a number of cabins hidden in the forest. The cabins and Lodge are owned by the state but operated on lease by a private concessionaire. Each cabin is furnished with a refrigerator, stove, bedding, and kitchenware. They also have hot water for sink and showers and a fireplace.

An interesting tale from this area of Kaua'i concerns the adventures of Ko'olau, a victim of leprosy (Hansen's disease), who became the island's most famous fugitive. He had been born in Kekaha in 1862 and educated in Waimea. At the age of 17 he became a *paniolo* and a few years later married an island girl named Pi'ilani. They settled down in Waimea to raise a family.

In 1889, however, a rash developed on Ko'olau and his son, Kaleimanu. It was diagnosed as leprosy and the authorities then tried to relocate the father and son to the isolated leper colony on Moloka'i. When government officials refused to allow his wife to accompany him, the family fled through the Koke'e mountains, past Waimea Canyon and into Kalalau Valley. Here they joined other lepers who were also evading the government's efforts to capture them.

The lepers were left alone in the valley until an overzealous deputy sheriff decided to hunt them down. When he was shot during a confrontation with Ko'olau, a well-armed patrol, including a band of National Guard soldiers, arrived by sea. The guardsmen set up their camp at the base of the valley and within a few days had captured most of the lepers.

Only Ko'olau, his wife, and their son, continued their resistance. They escaped again after killing a couple more soldiers on his trail. The patrol finally gave up and returned to Honolulu empty handed. For years Ko'olau and his family lived by themselves, deep in Kalalau Valley. Not until both Ko'olau and his son had died of the disease did Pi'ilani emerge from their jungle hideout.

Pi'ilani wrote a book about her husband and the outlaw life they shared but it has never been fully translated from the Hawaiian. The most famous fictional account is "Koolau the Leper," a short story by Jack London which was included in his 1916 book, *The House of Pride*.

*W*aimea and Koloa were the population centers of Kaua'i during the mid-19th century. Koloa, home of the island's first successful sugar cane plantation in 1835, became a provisioning port during the peak whaling period. The town never rivaled the popularity of Lahaina on Maui but as many as 60 ships a year anchored at Koloa Landing to take on preserved meat, salt, dried fruit, and fresh vegetables. The area was noted for its sweet potatoes. In recent years many of Koloa's old buildings have been renovated into tourist-oriented shops. Plaques on each renovated building describe its background.

Hanapepe, between Waimea and Koloa, was once a flourishing community of rice farmers but progress bypassed the town during the 1930s. Today Hanapepe remains almost frozen in an architectural time warp. Most of its buildings were built during its boom years, 1910 to 1930. A good example is Seto's Market, a wooden store structure built around 1915. Seto's Market is a third generation business, a family-type operation that's slowly vanishing from Kaua'i's rural communities.

Kaua'i's county seat is Lihu'e, a centrally located town that has the island's main airport and harbor facilities. Lihu'e began its slow but steady growth when two sugar plantations were started here, Lihu'e Plantation in 1849 and later Grove Farm Plantation in 1864. As the local sugar industry prospered the area

became increasingly important to the island's economy.

The deep water harbor at Nawiliwili, completed in 1930, established Lihu'e as the transportation hub of Kaua'i. By the end of the decade Lihu'e had also become the central point on the new "belt road" that linked Waimea with Hanalei. Lihu'e, having been born in the age of the automobile, made its streets wide enough to accommodate the increased flow of traffic. The automobile, in turn, allowed Lihu'e to grow larger than other island towns built during the horse and buggy days.

At the height of the sugar boom, there were eight sugar mills on Kaua'i. Today there are four with the largest being the Lihu'e Mill in the center of town. It produces over 80,000 tons of sugar each year and, during the harvest, is kept operating weekdays around the clock.

Kaua'i's plantation era lifestyle is easily imagined at Grove Farm Homestead, a plantation complex in Lihu'e that's recently been turned into a historical museum. Grove Farm was bought in 1870 by missionary descendant George N. Wilcox, then 25, who built his original home on the flat plain of a hill above Nawiliwili Bay. This home, redesigned in 1915, is the heart of the present historical museum.

Until his death in 1933, Wilcox continued to add additional buildings to his operation, including a plantation office, his own separate sleeping quarters, a guest cottage, and a base camp for his workers. The main houses were enclosed by a stone wall. Mabel Wilcox, a niece

Kāua i ka holo wa'apā
Lawe mālie ka lima i ka hoe
I mua a i hope pa'a ke kulana
Mea 'ole nā 'ale i ka luli mālie

Kō mai 'oe a paā i ka hoe
Kohu manu 'iwa i ka pi'i mau i mua
Inā 'o Mine, ku'u lio holo nui
Kupaianaha e ka hana a nā 'ale

Hō a'e ka ihu i ka makani
Nowiki, Noweke, Kauweke
'O ka hana ia lā o ka moku
Port hard mai 'oe i ka hoe

Hā'ina 'ia mai ka puana
Lawe mālie ka lima i ka hoe
I mua a i hope pa'a ke kulana
Mea 'ole nā 'ale i ka luli mālie

Holo Wa'apā
Lena Machado

Let's you and I take a rowboat ride
Carefully take up the oars
And now forward then back, steady as she goes
Don't mind the gentle swaying of the waves

Draw and hold the oars steady
As she pitches ever forward like the 'iwa bird
And oh if I was riding
Minnie my galloping steed
What wonders I could feel through
the wave action

Turn the bow into the wind
Northeast, Northwest, Southwest
As the boat makes its turns
Port hard on the oar

Tell this story
Carefully take up the oars
And row forward then back, steady as she goes
Don't mind the gentle swaying of the waves

At left: Kalalau Valley, haven for hidden beaches, valleys, and waterfalls, and the former hideaway for Ko'olau the Leper and his family. Above: progress has bypassed Hanapepe, a once flourishing town of Japanese rice farmers. Its wooden buildings are functioning museum pieces that have vanished from Hawai'i's other rural towns.

of George N. Wilcox, began planning for the museum before her death in 1978 at the age of 94. Grove Farm represents over a century of sugar plantation history on Kaua'i. The Wilcox family has preserved the business records, household furnishings, and even the original landscaping plan of the 80-acre estate.

The Wailua River, outside of Lihu'e, is the only navigable river in Hawai'i. It is fed by the streams flowing down Mount Wai'ale'ale, the wettest location in the islands with an average rainfall of over 450 inches a year. In ancient times the Hawaiians built a series of *heiau* at intervals from the mouth of the Wailua River to the summit of Mount Wai'ale'ale. A path connecting these temples was used during religious processions.

In 1947 the Smith family began a boat service to transport visitors up the river to the Fern Grotto, a natural lava tube cave hidden among lush foliage in the side of mountain. Ferns cascade from the ceiling and walls of the cave and colorful flowers grow throughout the area. Today the Smith Motor Boat Service and Waialeale Boat Tours operate a couple dozen large boats and about 1,000 couples a year ride to the Fern Grotto for their wedding ceremony.

Kaua'i has several resort hotel areas. The island's only "skyscraper" is the 11-story Kauai Surf Hotel on Kalapaki Beach in Nawiliwili. The major concentrations are between Wailua and Kapa'a, and at Po'ipu Beach. The Wailua hotels include the Coco Palms, Sheraton Coconut Beach, Islander Inn, Kauai Beachboy, Kauai Sands, and the Kauai Resort Hotel. Po'ipu, on the coast near Koloa Landing, has several popular hotels. Included are the Waiohai, the Poipu Beach, and the Sheraton-Kauai.

The road from Kapa'a to Hanalei and Ha'ena is almost as celebrated as the road from Pa'ia to Hana on Maui. Around each bend in the road are lovely scenes of mountains, valleys, and beaches. One of the most famous views in Kaua'i is from the Hanalei Valley Lookout, just before entering the town. From the top of the hill there is a panoramic view across hundreds of acres of green taro fields. Hanalei River flows through the center of the valley and in the distance the mountains sleep like a curling dragon on the horizon.

Hanalei, one of Kaua'i's true treasures, has changed little in the past half-century. It is a small-town collection of friendly farms and wooden buildings that supports a slower lifestyle than the rest of the island. One of the most interesting places to visit is the Waioli Mission House which was built by missionaries in 1836. The stately white house and its manicured lawn were also restored by the Wilcox family. The one-lane bridge into town was erected in 1912 and residents have refused all pleas to widen it. As long as the bridge stays in place Hanalei will likely remain a relatively unspoiled paradise.

During the recording of *Ho'ala,* Robert and Roland Cazimero spent much of their free time exploring Hanalei and the scenic road that leads

through the town to Ha'ena. There is a good beach along Hanalei Bay and an even more beautiful stretch of sand at Lumahai Beach where the movie version of James A. Michener's *South Pacific* was partially shot in 1958.

There are three well-known caves along this route, each more important to local legends than they are attractive in reality. One is the Maniniholo Dry Cave which is named after a *menehune* chief whose followers dug the cave in search of evil spirits. It is actually the mouth of a long lava tube that spreads out under the hillside. Just past Haʻena are two more caves associated with Pele, the volcano goddess. These are named Waikapalae and Waikanaloa and are both wet caves. While recording the Brothers Cazimero's album in Hanalei, Roland Cazimero spent his "free" time writing the songs for his own *Pele* album. In the course of his research he paid a visit to each of the cave sites as well as the nearby Kaulu-a-Paʻoa *heiau*.

"According to legend," Roland says, "Pele dug both of these caves trying to find a home but each time

hit water. She continued her travels south across the island chain until finding Hawaiʻi and settling down at Kilauea. Haʻena was also the home of Lohiʻau, the handsome young chief that figures so prominently in the mythical stories of Pele and Hiʻiaka."

The road ends at Keʻe Beach and the cars must turn around. If they want, hardy hikers can walk the 11-mile trail along Kauaʻi's rugged Na Pali Coast to Kalalau Valley. The spectacular beauty of this rugged shoreline features hidden beaches, valleys, and waterfalls.

Opposite page: Wailua Falls, east of Lihuʻe and at the end of narrow, four mile road, you'll find this double waterfall among the cane fields. Above left: the Na Pali Coast. Top to bottom: Princeville at Hanalei, a 1,000-acre recreation community; waterfalls scrape the face of Waiʻaleʻale; and Haʻena, where the road ends and the 11-mile trail to Kalalau Valley begins.

A trail from Keʻe Beach leads to Kaulu-a-Paʻoa, a *heiau* situated directly against the cliffside. Legend says this temple was founded by Paʻoa, a friend of Lohiʻau, and was once the most renowned hula seminary on Kauaʻi. Up from the *heiau* is Ke-ahu-a-Laka, the actual platform site of the *halau hula*.

"Today," Roland Cazimero explains, "There is just an earth-filled terrace on the site. "But in ancient times a large grass house probably stood on this spot. Inside this house, students were taught the art of hula by the resident teacher or *kumu hula*. A few hundred feet east of the *heiau* is a house platform believed to have belonged to Lohiʻau."

During the recording of *Hoʻala* in Hanalei, Jon de Mello says there were was an average of about 10 people in the house at any one time. The kitchen duties fell to Wayne Chang, then Robert's *halau* partner, and Leinaʻala Kalama Heine. When neither was around, the crew was forced to survive on rice and salad.

It was not the lack of food, however, but too much of it that caused one recording problem during the *Hoʻala* taping. When it came time for Robert to sing on "Muʻolaulani" he could hardly move. He had too much to eat. "It's hard for me to sing when I'm full," Robert says good humoredly, "and I was just stuffed. Wayne Chang had made chopsteak that night and ʻAla had prepared a pot of pork tofu.

"After dinner I wanted to take a nap but Jon wouldn't let me. He insisted that we record. Some of my friends told me afterwards that they liked my voice on that song. They wondered how I managed to get such a nice, rich sound."

Jon de Mello laughs at Robert's "story behind the song" but he believes that the environment of Kauaʻi, and not over-eating, made *Hoʻala* into a remarkable album. "I think we achieved something much more significant than notes and words at that house in Hanalei. We tapped into the spirit of a special place at a special time in our lives."

Before coming to Kauaʻi, de Mello says, both Robert and Roland were seriously thinking about separate careers. Roland had his *Pele* album underway and Robert had recently finished his own solo album. During the recording of *Hoʻala,* however, they finally came to terms with their partnership. On Kauaʻi they put aside their differences and found they had a destiny to share, for once and for always, as the Brothers Cazimero. ■

142

The Na Pali Coast, where Pele's sister Hiʻiaka found Lohiʻau's spirit wandering in sadness among the cliffs. She captured it and returned it with a prayer to his body. Lohiʻau awoke from his deadly sleep.

Ocean Of Memories

Roland Cazimero/Danny Kaninau

Memories return to me
   Like drifting sand to the sea
Swirling in endless motion
   Revealing thoughts of emotion

   Washed against the lonely shore
     Reliving thoughts just once more
       Imprinted mirages that recede
     A hope and a dream I need

     An endless ocean of memories
     Shaded moments of infinity
      On a crest of a wave
     Though my mind
       If you search too
        what will you find

Moloka'i & Lana'i

Ua ala 'oe e ku'u ipo
Kāhea ana au iā 'oe
I ka lipolipo o ka pō
Pane mai, pane mai

Ho'omaha 'oe i ku'u poli
Honi aku au, honi mai
He aloha wau iā 'oe
Pane mai, pane mai

(chorus)
Huli huli kou kino
Pumehana i ka la'i
Kipuni'ia kāua me ke aloha
Pane mai, pane mai

'Olu'olu 'oe e ku'u ipo
I kēia ho'oipoipo nei
I ka wai welawela nui
Pane mai, pane mai

Pane Mai
Robert Cazimero

Where are you my love
I call unto you
in the darkness of the night
answer me, answer me

Come closer into my arms
I kiss you, you kiss me
For I love you
answer me, answer me

Turn, turn your body (to me)
My love in the calm
You and I, in love
answer me, answer me

Are you comfortable, my love
here, we are in this great
feeling of surging
answer me, answer me

Although they have spent relatively little time on Moloka'i and Lana'i, Robert and Roland Cazimero are always looking for an opportunity to return. They have made many friends on both islands during their recent concert performances.

"When we play on these smaller islands," Roland says, "we get a real feeling for Hawaiian country life. The local residents have a strong sense of family and are as friendly and generous as any people we've met."

During ancient times both Moloka'i and Lana'i were isolated from the main Polynesian community. Lana'i, in fact, did not have a permanent population until at least a thousand years after the first settlers arrived in Hawai'i. It was considered an island crawling with evil spirits until Kaulula'au, the son of a Maui chief, chased the ghosts away around the beginning of the 15th century. From that time on it was ruled as an outer island of Maui.

The oldest recorded habitation site on Moloka'i is in the fertile Halawa Valley on the eastern end of the island. Archaeologists have dated the settlement back to at least 650 A.D. For centuries the valley was home

for a large agricultural-based community. Halawa Stream, which flows from the Moa'ula and Hipuapua waterfalls and winds through the center of the valley, provided the primary irrigation for the crops.

Besides its reputation for farming, Moloka'i was celebrated for the learning and power of its *kahuna* or priests. Because of the island's reputation as a religious center, it was spared from the frequent fighting that raged elsewhere in Hawai'i. During the

Above: three miles back into Halawa Valley hikers will find Moa'ula and Hipuapua Falls, where some say a legendary sea dragon still lives. At left: Siloama Congregational Church at the abandoned leprosy settlement of Kalawao on the Makanaula Peninsula.

latter half of the 16th century, a famous prophet named Lanikaula resided on Moloka'i. He lived in virtual seclusion but Hawaiians from all of the islands visited him for advice.

Lanikaula, however, made a fatal mistake when he became overly friendly with Kawelo, a rival *kahuna* from Lana'i. The Moloka'i priest gave away too many of his secrets to the younger man. Kawelo used this new knowledge, and a formidable talent for sorcery, to kill Lanikaula. When the old prophet was on his deathbed, he told his son to hide his bones so that Kawelo's followers could not find them. The son buried his father's bones without a gravestone and instead planted the surrounding area with silvery-leafed kukui trees.

Years passed, the trees grew and this grove, on the East end of the island, became known as Ka Ulu Kukui o Lanikaula (The Kukui Grove of Lanikaula). It was the most venerated spot on Moloka'i. Today the grove still stands but many of its trees are slowly dying.

Another well-known sacred site on Moloka'i is 'Ili'ili'opae, a large *heiau* also located on the east end of the island. It is one of Hawai'i's largest *heiau* and, due to its being on private land, is also one of the best preserved. It consists of three platforms and is 286 by 87 feet. The height of the walls vary from 11 to 22 feet. According to legend, the stones for the *heiau* were transported by *menehune* in a single night from the seashore at Wailau Valley.

Moloka'i was named after a child of Hina, the legendary moon goddess, and Wakea, the father of all the Hawaiian islands. The island was formed geologically by two volcanoes which rose out of the sea aligned with each other. Mauna Loa, which

At left: a kukui grove at Lanikaula, where the sons of a Moloka'i
kahuna hid their father's bones after he was killed by a Lana'i sorcerer.
Above: Kaloko'eli, one of 62 fishponds that the ancient
Hawaiians built along the Moloka'i coast.

148

Above: the north coast of Moloka'i, where isolated valleys and the ocean still support small colonies of people. At right: the Makanaula Peninsula, home for the Islands' diminishing population of leprosy patients who live at Kalaupapa.

shouldn't be confused with the Big Island mountain of the same name, is the West Moloka'i volcano. It emerged first and eventually developed into a dry, hot plateau. Pu'unana, its highest peak, is 1,381 feet above sea level.

East of Mauna Loa is a low saddle-land joining the East Moloka'i volcano, Kamakou. This wetter end of the island is characterized by a semicircular ridge of jagged mountains nearly a mile in height. On the windward coast the pounding surf has managed to carve out great sea cliffs while streams have eroded deep into the valleys.

Jutting out from north central Moloka'i is Makanalua Peninsula, the result of a third and smaller eruption by the Kauhako Volcano. Here, isolated from the rest of the island by nearly perpendicular cliffs, are the leprosy settlements of Kalawao and Kalaupapa. Today, the entire peninsula is designated the Kalaupapa National Historic Preserve.

Captain James Cook sighted Moloka'i on Nov. 26, 1778, but did not stop for a visit. He missed Lana'i altogether and the initial sighting of this island was left to his successor, Captain Charles Clerke, who took over command of the voyage after Cook was killed at Kealakekua Bay on Feb. 14, 1779. Clerke's crew spotted Lana'i on Feb. 25, 1779 as they were leaving the Hawaiian island chain.

Face-to-face foreign contact came later, in 1786, when Captain George Dixon anchored his ship, *Queen Charlotte,* offshore and met with the natives of Moloka'i and Lana'i who approached in their canoes. Dixon had sailed with Cook and Clerke on the earlier voyage.

Kamehameha the Great landed his war fleet on Moloka'i in early 1795 but did not overrun the island. His obvious military strength was enough to bring the chiefs of Moloka'i and Lana'i under his control. From Moloka'i in April, 1795, he launched his final, decisive attack on O'ahu. His victory there, at the Nu'uanu Pali, broke the will of his enemies and led to the establishment of the Hawaiian Kingdom.

Christian missionaries were among the first outsiders to construct permanent residences on Moloka'i and Lana'i. Reverend Harvey R. Hitchcock founded the Kalua'aha Congregational Church on Moloka'i in 1832, and in 1835 both Reverend Dwight Baldwin and Reverend William Richards of the Lahaina mission station made visits to Lana'i.

In 1848 a land division known as The Great Mahele was signed into law by Kamehameha III and from this time on certain tracts of land could be owned

by private individuals. Some of the high chiefs on Moloka'i got together and hired Rudolph W. Meyer, a young German surveyor, to manage their properties.

Meyer had originally stayed on the island with Rev. Hitchcock and through him had met one of his students, High Chiefess Kalama Waha. They were married in 1851 and in time raised a family of 11 children. One of Meyer's daughters eventually married one of Rev. Hitchcock's sons.

By the late 1850s Meyer had helped to turn much of West and Central Moloka'i into pastureland for cattle and sheep. He also operated a dairy farm and a sugar cane mill. During this mid-19th century period, potatoes were exported to California's gold rush population and cotton was cultivated for the Northern side during the American Civil War.

In 1865 the Hawaiian Legislature passed an Act to Prevent the Spread of Leprosy. To combat the outbreaks of leprosy (Hansen's disease), the government decided to resettle and isolate its victims on Makanalua Peninsula. The government bought 800 acres on the eastern side of the peninsula known as Kalawao. Later the western portion and its larger village of Kalaupapa was also annexed. Surrounded by the ocean on three sides and steep cliffs on the fourth, the natural environment made for easy population control. The first leprosy patients were dropped off at Kalawao in 1866.

Father Damien de Veuster, a Belgian priest, came to Moloka'i in 1873. He was originally to be one of four priests rotated every three months to serve the colony but once he saw the savage conditions there he decided to stay permanently. Two days after stepping ashore, he wrote to one of his superiors that "I am willing to devote my life to the leprosy victims. The sick are arriving by boatloads. They die in droves."

Damien enlarged St. Philomena Church and improved hospital conditions at the settlement. For the next 16 years he ministered to the material and spiritual needs of the patients on Moloka'i. His final sacrifice was his very own life. He contracted leprosy himself and died on April 25, 1889.

After Damien's death his spiritual work was continued by others, the best-known being Mother Marianne, a Franciscan nun, and Brother Joseph Dutton, a Trappist monk. Both Mother Marianne, who died in 1918, and Brother Dutton, who died in 1931, seldom left the Kalaupapa colony.

One Small Favor

Robert Cazimero/Roland Cazimero

I have one small favor to ask of you
Can I have a friend
to see me through
Just to walk beside me
someone to talk to
Can I have a friend to see me through
I would've asked you sooner,
it just slipped my mind
Would it be too much trouble . . .
hope it doesn't take
too much of your time
I have one small favor to ask of you
Can I have a friend to see me through

You can have this favor
that you ask of me
You can have a friend to see you through
Just to walk beside you
someone to talk to
You have a friend to see you through
But you should've asked me
sooner even though it
slipped your mind
It's been a lot of trouble . . .
you've just wasted
too much of my time

You can have this favor
that you ask of me
You have a friend to see you through

I am this favor you asked for
I am the friend to see you through
Just to walk beside you
someone to talk to
I am the friend to see you through
I am this favor you asked for
I am the friend to see you through

Each April the memory of Father Damien is honored throughout the Islands. When the Belgian priest arrived at Kalaupapa, the leprosy patients were savages without hospitals, crops, homes, or God. He helped them and, in doing so, died from their disease. The priest's lei-covered sculpture by Marisol is at the State Capitol on O'ahu.

It was also Brother Dutton who was responsible for arranging the peninsula's most dramatic ship visitations. The year was 1907 and President Theodore Roosevelt had decided to demonstrate the naval strength of the United States. He dispatched 16 huge battleships, and their auxiliary cruisers and destroyers, on a round-the-world cruise.

Roosevelt's "Great White Fleet" left Virginia in late 1907 and circled South America, entering the Pacific through the Strait of Magellan. Through the office of Hawai'i's then-Governor Walter Frear, who had been appointed by the President, Dutton requested that the fleet change its scheduled course and sail past the Kalaupapa settlement so that the patients, though isolated from society, could experience a sense of pride in their country.

On the morning of July 16, 1908, the "Great White Fleet" sailed past the peninsula and came within a mile of land. While hundreds of patients waved American flags from Kalaupapa, the ships went through their maneuvers. Afterwards they broke off into four groups and sailed away, three to Honolulu and the fourth to Lahaina. From Hawai'i the fleet continued on to New Zealand and Australia.

Today the Makanalua Peninsula, its present town at Kalaupapa, and its abandoned village at Kalawao, are popular tourist attractions, which—as a preserve—are protected from development. The Hawaiians who lived on the peninsula before the patients arrived built a three-mile-long switchback trail through the rain forest and down from the 1,600-foot high cliffs. Visitors can now arrive by airplane but most choose to ride mules down the improved switchback trail.

By the time of Damien's death most of the island's large west and central land parcels had been combined by Kamehameha V into what was referred

*Top: the Hop Inn in Kaunakakai; King of Kings and Lord of Lords
Protestant church in Halawa Valley; and riding the mules down the trail to
Kalaupapa. Above: Ua (rain) falls across the hills of Moloka'i.*

to as His Majesty's Moloka'i Ranch. After being passed down through the royal family, a group of four Honolulu businessmen bought the ranch in 1897 and renamed it the American Sugar Company. Their plans to raise sugar cane, however, were aborted when the irrigation water turned brackish and ruined the crops. The company turned to honey production and found success. From 1898 to 1920 there were more than 2,000 hives in production and for awhile Moloka'i was the largest producer of honey in the world.

Charles M. Cooke bought out his partners in 1908 and Molokai Ranch brought in more cattle. George P. Cooke, the owner's son, served as manager for 35 years and built the ranch into the territory's second largest beef producer. Only Parker Ranch on the Big Island did more cattle business.

Lana'i lies seven miles south of Moloka'i and contrasted to the larger island, which is long and lean, it is compact and shaped somewhat like the shell of a clam. The name, Lana'i, means a "swelling" or "hump." It was formed by a single volcano, perhaps the oldest among Hawai'i's major islands.

The summit of Lana'i is Lana'ihale in the east central region which is 3,370 feet above sea level. High ridges radiate to the north and northeast and to the southwest there are steep cliffs.

In 1922, the Hawaiian Pineapple Company bought the Lanai Ranch Company (which by then owned most of the island) from Frank and Henry Baldwin for $1.1 million. Two years later new owner Jim Dole laid out Lana'i City to house the foreign laborers that he'd brought to the island to work in his pineapple fields. It became a model town with its individual family homes and well-landscaped yards.

One of Lana'i's symbols has become the Norfolk Pine. It was Lanai Ranch manager George C. Munro, a New Zealander, who planted the first Norfolk Pines on the island around 1910. Reports say he used to sow the pine tree seeds from horseback as he rode around the hillsides. On an environmental level the pines collect moisture from the air and increase the island's supply of ground water.

Today, approximately 98 percent of Lana'i is privately owned by Castle & Cooke through a subsidiary, Dole Company, which operates a 16,000-acre pineapple plantation on the island. The first

At left: summer workers at Dole's Lana'i pineapple fields: irrigating the fields; and the pineapple harvest is still done by hand. Above: a petroglyphed rock above Lana'i's fields; Norfolk pines were planted all over Lana'i to attract moisture from the air; and Manele, the island's boat harbor.

155

He Punahele

Albert Nahalea

He punahele nō ʻoe
Na ka makua
Pūlama ʻia nō ʻoe
Me ke aloha

You are a beautiful baby
Pride of my heart
You are my dear little lady
Right from the start

He wahine uʻi
A he pua nani
Ma kuʻu poli mai ʻoe
Kuʻu lei   Kuʻu lei   Kuʻu lei

You're so sweet and lovely
Like a pretty flower
Close to my bosom I hold you
Baby mine   baby mine   baby mine

156

morning work whistle sounds at 4 a.m. (5:30 a.m. in winter) and by 6 a.m. the workers are out in the field and the irrigation machines are turned on. The big harvest is in summer and all picking of the pineapple is done by hand. The fruit is then dropped on long conveyor belts which move it off the field to waiting trucks. These trucks, in turn, take their cargo to Kaumalapau Harbor for shipment to the Honolulu cannery.

Moloka'i also has proved ideal for pineapple farming and during the 1920s the firm of Libby, McNeil and Libby joined the California Packing

Today the 66,000-acre Molokai Ranch is still the second largest cattle ranch in Hawai'i. Its pastures are home for over 6,000 head of Santa Gertrudis cattle, a hardy breed that was started on the King Ranch in Texas. Molokai Ranch is also a developer of real estate and owns commercial properties throughout the Mainland.

In the mid-1970s the Molokai Ranch Wildlife Park at Kaluako'i was begun as an environmental project to control grass and brush growing. African and Asian animals were introduced which fed on the same kind of vegetation in their native habitat as was

Corporation (Del Monte) in leasing part of Molokai Ranch for pineapple plantations. Later the Dole Company took over the Libby lands.

Everything went fine during the four decades that followed. Then, crippled by battle scars of fighting a fluctuating market, Dole ended most of Moloka'i operations in 1976. Del Monte lasted another eight years before closing down its plantation on Moloka'i in 1983. While its neighbor, Lana'i, continues to profit from pineapple farming, Moloka'i has started searching for new ways to diversify its economy.

found on Moloka'i. The imported animals adapted easily and their numbers increased. In 1978 the ranch opened the Wildlife Park to visitors and now gives regular tours of the mile square reserve. Among the over 400 animals which now roam free in the park are giraffes, greater kudus, antelopes, black bucks, Barbary sheep, elands, rhea, sitka, ostriches, and axis deer.

Kaunakakai, on the southern coast of the island, is the main town on Moloka'i. Its main street, Ala Malama, is a wide three-block-long thoroughfare

At left: a fern lei crowns this wahine. Above: the Molokai Ranch Wildlife Park at Kaluako'i is home for 400 Asian and African animals, who have found that the Friendly Isle is just like home. Following pages: Malihini, astroturf, and hotel pool.

flanked by a colorful parade of wooden, false-front commercial buildings. Moloka'i has only recently begun to think of itself as a tourist destination. Two country-style hotels, the Pau Hana Inn and the Hotel Molokai, are close to Kaunakakai. The Sheraton Molokai, opened in 1977, anchors the Kaluakoi Resort near Molokai Ranch.

Not far from the Sheraton Molokai is Kepuhi Beach, an attractive stretch of shoreline long favored by the Hawaiians. The waters were full of sealife and there was once a small fishing village here. A French naturalist and traveller, Jules Remy, visited the Kaluako'i district in 1845 and talked with some of the local people. He asked them how they liked living on this side of the island.

"What place could be better than right here," a Kaluako'i resident asked Remy, "the sky almost never sends us rain, and where the sea gives us fish in abundance?"

Moloka'i. Even today, for many people, the "Friendly Isle" comes the closest to being the perfect Hawaiian Island. The pace is slow and the land is rich. "What place," they still ask now, "could be better than right here?" ■

There's No Love

Robert Cazimero/Jack de Mello

There's no love
without loving you
Empty rooms when the
day is through
Take the color from the sky
And the passion of a sigh
There's no love
without loving you

I have loved and I shall love again
But when you're here with me,
I know contentment

Give me hope answer honestly
Take a breath,
breathe it into me
Know the twinkle of my eyes
Happen just as you pass by
There's no love without loving you

O'ahu, The Gathering Place

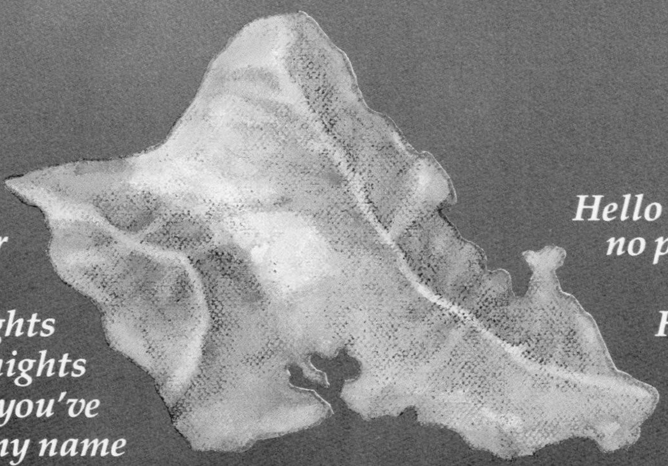

Hello Honolulu love you
Have you changed or
stayed the same
Your bright beckoning lights
Fill my heart lonely nights
Don't blame you if you've
forgotten my name

Need to ask you Honolulu
(what's new?)
From what I hear
you're looking swell
Is Mānoa still kissed
by your sweet evening mist?
Does the moon still dance
to music at the Shell?

Hello Honolulu
Margo "Doolin" Samuels/John K. Spencer

Hello Honolulu,
no place makes me feel
the way you do
Honolulu,
I miss you so, it's true

Yes I know, my Honolulu
love you
I never should have gone away
And the truth is I find
I've made up my mind
I'm going to follow
my heart home today

Going home to stay

I laila i nā pali i'ike ai
Ka wailele o Nu'uanu
E ho'okahe pau 'ole
E ka'aka'a kou maka
E 'ike a'
He wai nō ia e iho ai
Ke kahe nei ka wailele
Pāhihi'ole mai nō
He kahe mau nō ia

Ka Wailele O Nu'uanu

Jay Kauka

There on the cliffs can be seen
The waterfall of Nu'uanu
It never stops flowing
It just keeps coming down
The waterfall is flowing
Never locked
It flows forever

Although the Brothers Cazimero may sing about the beauty of rural landscapes of the Big Island or Maui or Kaua'i, they are still big city boys at heart. Robert and Roland were born, raised, and schooled in Honolulu and its quickened pace and wealth of opportunities put its stamp on them from the very beginning.

"O'ahu," says Robert, "has been the major influence in our lives. We are the products of its environment. If mama and daddy had stayed on the Big Island and raised us with the rest of the family in Kohala we would be a lot different than we are now. We might not have even turned out to be musicians. Or if we had we might still be playing at backyard parties instead of at the Waikiki Shell or the Royal Hawaiian Hotel."

On a recent afternoon Robert and Roland drove out from downtown Honolulu to the Nu'uanu Pali Lookout. The view from this point, looking toward the windward side of the island and over 1,000 feet above sea level, is one of the most famous in Hawai'i.

"This is one of my favorite spots on O'ahu," Roland says. "During the period of *Hokule'a* I would drive the other members of the group up here at night in my van. We'd sit out under the stars and play music. This place seemed to put us back in touch with ancient Hawai'i.

"Later, during the time I was writing *Warrior,* I got into the habit of coming up to the lookout again, this time to do a bit of exploring. It was here in 1795 that Kamehameha attacked and defeated the enemy O'ahu forces during the Battle of Nu'uanu. His large fleet of canoes had crossed from Moloka'i, coming in over the reefs and landing on the leeward coast. The men drew up their canoes between Wai'alae and Waikiki."

Kamehameha's *peleleu* canoes were a class of large double-hulled war canoes which featured a quasi-European sail plan. Their hulls were carved from gigantic *koa* logs and freeboard was built up on the sides. Often they were decked over the stern and had shelters on top. Some also mounted swivel guns which the chiefs had obtained through trade with the Europeans. A canoe of average size might have been 70 feet long with a hull depth of five feet or more. Several hundred *peleleu* were included in Kamehameha's fleet, along with single-hulled outriggers and a few schooners constructed in the European style.

Preceding pages: downtown Honolulu, Aloha Tower, and the harbor; Waikiki at night; a pink tecoma blossom; and palm trees at dusk. At left: the Nu'uanu Pali. Above: "Peleleu,"Herb Kawainui Kane's painting of Kamehameha's invasion canoe with a European swivel gun mounted on the bow.

Ua hala aku nā lā hanohano	The glorious days
O ko mākou mau ali'i aloha	Of our beloved nobility have gone
Hā'ule nō nā kupa 'aiau	The old-time people have passed on
A mākou i pūlama mai ai	Those that we have loved
No ke aloha ana 'ole	It's for immeasurable love
I ka lāhui kulaiwi	For the nation of the land
E ola mau ai kou inoa	That your name
E Hawai'i, he 'āina aloha	will live on forever
	O Hawai'i, a beloved land
He pae moku i ho'omaika'i 'ia	This is a group of islands blessed
Na ke Akua mana loa	By the almighty God
He wahi aloha e pili mau ai	A beloved place that will always be close
I ka na'au o nā kupa	To the hearts of the people of that nation

No Ke Aloha Ana 'Ole

John Mahelona

Estimates of Kamehameha's invading army vary from 10,000 to 16,000 men. They advanced over the plains, across Kaimuki and Manoa, and on to the lush Nu'uanu Valley. Here the main force split off two flanking detachments. Following a series of minor confrontations, Kamehameha's men pursued the last of the O'ahu soldiers to the Pali Lookout area. Hundreds were killed in hand-to-hand combat or were pushed over the cliff's edge to their deaths.

"Following this important victory," Roland continues, "Kamehameha ordered his men to stop fighting and granted amnesty to the losers. After setting up his O'ahu headquarters at Waikiki he returned to the Big Island to consolidate his power over the Islands."

Kamehameha came back to O'ahu around 1804 and five years later moved his new capital from Waikiki to Honolulu to take advantage of the increased visits of foreign trading ships to the village's natural harbor. At this time perhaps a hundred thatched houses were spread out along the beachfront from Nu'uanu Stream to Kaka'ako. The royal court ruled from a compound that was situated at Pakaka, a canoe landing at the inner curve of the bay. This was near the present junction of Nimitz Highway and Queen Street.

The main palace building, where Kamehameha and his high chiefs gathered to talk and eat, was called Halehui. Just to the north was the women's eating house. Queen Ka'ahumanu and the king's lesser wives slept in three separate houses close by. The compound also included a number of other residences, guard

shacks, and storage houses. Nearby, where Aloha Tower now stands in Honolulu Harbor, was docked the *Lelia Bird,* a three-masted sailing ship owned by the government.

In 1812 the king moved his court to Kailua-Kona on the Big Island. He left the island of O'ahu under the charge of Governor Boki, a well-liked and skilled administrator. Kamehameha remained on the Big Island until his death in 1819.

A year later, on April 4, 1820, seven men, their wives and five children arrived in Kailua-Kona aboard the brig *Thaddeus.* These men and women, the first Christian missionaries to Hawai'i, had been sent to the Islands from Boston by the American Board of Commissioners for Foreign Missions.

Only two members of the pioneer company were ordained ministers: Asa Thurston, who stayed in Kona, and Hiram Bingham who sailed on to Honolulu. The other men in the party included a doctor, a printer, a farmer, and two school teachers.

At left: the statue of King Kamehameha in front of Ali'iolani Hale was unveiled by King Kalakaua in 1883. Above: a modern Hawaiian wears replicas of the ancient ali'i cape and helmet.

The Lake

Wendell Ing/Traditional

You've got to go down to the lake
To see what man has done
again, done again
There's still some hill to be seen
between the blue
But we know the lake is dying

There's a one lane dirt road
leading down
Through kiawe trees and few old cars
You'll see the remains of our ways
And countless scores of
deadlife all around

(chorus)
Sometimes I have to wonder
If they really see
Or, if they do
They just don't care about me

Try tripping and seeing back
It'll turn you right around
Eh, it'll turn right around —
right around
Eh, turn you right —
Eh, turn you right around

Mai Poina ʻOe Ia ʻu

(chorus)
Mai Poina ʻoe ia ʻu
E kaʻu mea e liʻa nei
E hoʻomaumau ka ʻikena
I mau ai ke koʻiʻi a loko

Above: moonlit Olomana Peak on Windward Oʻahu, named for the
giant who jumped from Kauaʻi to the peak. At right:
restored turn-of-the-century buildings stand next to Honolulu's newer
cement, glass, and steel towers.

Most of the then native houses in Honolulu were low, windowless structures. They were erected near the water for easy access to their canoes. Built of thatched grass over a wooden frame, they usually consisted of one room with a crawl-through entrance. *Lauhala* mats covered the floors. Only in the houses of the chiefs could a person fully stand up.

In the beginning the Christian missionaries were quartered in these low huts. Governor Boki, acting on the orders of Kamehameha II, arranged for a row of four large thatched houses to be built on empty government property that was about half-a-mile from downtown Honolulu on the narrow dirt road to Waikiki.

On March 20, 1821, permission was received from the king to assemble a prefabricated frame house that had been shipped to Honolulu around Cape Horn from Boston. Daniel Chamberlain, a farmer, moved in first with his wife and five children. Over the years the Frame House, the oldest surviving wooden building in Hawai'i, sheltered many of the mission families.

The Chamberlain House was built in 1831. Levi Chamberlain, the accountant and business agent for the mission, used the structure to store food, clothing, and furnishings. Ten years later the building today called the Printing House was constructed of coral blocks between the two already existing structures. The mission press at Honolulu was the first in this country to operate west of the Rocky Mountains.

On July 21, 1842, the present Kawaiaha'o Church, its walls built of coral quarried from the reefs off Waikiki, was dedicated after six years of steady construction. It had been designed by Hiram Bingham and quickly became a preferred meeting place of both church and state officials. The next year, at a special thanksgiving ceremony marking the end of a brief British occupation and the restoration of Hawaiian sovereignty, Kamehameha III used the expression, *Ua mau ke ea o ka aina i ka pono* ("The life of the land is perpetuated in righteousness"). These words were later adopted as Hawai'i's official motto.

Before the missionaries and whalers arrived, Hawaiians were content with their one room hale pili (grass houses). They weren't tall enough to stand in, but they were within walking distance of the surfing beaches.

During the 1850s the appearance of downtown Honolulu took on a more orderly nature. The Great Mahele of 1848 had brought private land ownership and a movement was started to formalize streets and to register their proper names. The choices were reflections of the times.

King Street, of course, was named after the ruling monarch, Kamehameha III. Queen Street paid honor to his wife, Queen Kalama. Beretania Street commemorated the British influence and Merchant Street the presence of new business interests. Hotel Street, which ran through a popular boarding house area, acknowledged the arrival of foreign travelers.

Nuʻuanu Street got its name from the Nuʻuanu Valley. From the earliest of times there had been a foot trail across the Nuʻuanu Pali but it had not been much improved since the Battle of Nuʻuanu. In 1845 government funds were allotted to make the path usable for riders on horseback. It was then paved with large, flat rocks. Kamehameha III christened the new trail himself and led a group of riders from Honolulu to the windward side.

Pack animals soon began crossing the *pali* and trade was established on a regular basis between Honolulu and Kailua. During the decades that followed the mountain trail became one of the island's busiest thoroughfares. The first known automobiles arrived on the island in 1899 and the next year work was begun on a full-scale road across the *pali*.

Contemporary reports indicate that some of the road workers, scaling their way down the face of the *pali*, found human bones scattered along the steep cliffsides. These bleached bones, possibly dating back to the days of Kamehameha the Great and the Battle of Nuʻuanu, were reburied under a landslide of rocks.

The missionaries brought Christianity, printing presses, double-wall construction, windows, prefabricated homes, and the engineers to build the Kawaiahaʻo Church (lower right) from coral. The state seal (center) contains the Islands' motto—"The life of the land is perpetuated in righteousness."

170

Clockwise from top: Mokapu Peninsula, the Pali golf course, and Kaneohe Bay can be seen from the Pali Lookout; the Pali Highway snakes up the Koolau Mountains from Kailua; Kamehameha drove O'ahu's armies up the Nu'uanu Valley (as it looks today) to the Pali Lookout, where hundreds escaped his army's wrath by plunging to their deaths on the rocks below.

Haʻalele mākou iā Honolulu	We left Honolulu
I ka hapahā o ka hola ʻekolu	At a quarter to three
Hāʻawi ke aloha lūlū lima	We extended our aloha and handshakes
Me nā huapala o ka E.S.	With the belles of the E.S.
A uka mākou o Haukomo	When we got up to Haukomo
Pā ana ke ʻala o ka ʻawapuhi	The scent of ginger filled the air
A uka mākou o Nuʻuanu	When we got to Nuʻuanu
Huli aku nānā iā Koʻolau	We turned and saw the Koʻolau district

Maunawili

J. Kukolia/A. Koko

ʻAlawa i ka wai o Silosia	We gazed upon
I ka neʻe mālie i ke alo pali	the waters of Silosia
	As we made our way slowly
	on the face of the cliff
ʻEwalu mākou i ʻalo aku	There were eight of us who traveled
Ma nei kula loa o Maunawili	On the expansive plains of Maunawili
A lalo mākou o Maunawili	When we were below Maunawili
Pā ana ka makani wili ʻāhihi	The wind that twists the ʻāhihi blew
ʻĀina maikaʻi o Maunawili	Maunawili is a great place
Hoʻokahi nō hewa he elua ʻole	There's only one thing wrong—
	there are no sweethearts
Hāʻina ʻia mai ana ka puana	Tell the story
ʻEwalu mākou i ʻalo aku	There were eight of us who traveled

This 1908 road runs down Nuʻuanu Valley toward Honolulu. Planting and
reforestation were done to stop the valley's erosion by wind and rain.
Following pages: the Koʻolau Mountains at dusk.

Nani Koʻolau a he pō anu
Ka ʻiniki welawela
o ka Makasila
I laila kāua i walea ai
Me ka wai o ka ʻulala e hō

A hiki kāua i Nuʻuanu
A inu i ka wai o Silosila
I laila kāua i hiʻolani ai
Me ka wai o ka pali Koʻolau

I laila aku wau i ka pō nei
Ua paʻa ko puka i ka laka ʻia
Wehe akuau he ʻole e ka hemo
Me ka wai o ka ʻūlala e hō

Hāʻina ʻia mai ana ka puana
Kuʻu hoa o ka nani o ke Koʻolau
Me ʻoe hoʻi au hoʻoipo ai
Me ka wai o ka ʻūlala e hō

Nani Koʻolau
Traditional

A cold night with the
beautiful Koʻolau mountains
I felt the passionate
nip of the Makasila wind
It was there that you and
I whiled the time away
With the waters of song

We arrived at Nuʻuanu
And drank the waters of Silosila
It was there that you
and I rested pleasantly
With the waters of song

I was there last night
Your door was locked
I tried to open it but it would not open
With the waters of song

Tell the refrain
My companion of the beauty of the Koʻolau
I was with you in sweet love
With the waters of song

The historic heart of Oʻahu is today centered in old downtown Honolulu near the Mission Houses, Kawaiahaʻo Church, ʻIolani Palace, and Aliʻiolani Hale. In front of Aliʻiolani Hale is the statue of Kamehameha I, a duplicate copy of the Big Island statue.

ʻIolani Palace, the only royal palace in the United States, was built by King Kalakaua to replace a smaller building on the present grounds. The cornerstone was laid in 1879 and the Merrie Monarch took up residence in 1882. He lived there until his death in 1891. His sister and successor, Queen Liliʻuokalani, occupied ʻIolani Palace until the overthrow of the Monarchy in 1893. In 1895 she spent nine months as a prisoner in the palace following a failed insurrection that had tried to put her back on the throne.

When the Hawaiian Kingdom was overthrown, the Provisional Government made the palace its Executive Building. The ceremony marking the annexation of Hawaiʻi to the United States was held on the front steps of ʻIolani Palace on August 12, 1889. The American flag was hoisted up the flagpole on the central roof turret. In 1969 the new State Capitol was completed and ʻIolani Palace was emptied of government offices. In 1970 the Department of Parks and Recreation, advised and assisted by the Friends of ʻIolani Palace, began a complete restoration of the structure.

Across the street from ʻIolani Palace is Aliʻiolani Hale, a building that has housed members of the Hawaiʻi Supreme Court since being completed in 1874. It was the first major office building built by the monarchical government. On its front steps the Republic of Hawaiʻi was proclaimed on January 17, 1893. The interior of Aliʻiolani Hale has now been restored to its appearance in 1911, the date of the building's first major reconstruction. The exterior has been restored to how it looked on opening day, 1874.

Outside in front of Aliʻiolani Hale, is one of the most photographed objects on Oʻahu, the bronze and gold statue of Kamehameha the Great. The idea for the statue was originally voiced in 1878 by the controversial Walter Murray Gibson, then a freshman legislator from Lahaina, Maui, and later premier of the kingdom. Gibson made his proposal during the centennial year of Captain James Cook's first visit to Hawaiʻi. Gibson, a strong supporter of the "Hawaiʻi for Hawaiians" movement, sought to change the emphasis of the centennial away from the *haole* discoverers to the Hawaiians who welcomed them. Kamehameha, of course, had met Cook first as a curious young chief and later witnessed the tragic death of the famed British explorer at Kealakekua Bay.

Gibson's proposal found popular acceptance and he was chosen to head the statue committee. The primary requirements were that the statue be as accurate as possible in its facial likeness, have a well-formed Hawaiian body, and be dressed in appropriate garments.

Thomas R. Gould, an American sculptor who lived in Boston, got the commission. He did the modeling in Florence, using full-body photographs taken of John Timoteo Baker and his half brother, Robert Hoapili Baker. The face was adapted from an engraving which was based on an 1816 portrait by Louis Choris.

Gould decided to give Kamehameha a classical Western pose, inspired by a statue he admired of the young Augustus Caesar, a warrior from a different land and age who had united his own Roman Empire. He dressed Kamehameha in a simple *malo* or loincloth and draped a full-length feather cloak over his shoulders. A feather helmet was placed on his head and a hardwood spear in his left hand.

Above: ʻIolani Palace, the only royal residence in the United States was built by King Kalakaua. Its entrance hall staircase is made of koa.
At right: the Honolulu statue of King Kamehameha is covered with leis on June 11—Kamehameha Day, a state holiday celebrated with a parade, luau, hula, parties, and fairs.

Honi ana i ke anu
i ka mea hu'ihu'i
Hu'i hewa i ka 'ili i ka
ua Pō'aihala
Lei ana i ka mokihana
i ka wewehi o Kaiona
Līhau pue i ke
anu hau'oki o Kaleponi

She smells the cool
and refreshing air
Chilled is her skin by
the Pō' aihala rain
She wears the mokihana,
the adornment
of Kaiona
She shivers in the cold,
the chilly cold of California.

Hia'ai ka welina ka nene'e a ka 'ōhelopapa
Pupua i ka noe
mōhāhā i ke anu
Noho nō me ka 'ano'i ka manao
(o) ia loko
'O loko hana nui
pau 'ole i ke ana 'ia

She delights and is pleased with
the creeping strawberries
Profuse with bloom in the mist
and spreading so full
in the chilly air
She remains with great love
that comes from within
From her great heart whose depths
cannot be measured

He Inoa No Pauahi
Traditional

A ka wailele 'o Niakala
'ike i ka wai ānuenue
I ka pō'ai'ai a ka 'ohu hāli'i
pa'a i laila
Pue ana i ka 'ehu wai
pupu'u i ke ko'eko'e
Eia iho ka mehana o ka poli o Hi'ilei

At the waterfall of Niagara
she saw the rainbow arch
And the mist that spread all around there
She shrank from the water spray
shivered in the cold
And found warmth
in the bosom of Hi'ilei

E ō e ka wahine hele lā o Kaiona
Alualu waili'ulā o
ke kaha pua 'ōhai
'O ka ua lani pōlua pō anu o ke Ko'olau
Ku'u hoa o ka malu kī malu
kukui o Kaho'iwai

Answer, O lady who walks
in the sunshine of Kaiona
Where mirages dance
on the 'ōhai-covered plain,
In the very foggy rain
on the cold night of Ko'olau
My companion of the kī and kukui
groves of Kaho'iwai

The bronze statue was cast in Paris in 1880 and then taken to Bremen, Germany. It was put on the *G. F. Haendel* for shipment to Honolulu. The ship, however, caught fire during a storm in the South Atlantic. It broke up on a reef off the Falkland Islands and sank to the bottom.

Luckily for Hawai'i, the cargo was insured and the money collected was sufficient to pay for a duplicate of the statue made from the cast which was still intact in the Paris foundry. While the second statue was being cast, the first was pulled from the ocean and brought to Honolulu by a British sea captain. It was purchased by the Hawaiian government, repaired and sent to Kohala, the birthplace of Kamehameha on the Big Island. Later, in 1912, it was moved from 'Ainakea to its present location at the Kohala Court House in Kapa'au. The second statue was unveiled at its present location in downtown Honolulu by King Kalakaua on February 4, 1883, two days after his coronation at 'Iolani Palace.

Over the years the twin statues of Kamehameha the Great have proven to be more than decorative pieces of art. Together they have inspired several generations of islanders and have become symbols of Hawaiian pride. A third Kamehameha statue is in Washington, D.C. It was cast from molds taken of the Honolulu statue, and dedicated in the Hall of Columns (along with the Father Damien statue) at the U.S. Capitol in 1969. Every June 11, on Kamehameha Day, the three statues are draped with flower leis to show respect and *aloha* for the first king of all Hawai'i.

R obert and Roland Cazimero have recorded more songs about O'ahu than any other island. Starting with "Maunawili" and "Aloha Tower" on their fine debut album, *The Brothers Cazimero* (1976), and continuing through their most recent albums, they have painted a captivating musical portrait of their home island. The meaning of O'ahu has long been forgotten but its nickname, "The Gathering Place," seems quite appropriate to this most populated of the Hawaiian Islands.

There are many places on O'ahu that hold special meaning, for one reason or another, to Robert and Roland. Some are merely fun places to visit, like Kailua, Waimanalo, and the North Shore. Others hold a deeper significance. Kalihi, for example, is where the Brothers were raised and went to elementary school. Many of their childhood friends still live here. Later they attended the Kamehameha Schools in nearby Kapalama Heights.

During their 1984 Lei Day Concert, an evening spotlighting the theme of "Song of Old Hawai'i," the Brothers paid tribute to Kamehameha the Great by performing several songs from Roland's *Warrior* album. This segment of the program then faded into a salute to Kamehameha Schools featuring a young woman on stage dressed to resemble Bernice Pauahi Bishop

Princess Pauahi, a great-grandchild of Kamehameha the Great, was born in 1831 in Nu'uanu Valley. Her mother was the Chiefess Konia and her father was High Chief Abner Paki, a future supreme court judge and an acting governor of O'ahu. Soon after birth, however, she was adopted by Kina'u, a daughter of Kamehameha the Great.

In 1839 the young princess was one of the first students enrolled in the Chiefs' Children's School which had been founded earlier in the same year by Reverend and Mrs. Amos Starr Cooke. Princess Pauahi developed into an excellent student, fond of history and literature. At the age of 18 she married Charles Reed Bishop, a talented young man 10 years her senior.

T he Bishops soon established themselves as pillars of the Honolulu community. Charles became one of the town's leading businessmen and eventually started a successful bank close to the waterfront on Honolulu Harbor. This bank is known today as First Hawaiian. Princess Pauahi became interested in charitable causes, social work, and the educational betterment of her Hawaiian people.

At daybreak on December 11, 1872, the bachelor king, Kamehameha V (Lot Kamehameha) summoned

At left: Bernice Pauahi Bishop turned down the throne so she could better serve the Hawaiian people. Revenues from her vast land holdings still support the Kamehameha Schools. Above: the Bernice Pauahi Bishop Museum in Honolulu was built by her husband, Charles Reed Bishop, after her death. It is one of the finest natural history and anthropology museums in the world.

177

He beauty wale 'oe e ku'u pua 'ula
I Mānoa i ka ua
Ka nani loa o ka nahele
E 'ume mai 'oe ia'u nei
Me kou 'ala anuhea
E kilipue kāua i ka ua Tuahine
He ipo ahi kāua
Ua la'i ke kaunu
He kipona kaunu kēlā

He Beauty Wale 'Oe

Jay Kauka

You are a beauty, my sacred flower
In Mānoa, in the rain
The beauty of the forest
You are enticing me
With your cool soft fragrance
Let's embrace in the Tuahine rain
We are ardent lovers
The passion is calmed
That is a deep passion

Princess Pauahi to his deathbed and offered her the chance to be his successor. She refused his offer, reasoning that she could help the Hawaiians more by influencing affairs behind the throne. In time Princess Pauahi willed her lands, part of which had been inherited from her wealthy cousin, Princess Ruth Ke'elikolani, to the creation and maintenance of a school for Hawaiian children.

Princess Bernice Pauahi Bishop died shortly after noon on October 16, 1884. The rain outside continued until the morning of her funeral. As the cortege wound its way up Nu'uanu Valley the storm clouds finally parted. The sun broke through as the procession reached the Royal Mausoleum. In a sermon a few days later at Kawaiaha'o Church, the Reverend J. A. Cruzan called Princess Bernice Pauahi Bishop "the last and the best of the Kamehamehas." He said that by "refusing to rule her people, she did what was better, she served them, and in no way so grandly as by her example."

The Kamehameha School for Boys was formally dedicated in 1887 and the five-building school opened in Kalihi, two-and-a-half miles northwest of town. The first class enrollment consisted of 37 students. In 1894 the Kamehameha School for Girls opened next door.

At the same location, in 1888, Charles Reed Bishop began construction of another memorial to his late wife, the Bernice P. Bishop Museum. The main Entrance Hall building was opened in 1891, the Polynesian Hall in 1894, and the Hawaiian Hall in 1903. All were faced with cut-stone that had been quarried on the site. Koa wood was used for the interior paneling, staircases, and cabinets. The museum originally housed collections of Hawaiian artifacts and "curiosities" belonging to Princess Pauahi, Princess Ruth, and Queen Emma.

In 1932 the Kamehameha School for Girls moved to Kapalama Heights on a site overlooking the museum. The Kamehameha School for Boys followed in 1948. Today the Kamehameha Schools have classes from kindergarten through 12th grade, and all the students are of Hawaiian ancestry.

Above: although close to a million people live on O'ahu, its natural beauty still makes busy locals stop to admire. The inset is the blossom of the monkeypod tree. At right: the Kaimuki-Kalihi trolley, 1940.

Manoa Valley is another favorite area of the island for Robert and Roland Cazimero. It was as The Sunday Manoa, of course, that they achieved their first widespread recognition during the early 1970s with bandleader Peter Moon. The Sunday Manoa name was chosen because it conjured up romantic happy-go-lucky images of the past.

During the time of the monarchy, Manoa Valley, like Nu'uanu Valley, was another favored spot for the summer homes of royalty. The most respected resident was Ka'ahumanu, the widow of Kamehameha the Great. During the 1820s her home was visited frequently by government officials and the newly arrived Christian missionaries. On an 1882 map it was located about where Loulu Street now crosses the end of Kumukoa Street.

Chief Boki, later governor of O'ahu, owned an extensive section of land in Manoa Valley. He and his wife, Liliha, gave missionary Hiram Bingham a tract of land known as Kapunahou on which to build a home and a school for missionary children. In time it became known as Punahou School.

Agriculture played an important role in the history of Manoa Valley. The first sugar cane brought to the Islands was grown here in 1825 by John Wilkinson, a former West Indies planter. Chief Boki loaned him about 100 acres for his plantation in the center of the valley. Wilkinson's death, coupled with the high cost of labor, brought the sugar plantation to a stop.

Taro, pineapples, bananas, and sweet potato farms took over from the sugar cane. Dairy cattle also thrived in grassy Manoa and at one time there were eleven dairies in the valley. Eventually the dairies folded and the fertile pastures gave way to housing tracts. Manoa Valley, which is also the home of the University of Hawai'i's main campus, is heavily residential today.

'O ke ka'a rapid transit Ka'u aloha
I ka nome mālie I ke ala hao

Hao ana e ka mana O ke kalaiwa
Ehuehu i ke kula Loa o Kalihi

Ho'olale mai ana E huli ho'i
E 'ike i ka nani O ke kapitala

Ka ihona o ke kula O Kalihi
Pā ana ka makani Pō'aihale

'O ka hana 'ana ia A ka uila
He pakika he pahe'e Kahi o nā pali

Rapid Transit Hula

Traditional

The rapid transit is my delight
As it rolls gently along on the rails

The driver turns on the power
Kicking up the dust on the plains of Kalihi

Hurry now and turn about
And see the beauty of the capital town

Moving down the slope of Kalihi's plain
The Po'aihale winds blow gently

The energy of the electricity
Causes us to slip and slide on the inclines

Separating the valleys of Manoa and Nu'uanu is Mt. Tantalus, a 2,000-foot-high mountain directly behind the center of Honolulu. It is on Tantalus that the Brothers Cazimero have recorded their most recent albums, in a hilltop home and studio built by Jon de Mello. On one side of Mt. Tantalus is Puowaina, the "Hill of Sacrifice." It is more commonly called Punchbowl. Inside this extinct crater is the National Memorial Cemetery of the Pacific.

On the other side of the mountain, a short road leads into Pu'u'ualaka'a State Park and an observation point that provides a spectacular panoramic view stretching from Diamond Head to Pearl Harbor. To the near right is downtown Honolulu, Honolulu Harbor, and Aloha Tower. Below to the left is Manoa Valley and straight ahead is Waikiki. As recently as a decade ago it was still quite easy to spot the gracious Royal Hawaiian Hotel, spreading its pink wings out along the famous beach. But those days are past. Today the "Pink Palace" is nearly lost amidst the towering hotels, condominiums, and shopping centers that comprise this modern and very dramatic O'ahu skyline. ■

Oheohe Aloha Tower a'e kū nei
Kilakila i ke awa a'o Honolulu

'O ka ipukukui e 'ānapanapa
Kou mālamalama u'i kelakela

Nāu e mālama a'e helu pono
I ka manawa pololei
a'o ke kaona

Hā'ina ka puana me ka maluhia
Oheohe Aloha Tower a'e kū nei

Aloha Tower — Traditional

Aloha Tower stands tall
So majestic in appearance
at the harbor of Honolulu

Your beacon light shines bright
Beaming with a beautiful glow

It's you that keeps a careful watch
And maintains
the accurate time for the town

Here now the refrain with peace
Aloha Tower stands tall

Above: Honolulu's harbor was the best natural port in the Islands for foreign ships, so this humid, dusty plain where few people lived 200 years ago—became the state's largest city and busiest port. At right: Honolulu's Aloha Tower, once the tallest building in Hawai'i, is reflected in a glass tower that now dwarfs it.

On The Beach At Waikīkī

That's where I'm going
To my castle by the sea
Coconut trees
wave their palms to me
Sweet Leilani
with gingers so fair
Run your fingers
through my hair
Walk with me
talk with me Waikīkī

Talk With Me Waikīkī

Ron Kaipo

That's where I'm going
To the place
where I was born
Tradewinds they call—
softly come to me
What will I do
if you leave me
What can I say
Walk with me
talk with me Waikīkī

For many years Robert and Roland hesitated to play their music on a regular basis in Waikiki. They had built up a strong local identity and feared that they would lose their loyal following if they started performing primarily for a tourist crowd.

In 1979 the Brothers Cazimero tested the waters first with a record album, *Waikiki, My Castle By the Sea.* The jacket cover, as well as the actual record label, pictures a nostalgic-styled photo of the Pink Palace, the Royal Hawaiian Hotel. The back cover contains a portrait of Robert and Roland wearing pink leis with Diamond Head in the background.

"That album jacket," explains Robert with a laugh, "probably reflected our unconscious desire to perform in Waikiki and, more specifically, at the Royal Hawaiian Hotel. Unfortunately, nobody took the hint. It took us four more years and a few more albums before we were ready for the Royal and luckily the Royal was waiting for us."

The success of *Waikiki, My Castle By the Sea* did, however, serve to associate the Brothers with Waikiki and many of those fans who bought the album probably thought they were already playing at the Royal. It certainly looked like it and sounded like it. The album, recorded with acoustic instruments, leads off with a medley of the songs "Talk With Me Waikiki" and "Sweet Memory," a combined tribute to the

Waikiki of yesterday. "Kaimana Hila" on side two is a beautiful salute to Hawai'i's most famous natural landmark, Diamond Head.

This album also contains "Rainbow Connection," a song from "The Muppet Movie," with Hawaiian lyrics by close friends Kaipo Hale and Larry Lindsey Kimura. Few singers have less Hawaiian blood than Kermit the Frog but the Brothers' daring recording of this song has nearly turned it into a Hawaiian classic. The album also features a vocal appearance by Betty Cazimero on "Kaimana Hila" and the expert touch of Bill Cazimero's steel guitar on "Kalihi."

At left: the Royal Hawaiian Hotel. Above: the Kodak Hula Show.
At right: the Brothers Cazimero, Robert and Roland. Following pages: the
Moana (at left) and Royal Hawaiian hotels on Waikiki Beach in the
1930s; and Waikiki Beach in the 1980s.

During the summer of 1982 the Brothers Cazimero finally made the transition to Waikiki, opening in the Monarch Room of the Royal Hawaiian Hotel. One of the first songs they tried out on their new audiences was "Royal Hawaiian Hotel" which they had recorded on their first album. "Finally," Robert says, "we were able to perform the song in the place it belonged. Now it's hard to sing it anywhere else."

"We resisted Waikiki for a long time," Roland adds, "but now we feel quite at home. Our following has not gotten smaller but bigger and we sing to at least 10,000 new faces each month. Every night visitors come up after the show and tell us that they are happy to find something truly Hawaiian in the heart of Waikiki."

Contemporary Waikiki is, indeed, a remarkable place. It has probably the most famous stretch of sandy beach in the world and is the home of a dozen first-class hotels that shelter nearly four million tourists to the Islands each year. Some of these visitors just come to lay on their backs in the sun. Others spend their time shopping, eating, and generally enjoying the sights. By the time they leave most of them are already thinking about how soon they can get back.

Uluwehiwehi ‘oe i ka‘u ‘ike la,
E ka Royal Hawaiian Hotel.

A he nani la, ke hulali nei,
A he nani māoli nō.

Ka moena weleweka moe kāua la,
He pakika he pahe‘e maika‘i nei.

Ka paia māpala ‘ōma‘oma‘o la,
He pipi‘o mau e ke ānuenue.

‘O ka hone a ke kai i ka pu‘u one la
Me ke ‘ala līpoa e moani nei.

‘O ka holunape a ka lau o ka niu la
I ke kukulu aumoe.

Ka Hōkū-loa nō kou alaka‘i la,
‘O ka mana kahikolu kou home.

E ō e ka Royal Hawaiian Hotel.
Kou inoa hanohano ia la.

Mary Pula‘a Robins

You are festive to see,
O Royal Hawaiian Hotel

Beauty gleaming,
True beauty.

Velvet beds we sleep upon,
Smooth, soft and good.

Green marble walls,
Rainbow constantly at arch.

Soft song of sea on sand dunes
Wafting in fragrance of seaweed.

Leaves of coconut sway
In the late night.

The morning star your guide,
Power of the trinity your home.

Answer, o Royal Hawaiian Hotel.
This is for the glory of your name.

A person can stand almost anywhere along the miracle mile of Waikiki to watch the parade of humanity pass by. Every color of skin is represented here, from brown to black to yellow. If there's any white at all it belongs to the first-day visitor. Soon those white arms and legs will turn to lobster red. What people wear in Waikiki is just as varied. Colorful shirts, shorts, and bathing suits dominate the day but after dark Waikiki's nightspots are full of the latest fashions.

James A. Michener, the bestselling novelist, worked in Waikiki during the late 1950s. He and his Japanese wife, Mari, lived for a time in a small apartment, just off the beach. After his morning exercises at the typewriter, Michener took frequent walks along the streets clad in long shorts and a bright aloha shirt. He enjoyed looking for people and places that he could later incorporate into his fiction.

While he was living in Waikiki, Michener developed a special fondness for what he called the beach's "Golden Men" and Kelly Kanakoa, a beachboy in his novel *Hawaii* (1959), is one of the book's most attractive characters. He is described as being over six feet tall, "unusually handsome," and possessing "a powerful body whose muscles rippled in sunlight as if smeared with coconut oil."

If that weren't enough, this young man was a surfer, a singer, and a talented slack key guitarist. Ladies vacationing in the Islands were always falling in love with him.

There was no real Kelly Kanakoa, of course. Michener combined several of Waikiki's legendary beachboys into a single person to help capture the lifestyle of Honolulu in the 1920s and 1930s.

These decades make up a particularly exciting period in the story of Waikiki and one of continuing interest to Robert and Roland Cazimero. Many of the older songs in their repertoire were made famous during the glory years of Waikiki. And their stage performances, when showcased at a nightspot as legendary as the Royal Hawaiian Hotel, enables the Brothers Cazimero to take audiences back to those days when the entire world considered Waikiki a synonym for music and romance.

Waikiki's human history, however, begins much earlier than the 1920s. It started centuries ago when only a handful of ancient Hawaiians lived on O'ahu's south shore. Here, under the impressive shadow of Diamond Head, they cultivated a swampy lowland with duckponds, taro patches,

At left: a sunset surfer. Top: snoozing in the sun; and a 1930s look at the Moana Hotel's pier as seen from the old Outrigger Canoe Club.

189

and rice paddies. Several natural springs watered this district year-round and the area became known as Waikiki or "spouting water." During the rainy season the area's narrow Manoa and Palolo streambeds tended to overflow and flooding was a frequent problem for the farmers.

From almost the beginning Waikiki was the playground of Hawaiian royalty. Kamehameha the Great landed here in 1795 to begin his successful invasion of O'ahu and afterwards he built a small palace near the beach. Only later did he move his headquarters near the harbor in present downtown Honolulu.

In the years that followed, Waikiki became a summer resort for the monarchs and most of Hawai'i's royal families maintained second residences here in an area called Helumoa. When David Kalakaua became king in 1874, he built a cottage next to the house of Kamehameha V, on the site of the present Royal Hawaiian Hotel.

On June 11, 1877—Kamehameha Day—King Kalakaua donated almost 200 acres of land at the eastern end of Waikiki to the kingdom. Named for his queen, Kapi'olani Park became Honolulu's first public park. During the king's waning years, Kapi'olani Park was used regularly for horse racing, polo, and various musical events.

Above: King Kamehameha V's house at Waikiki in 1866.
At right: a Waikiki sunset. Following pages: polo at Kapi'olani Park
in the 1920s; and today's Kapi'olani Park and the Waikiki Shell.

My Wahine And Me

Don McDiarmid Sr.

Where ever you go in the islands
Where ever you happen to be
Chances are that you won't be far
From my wahine and me

Strolling along in the islands
Walking along by the sea
We're here, we're there
We're everywhere,
my wahine and me

I don't know whether it was meant
I only know that it's nice
Here together we're content
In our Hawaiian paradise

So riding along on a surfboard
Or under a coconut tree
We're satisfied to be side by side
Cause I love her and she cares for me
My wahine and me

oday the acreage is home of the Honolulu Zoo, Hawai'i's first bandstand, tennis courts, ball fields, plenty of picnic tables, and the island's largest outdoor concert theater the Waikiki Shell. Here, on every May 1, the Brothers Cazimero stage their annual Lei Day concert, an event that has become as much an island tradition as the day itself.

King Kalakaua's park supervisor was a Scotsman, Archibald Cleghorn. He had married one of the king's sisters, Princess Likelike, and they had one daughter, Princess Victoria Ka'iulani. Since the king did not have children of his own, this infant was designated the heiress to the throne after another sister, Princess Lili'uokalani.

At her christening, Princess Ka'iulani was given a part of the royal estate by her godmother Princess Ruth. It was a simple country house set in a coconut grove close to the beach named 'Ainahau. It was not far from where the present-day Princess Ka'iulani Hotel is located in Waikiki. While growing up, Ka'iulani frequently rode her white saddle pony, Fairy, over the bridal paths in Kapi'olani Park.

It was in 1884 that Allen Herbert purchased several acres of seafront land adjoining Kapiʻolani Park. Here he built a small bungalow-styled hotel and called it Sans Souci. It was not the first hotel in Waikiki. As early as 1837 a hotel had been advertised in the newspaper, *Sandwich Islands Gazette.* The name Sans Souci was borrowed from the Potsdam Palace of Frederick the Great and translated means "without a care"—a slogan that Herbert's guests learned to appreciate.

Robert Louis Stevenson and his family, returning from a South Pacific cruise, arrived in Honolulu with his family in 1889. The celebrated author of *Treasure Island* anchored his chartered yacht, the *Casco,* in Honolulu Harbor but preferred the Waikiki area to downtown.

While in Waikiki, Stevenson lived temporarily in a number of small wooden cottages while working on a new novel, *The Master of Ballantrae.* The first of these haunts was a comfortable little bungalow located along Waikiki Road near Sans Souci. After a short stay here, Stevenson had to move to another private estate,

a half-mile down the beach. There were a couple of small houses here, bare-walled and cockroach infested, and the author jokingly referred to his joint bedroom and study as a "grim little shanty."

Besides being a novelist and poet, Stevenson was also a fairly good amateur musician. One photograph from this period shows the novelist in bed playing the flageolet. In another he is playing the flute-like instrument at a party with his wife, Fanny. His step-daughter, Isobel, wife of the artist Joseph Strong, is at the piano and a couple of friends are playing flutes and violins.

While in Honolulu, Stevenson was introduced to King Kalakaua and Princess Lili'uokalani. He and the King, himself an author and musician, became fast friends and they often sat talking far into the night. King Kalakaua had written a book, *The Legends and Myths of Hawaii,* published in 1888, and it was a common interest in Hawaiian and Polynesian culture and folklore that drew them closest together.

At this time you could ride downtown to Kapi'olani Park for only 5 cents on a mule-drawn tram

car. Stevenson and his family often rode the tram and waved to pedestrians along the route. Around the turn of the century the mules were replaced by electric street cars that ran until 1941.

Rail sections from this narrow gauge track can be seen today at the covered "Jogger's Rest" near the Kapi'olani Park tennis courts. This green and yellow shelter resembles the old street car station which marked the end of the line here.

During his stay in Waikiki, Stevenson also met Archibald Cleghorn and his daughter, Princess Ka'iulani and would often stroll over to 'Ainahau. It was still a sad time for Ka'iulani since her mother, Princess Likelike, had died only two years before at the age of 36.

Stevenson and Ka'iulani would walk around the grounds, often feeding the peacocks that the princess had been given as a present. The Hawaiians had no word for peacock so they used their own language and the name came out "pikake." Ka'iulani's favorite flower, the jasmine, is also called "pikake" by Hawaiians in her memory.

Stevenson read poetry to the young princess beneath the great banyan tree for which 'Ainahau was noted. Sometimes they would sit on the ground below a spreading banyan tree.

Before Ka'iulani left in May 1889, for school in England, Stevenson wrote this poem in her personal autograph book:

194

Left to right: electric street cars replaced the mule-drawn trams, whose last stop was Kapi'olani Park; seated with a flageolet, novelist Robert Louis Stevenson plays with friends; Robert Louis Stevenson and King Kalakaua; Princess Ka'iulani befriended Stevenson at her 'Ainahau home in Waikiki.

Forth from her land to mine she goes
The Island maid, the Island rose,
Light of heart and bright of face,
The daughter of a double race.

Her Islands here in Southern sun
Shall mourn their Kaiulani gone,
And I, in her dear banyan's shade,
Look vainly for my little maid.

But our Scots Islands far away
Shall glitter with unwanted day,
And cast for once their tempest by
To smile in Kaiulani's eye.

Underneath the poem, Stevenson added the following note:

"Written in April to Kaiulani in the April of her age; and at Waikiki, within easy walk of Kaiulani's banyan! When she comes to my land and her father's, and the rain beats upon the window (as I fear it will), let her look at this page; it will be like a weed gathered and pressed at home; and she will remember her own islands, and the shadow of the mighty tree; and she will hear the peacocks screaming in the dusk and the wind blowing in the palms; and she will think of her father sitting there alone.
—R. L. S."

Stevenson left Honolulu after six months, returning for five weeks in 1893 from his home in Samoa aboard the passenger liner *S.S. Mariposa.* On this second visit he stayed at Sans Souci, then owned by George Lycurgus. Stevenson found Waikiki had changed little since his 1889 visit but he greatly missed the company of King Kalakaua who had died in 1891. His sister and successor, Queen Lili'uokalani, was alive but had been deposed earlier that year. The monarchy had ended and Sanford B. Dole, a former judge in the kingdom's Supreme Court, was now head of the provisional government of Hawai'i.

Archibald Cleghorn was still around but his daughter, Princess Ka'iulani was away at school in England. The poet and the princess would never see each other again. Stevenson would die just over a year later in Samoa.

Upon leaving Honolulu in October, 1893, Stevenson wrote a note of appreciation in the Sans

195

Souci register. It was later used in a hotel advertisement.

"If anyone desire such old-fashioned things as lovely scenery, quiet, pure air, clear sea water, good food, and heavenly sunsets hung out before his eyes over the Pacific and the distant hills of Waianae, I recommend him cordially to the Sans Souci."

Stevenson, who spent a total of six and a half years in the Pacific, never forgot his friends or the kindness he experienced in the Islands. Especially noteworthy had been his 1890 public letter in defense of Father Damien de Veuster, the Belgian priest who had worked with the leprosy patients on Moloka'i. The letter was addressed to Rev. Dr. Charles M. Hyde, a Protestant missionary in Hawai'i who had attacked the priest's reputation for improving the conditions of the leprosarium.

A visitor to the Waikiki Library will find that most of the Hawaiian history books credit Dr. George Trousseau, Kalakaua's physician, with diagnosing, in 1885, that Father Damien had acquired the leprosy himself. There are few references, however, to the fact that this colorful doctor once started an ostrich farm in the Waikiki area.

Dr. Trousseau's first ostriches— one male and two female—arrived in the summer of 1890 and he immediately began exercising them in Kapi'olani Park. Soon they were getting as much attention by the residents as Ka'iulani's peacocks. The herd eventually grew to about 65 birds and their feathers commanded a high price overseas.

The good doctor died in 1894 and his ostriches subsequently vanished from Waikiki. Those that didn't die in the islands were shipped back to California. All that remains behind for sightseers today is a short street named for Trousseau near Diamond Head.

In 1897 the Seaside Hotel, used the former home of W. W. Dimond, opened in Waikiki. During the reign of King Kamehameha V, from 1863 to 1872, this had been the site of the monarch's summer home and for this reason many Hawaiians regarded it as sacred land.

At the start the Seaside functioned as an auxiliary to the downtown Royal Hawaiian Hotel for guests who preferred the beach and a more isolated location. Transportation between the two hotels was either by horse and buggy or street car.

The Seaside Hotel, like Sans Souci, gradually acquired a reputation on its own merits and travelers from around the world sought out its roomy cottages and friendly hospitality. It was here in the rotunda, contemporary newspaper clips say, that "Saturday night dancing was introduced to Honolulu."

The four-story Moana, built in 1901 of redwood in the shape of a rectangle, was the first modern resort hotel in Waikiki. There were originally 75 guest rooms, a lady's parlor, a saloon, a billiard room on the first floor and a dining room that extended out over the beach.

By the time the Moana opened its doors, however, Hawai'i's beloved "Princess of the Peacocks" was gone. Ka'iulani had died two years earlier, at the age of 23, in the early morning hours of March 6, 1899. Her friends in Waikiki knew the end had come when they heard her peacocks screaming into the darkness. The final hope to restore the monarchy was gone.

Waikiki changed with the death of Princess Ka'iulani and the opening of the Moana Hotel. Tourists began taking the place of royalty on the streets and the sandy stretch of seashore from the Waikiki Aquarium (opened in 1903) to Fort DeRussy (established as a military reservation in 1909) became one of the most famous beaches in the world.

A photograph, A calabash,
A paper lei
Are my Hawaiian
souvenirs.
Each token brings
back memories
All through
the day,

And may they last for many years.
When I am old and gray
I'll have the pleasure
to say to you,
A photograph,
a calabash,
a paper lei   Are my
Hawaiian Souvenirs.

Johnny Noble

Alice Roosevelt, the daughter of President Theodore Roosevelt, bypassed the up-scale Moana in 1905 and checked into the Seaside. Here, it was reported, she shocked the entire community when she lit up a cigarette on the hotel's beach-side, semi-circular *lanai.* Few women in Honolulu had ever been seen doing that before.

Jack London also came to Honolulu aboard his ketch, the *Snark,* in 1907. He had stopped at Waikiki briefly in 1904, on route to the Orient as an overseas correspondent in the Russo-Japanese War, but now had returned for a longer visit with his wife, Charmian.

With their boat moored at Pearl Harbor, London and Charmian commuted between a small cottage near Pearl City and the Seaside Hotel. The manager at the time was an old buddy from London's earlier days in the Yukon.

Much of London's mornings were spent at the beach. Two new Waikiki friends, Alexander Hume Ford and George Freeth gave him surfing lessons and he later wrote an article about the experience titled "A Royal Sport: Surfing at Waikiki."

On one occasion, London and his wife rented a pair of horses and rode to the base of Diamond Head crater. They climbed up the side and, once at the top, looked toward the Seaside Hotel in the distance. They then sat down to admire the vast panoramic view of the sea meeting the land at Waikiki.

During London's 1907 visit the Londons met a number of local dignitaries. During a Waikiki

My Sweet Gardenia Lei

My sweet gardenia lei,
 you gave to me
Upon a moonlit night
 at Waikīkī
A lover's melody
 just meant for two
A flower scented night
 when I met you

Fondest memories of you
 Are here haunting me now
Your faint perfume
 I cannot forget
'Til you return to me
again someday
 Bringing me a song
 And my sweet
gardenia lei

Danny Kuaana/Bernie Kaai

Preceding pages: a trip to Hawai'i isn't complete without some souvenirs.
Above: Waikiki's first visitors had to fend for themselves in the ocean.
Then a beachboy service was formed and snorkeling, swimming,
surfing, paddling, were taught. Here, an outrigger filled with tourists
is pushed off Waikiki Beach.

My tropical baby, my little empress
down at Waikīkī
Your hips they sway, like the
coconut trees
You're such a sweetheart to me

My tropical baby, your hair, your
body, always tickles me
To see you dancing, right in front of me
It's always more than what the
people see

Tropical
Baby
Noland
Conjugacion

The way you wink your eyes at me
It blows my senses, like the Kona breeze
Oh darling open your eyes and see
That I want you to belong to me

My tropical baby,
my little empress down at Waikīkī
I'm your Hawaiian boy,
waiting patiently
For you, to marry me

reception given for visiting congressmen by Hawai'i's delegate to Washington, Prince Jonah Kuhio Kalaniana'ole, they were introduced to the deposed Queen Lili'uokalani.

Later they had a Sunday breakfast with Sanford B. Dole at Aquamarine, the former governor's Waikiki home. Archibald Cleghorn also welcomed the Londons at 'Ainahau just as he had welcomed the Stevensons in 1889 and 1893. He took them into his garden and showed them the famous banyan tree where Stevenson had once read poetry to Princess Ka'iulani.

The Londons spent only five months in Honolulu during 1907 but returned again in March of 1915, this time on the passenger liner, *S.S. Matsonia.* They rented a cottage on Beach Walk and here welcomed visits from their many old Hawai'i friends.

Back in 1908, Alexander Hume Ford had helped to organize the Outrigger Canoe Club and the members had built several wooden, open-air pavilions at the beach between the Moana and Seaside hotels. London enjoyed visiting the club where he liked the company of Duke Kahanamoku. Three years earlier, in the 1912 Olympic Games at Stockholm, Kahanamoku had won the 100 meter swim in record time.

Photographer Ray Jerome Baker, a friend of both Ford and Kahanamoku, arrived in Hawai'i in 1908 and eventually established a studio in Waikiki. Baker took a number of photographs of the Londons during their 1915 visit and, on one afternoon, had lunch at the Hau Tree Inn to discuss collaborating on some magazine stories. These articles were still unfinished when London died at his California home in late 1916.

In 1917 the Hau Tree Inn became the Halekulani or "House Befitting Heaven." The main building, a former private residence belonged to Robert Lewers, and its five adjacent bungalows proved immediately popular for the new owners, Clifford and Juliet Kimball. Guests loved staying at the Halekulani where they could swim at nearby Gray's Beach or listen to the music meeting the waves while sipping tropical cocktails on the Hau Terrace. The Kimballs loved Hawaiian music and over the years hundreds of local singers and musicians were featured in the Halekulani's oceanside showroom.

Earl Dale Biggers, a mystery writer, stayed at the Halekulani in 1915 and during his visit read a newspaper article about the exploits of a local Chinese detective. He immediately conceived a series of fictional adventures starring Charlie Chan of the Honolulu Police Department and Chan's 1925 debut, in the novel, *House Without a Key,* was an instant success. Biggers completed six more books about Chan before his death in 1933. The Halekulani, for its part, renamed its popular bar and terrace area the "House Without a Key."

At left: Kanoe Cazimero, Robert and Roland's sister, strings a plumeria lei. Above: for a hundred years native musicians have romanced visitors and locals with Hawaiian harmonies.

Hawai'i's own brand of music had attracted world-wide attention in 1915 when the popular song, "On the Beach at Waikiki," was premiered at the Panama-Pacific Exposition. This was the first local song to score a hit on the Mainland. Waikiki became a hotspot almost overnight and soon everybody seemed to be on a ship bound for the islands.

Nightlife at the Moana Hotel proved especially popular. Three evenings a week dancers crowded into the lounge and *lanai* area, listening to Dan Pokipala and his Moana Hotel Orchestra. Johnny Noble joined the band in 1919, first as a drummer and, when Pokipala stepped down a year later, became its leader. He added modern, jazz rhythms to the band's sound and the dancers poured into the Moana.

One popular feature of the hotel was its wooden pier that stuck far out over the ocean and ended with a small pavilion. Tired dancers often strolled out on the pier to sit on its benches underneath the moonlight and listen to the music. On the nights that the orchestra wasn't playing the pier belonged to the beachboys who gathered there and strummed their 'ukuleles for the tourists.

When the band wasn't playing and beachboys weren't strumming, tourists and plantation workers alike often went down to Heine's Tavern (formerly the Waikiki Inn) at the *ewa* end of present-day Kuhio Beach. Here they could find Sonny Cunha, the father of *hapa-haole* music (English lyrics interspersed with a few Hawaiian words) at the piano. Cunha composed his first *hapa-haole* song, "My Waikiki Mermaid," back in 1903.

With the growing tourist popularity of Waikiki in the early 1920s the beachfront continued its slow change from agricultural lands to an urban resort area. The Waikiki Reclamation Project had begun as early as 1916 and hundreds of former swampland acres were drained and filled to provide new home tracts. The Ala Wai Canal was built and it successfully

The Ala Wai Canal (above) was built to drain mountain streams away from Waikiki, which was being reclaimed from a swamp. It was first used as a homeport for fishing boats. Now canoe paddlers stroke down it for practice.

203

204

channeled the runoff from the mountain streams into the ocean and away from the Waikiki business and residential district.

After the end of World War I, the people of Honolulu decided to honor those island men who had lost their lives in battle. A saltwater pool, extending into the ocean, was built near the Waikiki Aquarium and dedicated in 1927. Duke Kahanamoku officially opened the War Memorial Natatorium with an exhibition swim.

The Royal Hawaiian Hotel, the third of Waikiki's modern hotels, was opened in 1927. Today it is surrounded by modern, high-rise hotels yet remains more dignified than ever. It has not been lost—as some had feared—in the forest of concrete giants that have soared up around it. The Royal, in fact, has taken on a new aura with the coming of the large hotels. It has become, more than ever, the outpost of tradition and comfortable old ways.

The Royal Hawaiian was built in approximately a year and a half and opened on Feb. 1, 1927. Some 1,200 persons attended the grand opening party, remembered fondly by those who were lucky enough to attend. Members of the Honolulu Symphony formed a smaller concert orchestra and performed chamber music for dinner guests.

The architectural style of the Royal is Spanish, reflecting the interests of the mid-1920s, but the first manager was an Italian-American, Arthur Benaglia. The first registered guest was Princess Kawananakoa, who might have been Queen had the monarchy continued.

The idea for building the Royal Hawaiian is attributed to William P. Roth. He was a San Francisco stockbroker married to Lurline Matson, a member of the family that owned Matson Navigation Co. It was Roth's plan to build a hotel in Honolulu that would act as an extension of the Matson steamship fleet. With a luxury hotel in the Islands, the company's famous white liners could carry passengers as well as freight. A complete travel package to Hawai'i could thus be offered.

Roth approached E. D. Tenney, president of Castle and Cooke, and Conrad von Hamm, head of the Territorial Hotel Co. Together they raised $4 million to build the new hotel.

The pink stucco six-story Moorish styled hotel was designed by the architectural firm of Warren and Wetmore of New York. It is repainted every three years, taking about 1,300 gallons of paint per job.

Above: a reproduction of the original menu cover, February 1, 1927, "The Night They Opened The Royal." At left: Hawaiian swimming attire has gone from nothing, to loin cloths, to mu'u mu'u (after the missionaries came) and now—as this bikini wahine shows—it's going back to its beginnings.

I Waikīkī anuanu au
Hoʻi au i Kewalo, pumehana au

Aia i Kalihi kaʻu aloha
I ka hale kula nui ʻo Kamehameha

Mea ʻole ia loa i kahi manaʻo
Ma hope hoʻi au me kuʻu aloha

He loa ka ʻimina a ka huapala
ʻalo aʻe i ke kula o Kaiwiʻula

ʻŌlelo kauoha na kuʻu aloha
I ka hola ʻeiwa hiki aku wau

Kakali au a hala ka manawa
Pau ka manaʻolana o ka hiki mai

Ke huli hoʻi nei ʻo Lelesia
Keiki o ka pua lāʻī

Hāʻina ʻia mai ana ka puana
Hoʻi au i Kewalo pumehana au

Waikīkī Hula
Isaac Keola

At Waikīkī I am cold
I return to Kewalo and I am warm

There at Kalihi is my love
At Kamehameha High School

Traveling the distance doesn't bother me
Later I will be with my love

The search by this suitor has been long
Passing over the plains of Kaiwiʻula

My love requested of me
To be there at Nine O'clock

I waited way past the hour
I became disillusioned about her coming

Lelesia now is going home
Kid of the lāʻī flowers

Tell the story
I return to Kewalo and I am warm

Millionaires of the 1920s and 1930s found the Royal Hawaiian a perfect place to escape to, a sort of tropical Shangri-La. Some of them brought their own roadsters and phaetons to spin about the island of Oʻahu. After the stock market crash of 1929, the roaring of the 1920s ceased but the beach resort still managed to attract its share of guests.

In January 1942, the Royal was taken over by the Navy Department as a rest and recreation site for the men of the Pacific Fleet. For the duration of World War II there was a baseball diamond on the grounds, a dispensary in the current beauty salon area and cocktail bar that dispensed coffee and soft drinks.

The Navy released the Royal on Oct. 31, 1945, and it was refurbished by the Matson Navigation Co. at a cost of $1,250,000. It reopened to the public again on Feb. 1, 1947, its 20th anniversary. A $800,000 renovation program was again completed in 1958 when every room was redecorated. One year later, in June 1959, Matson sold its four Waikiki Hotels—including the Royal Hawaiian—to the Sheraton Corporation of America.

Still another renovation was completed by Sheraton in 1964 with all rooms and suites in the hotel redecorated and 250 guest rooms air-conditioned. A new kitchen was designed and completed for the Surf Room and the former Royal Ballroom was changed into the more adaptable and elegant Regency Room. By the middle of 1968 all of the original 410 rooms were air-conditioned.

One year later a new 16-story Royal Hawaiian wing was opened adjacent to the original pink structure. It contains 192 rooms and was designed by

the firm of Wimberly, Whisenand, Allison, Tong and Goo, Ltd. It retains the famous pink color, arches and pillars so familiar to five decades of travelers. Changes may have come to Honolulu and Waikiki over the past half-century but the Royal Hawaiian Hotel lives on as one of the Pacific's best-known landmarks.

The Monarch Room, where the Brothers Cazimero now hold court, is a centerpiece of the Royal and has long been Waikiki's most prestigious showroom. For the past half-century nearly every well-known Hawaiian entertainer from comic dancer Hilo Hattie to romantic balladeer Alfred Apaka has performed here.

During the late 1920s and 1930s the Moana and Royal Hawaiian Hotel orchestras had a friendly rivalry that involved everything from introducing new songs and dances to stealing musicians away from each other. Tourists and locals alike moved back and forth between the two hotels in search of the brightest musical highlights.

In 1932 an enterprising student of Hawaiiana, George P. Mossman, opened Lalani's Garden Poi Inn on the spot of the present Holiday Inn. The local-style restaurant was later joined by an entire complex of thatched huts and demonstration areas. Lalani Hawaiian Village was an ancestor, at least in theme

and spirit, to today's Polynesian Cultural Center.

Mossman's idea was to approximate an authentic Hawaiian lifestyle for visitors by including entertainment as well as classes in chanting, hula, conversational Hawaiian, weaving, and food preparation. At one point there were more than 50 people living at the village with the primary attraction being James P. K. Kuluwaimaka, the last living chanter from the court of King Kalakaua.

Although there had been beachboys in Waikiki since the first tourists arrived on horseback, James Michener's legendary "Golden Men" date from the middle 1930s. The three main Waikiki hotels had no organized beach services at the time and their guests were left, quite literally, out in the surf to either sink or swim. In 1934 members of the Outrigger Canoe Club responded to the problem by organizing the Waikiki Beach Patrol.

The carefully picked patrol crew aided the hotels by handing out towels, chairs, and umbrellas from their concession stations. Some of the beachboys also played guitar for the tourists and showed them how to surf and paddle a canoe. World War II put an official end to the Waikiki Beach Patrol but some of its members returned later and continued to hang around the beaches for the next two decades.

At left: Royal Hawaiian Hotel, a tropical Shangri-La for millionaires in the 1930s, a recreation post for the World War II Navy, and the grandest entertainment showcase in Waikiki today. Above: the Brothers Cazimero.

Harry Owens, a native of Nebraska, came to Honolulu in 1934 and became leader of the Royal Hawaiian Hotel Orchestra a year later. During 1935, while playing in the Monarch Room, he wrote his best-known song, "Sweet Leilani," for his new-born daughter. It was sung by Bing Crosby in the popular 1937 film, *Waikiki Wedding* and the record stayed on the Hit Parade charts for 28 consecutive weeks. It later won an Oscar for the year's best movie song.

On July 3, 1935, from under the famed banyan tree at the Moana Hotel, the first "Hawaii Calls" program was broadcast by shortwave to the West Coast. Webley E. Edwards, who created the show, hired Owens as the musical director of the band.

Al Perry took over the band in 1937 and remained its leader until his retirement in 1967. Until its demise in 1975 the band played once a week and its live program was broadcast, at its peak in 1952, to over 750 stations worldwide. Most of the programs originated in the Moana's Banyan Court but special performances were also broadcast from the Royal Hawaiian Hotel, 'Iolani Palace, at various locations on the Neighbor Islands and even from sea aboard the *S.S. Matsonia*.

Edwards explained that "Hawaii Calls" was launched "to give an accurate, faithful and authentic presentation of the music of the islands." From its first program in 1935 to its last 40 years later, over 300 Hawaiian musicians and singers made appearances on "Hawaii Calls."

World War II changed the face of Waikiki. The Royal Hawaiian Hotel was taken over as a rest and recreation post for the military forces and the surrounding area turned into a "honky tonk" district that entertained thousands of troops heading overseas. Miles of barbed wire were coiled along the beaches while curfews and blackouts were strictly enforced. By war's end, when the lights were turned on and the barbed wire rolled up, the loudest music in Waikiki was automobile traffic. With an increased population—not every sailor chose to go home—and a building boom, a modern Waikiki began to emerge.

Jet service came in the 1950s and Waikiki's first "skyscraper," the Princess Ka'iulani Hotel was completed in 1955 on the site of the former 'Ainahau estate. The main house at 'Ainahau had burned down in the 1920s and the banyan tree that had once sheltered Ka'iulani and Robert Louis Stevenson had been removed in 1949.

In 1956 both the Waikiki Shell and the

The Brothers Cazimero sing on a float during the annual Aloha Week parade that passes through Waikiki in October. At right: Waikiki in neon. Top right: Waikiki pumps with electricity, music, and dancing each night. The International Market Place is a collection of tourist shops, restaurants, and bars in the middle of Waikiki.

International Market Place, built on the original Outrigger Canoe Club parking lot, were opened. The Outrigger Canoe Club, itself, remained near the Royal Hawaiian Hotel until 1964 when increasing rents forced the members to move from the site it had occupied continuously for over half-a-century. It was relocated farther down the beach toward Diamond Head and next to the Elks Club.

Donn Beach introduced Don the Beachcomber's at the International Market Place soon after it opened and then presented a Hawaiian revue starring singer Alfred Apaka and hula dancer 'Iolani Luahine. Beach also presented the pianist Martin Denny whose combo soon had tourists standing in line to hear his own particular brand of South Seas music.

The original Don the Beachcomber was sold and renamed Duke Kahanamoku's in 1960. Denny's group remained along with a new show starring Ed Kenny. A few years later Don Ho and The Aliis took over and held center stage until 1970.

Waikīkī
Andy Cummings

There's a feeling deep in my heart
Stabbing at me just like a dart
It's a feeling heavenly
I see memories out of the past
Memories that always will last
Of a place beside the sea.

Waikīkī at night when the shadows are falling
I hear your rolling surf calling
Calling and calling to me

Waikīkī, tis for you that my heart is yearning
My thoughts are always returning
Out there to you across the sea

Your tropic nights and your wonderful charms
Are ever in my memory
And I recall when I held in my arms
An angel sweet and heavenly

Waikīkī, my whole life is empty without you
I miss that magic about you
Magic beside the sea
Magic of Waikīkī

Following pages: the Brothers Cazimero backstage at the Waikiki Shell, preparing for their annual May Day concert. At sunset, Waikiki (Royal Hawaiian Hotel in foreground) transforms from sun-drenched beach to entertainment capital of the Pacific.

209

Today there are still a handful of holdovers from Waikiki's glorious past. Diamond Head continues to guard Kapiʻolani Park and tourists return year after year to the essentially unchanged Moana and Royal Hawaiian Hotels. There is a fancier Halekulani and other new buildings but just as each unfolding decade brings changes to Waikiki they also bring new memories.

Waikiki Road, perhaps most significantly, is now Kalakaua Avenue, one of the most famous streets in the Pacific. It was renamed years ago in honor of David Kalakaua, the Merrie Monarch who walked on this beach and swam in this surf and, among so many other accomplishments, gave Hawaiian music and dance back to the Hawaiians. ▨

Preserving The Past

The Brothers Cazimero are modern musicians linked to the past. Robert and Roland are both students of Hawaiian culture and their unique contemporary sound remains rooted in the heritage of their musical ancestors.

In 1983 the Brothers gave four Christmas concerts in the Hawaiian Hall at the Bernice P. Bishop Museum. Here, in a three-level gallery that traces the history of Hawai'i from prehistoric times to the present, they performed their songs from a modest platform that was built in front of the museum's grass house display.

Only a handful of recent musical groups have been allowed to perform in the Hawaiian Hall, which was completed in 1900. The thatched house that the Brothers used as their backdrop was erected in 1902 by Dr. J. F. K. Stokes, then the museum's curator.

Stokes dismantled three separate grass houses on Kaua'i and reassembled them in Honolulu. The original *pili* grass roof, applied in the traditional manner, has not been changed since, except for occasional patchwork.

On a recent morning Robert and Roland Cazimero returned to the Bishop Museum and sat down again next to the grass house. Robert said that as kids growing up in Kalihi, and later as students attending Kamehameha Schools, he and Roland had visited the museum to look at its exhibits.

"We used to close our eyes," he says, "and try to imagine the days when all houses in Hawai'i looked like this. If you needed shelter you merely put together a framework of poles and sticks and then tied grass to the framework.

"If you wanted to eat you could go fishing or hunting. The ocean provided much of the food for people in the shoreline villages, but there was also basic farming for taro, sweet potatoes, and yams. Coconuts, breadfruit, and bananas were, of course, gathered from the trees."

Roland, who has researched ancient Hawaiian traditions, adds that the islands had a highly developed class society that was ruled by those of chiefly rank. There was also a strict religious system whose beliefs affected every facet of daily life.

"These spiritual laws unified the entire island community," Roland explains. "They covered everything from eating to canoe building to house dedications. If you wanted to marry, have a baby or go to war there were certain customs that had to be observed."

It is the chants, dance, and music of Hawai'i that interest Robert and Roland, and it is here, at the Bishop Museum, that much of the important research into their origins began. Since its founding in 1889 the museum has sponsored significant investigations into the field and has published numerous books, pamphlets, and scientific papers on the subject.

These studies have shown that during ancient times musical expression in Hawai'i was achieved primarily through chanting poems. These chants or *mele* preserved the legends, genealogies, and history of the people and were usually sung to the accompaniment of simple rhythm instruments. Chanted Hawaiian poetry is divided into two musical styles. Dancing accompanied *mele hula* while *mele oli* were chanted poems not accompanied by dancing.

At left: The Bishop Museum's Hawaiian Hall surveys the history of Hawai'i from prehistoric to contemporary times. Its grass house was erected in 1902. Above: Ray Jerome Baker photographed these Hawaiian girls eating poi in 1912. The girl at the left is playing a nose flute, a musical instrument said to have been used to convey the messages of lovers.

Some early Hawaiian musical instruments were brought in the canoes of the early Polynesian voyagers while others were created later by the native Hawaiians. Included in both categories were the *pahu* (drum), *ipu* (gourd), *'uli'uli* (gourd rattle), *papa hehi* (stone clappers) *kala'au* (resonant sticks), *'ili'ili* (clicking stones), *'ulili* (whirling rattle), and the *pu'ili* or split shafts of bamboo. Two woodwinds were also developed: the *'ohe hano ihu* (nose flute) and the *ipu hokiokio* (gourd whistle). The Brothers Cazimero have used all of these instruments, at one time or another, in their live stage shows and concert performances.

The Bishop Museum has two major collections of primary source recordings that can be studied for the sound of 19th century chants. One of these is the Helen Roberts Collection (1923–1924) and the other is the Kuluwaimaka Collection (1933–1936). Both are housed in the Division of Audio-Recording Collections and Research which is part of the Department of Anthropology.

Helen Roberts came to Hawai'i in 1923 under sponsorship of the government's Hawaiian Legend and Folklore Commission. The commission had the authority, under an act passed by the Territorial Legislature, to "collect, print, publish and . . . preserve for posterity the ancient songs, music and meles of the people of the Hawaiian Race."

Roberts, born in Illinois and a graduate of the Chicago Musical College, was already an experienced musicologist when she arrived in Hawai'i. She had an M.A. degree in anthropology from Columbia University and had previously made field trips to the Caribbean to record Jamaican music.

The Bishop Museum gave Roberts an office, a good research library, and the promise that her work would be published by the Bishop Museum Press. She was given an interpreter, Thomas K. Maunupau, and $5,000 to cover salary and expenses for the five-month project.

Roberts started her recording work on O'ahu, using an Edison phonograph with recording attachments. The bell-shaped tube attachment was held close to the mouth of the chanter and the sound of the voice was recorded onto a wax cylinder that was wound with a hand crank. Afterwards, some cylinders were sent to the Edison Laboratories in New Jersey where casts were made.

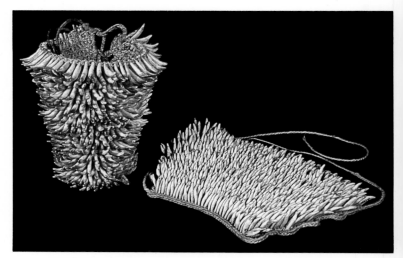

Upon arriving in Honolulu, Roberts began immediately collecting material on O'ahu. She recorded and interviewed nine elderly Hawaiians then living at the Lunalilo Home. From O'ahu she traveled to Kaua'i where she toured around the island by car from Lihu'e with her cylinders and recording machine. She spent two weeks in Hanalei and later visited the Big Island.

Roberts had a tough time in the beginning trying to find knowledgeable and cooperative chanters. She was, however, quite a personable young woman and her determination and smiles eventually gained the confidence of her informants, most of whom had been born between 1830 and 1870. Altogether she was able to collect nearly 700 different *mele* representing the chants and chanting style of the 19th century.

When she departed the islands on June 21, 1924, the *Honolulu Advertiser* printed a story about her

Voyaging artist Louis Choris drew these dancers (top) during his visit to the Islands in 1816. Dog-teeth leg ornaments (middle) were worn like anklets and produced sounds when shaken. Gourd nose whistles (bottom) had a hole for the nostril drilled near the stem end of the gourd and finger holes drilled on one side.

work that was amusingly, but rather accurately, head-lined, "Ancient Hawaiian Music Saved to Posterity by Haole Woman."

After leaving Hawai'i, Roberts went to Yale University. There she studied her notes, listened to the wax recordings, and wrote up her report, *Ancient Hawaiian Music.* This was the first scholarly and comprehensive examination of its subject and was published in 1926 as Bishop Museum Bulletin 29.

The museum's Kuluwaimaka Collection of recordings was made in 1933 by Theodore Kelsey working under the supervision of Kenneth Emory of the Bishop Museum. Emory hired Kelsey to record the chants of James K. P. Kuluwaimaka using a Dictaphone phonograph-recorder and wax cylinders.

Kuluwaimaka, born in 1845 on the Big Island, had been a professional court chanter for both King Kamehameha IV and King Kalakaua. His memory was still fairly sharp when Kelsey made his recordings of nearly 150 chants that were subsequently written down and annotated with Kuluwaimaka's own remarks. This collecting ended with the death of the chanter in 1936.

In addition to the Roberts and Kuluwaimaka material, the Bishop Museum also has other chant recordings and texts collected in the 1920s and 1930s by Emory, Kelsey, Charles Kenn, and Vivienne Haupala Mader. Jane Winne added recordings made during the 1940s, and Mary Kawena Pukui's collecting covered four decades, from the 1930s through the 1960s.

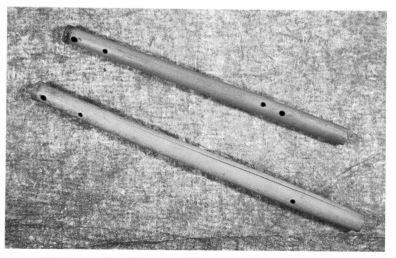

This total collection of sound material remained in the Bishop Museum Library until 1951 when the museum received an Ekotape recorder from 20th Century Fox. Fox's gift was in appreciation for help given by the museum during the film company's production of "Bird of Paradise," a Hollywood movie remake that starred Jeff Chandler and Debra Paget.

Kenneth Emory used the new machine to begin duplicating the post-1920s musical recordings onto newly developed magnetic tape. The wax cylinders used by Roberts were taken to Syracuse University in 1969 where they were also transferred to tape by the Thomas A. Edison Re-Recording Laboratory.

In 1981 the Bishop Museum released "Na Leo Hawai'i Kahiko: Voices of Old Hawai'i," an album of two long-playing records produced from material in the Roberts, Kuluwaimaka, and other collections. The project was directed by Elizabeth Tatar, the museum's ethnomusicologist. A year later the Museum Press published Tatar's *Nineteenth Century Hawaiian Chant,* a book that presents, among other things, a musical analysis of 19th century chants.

When Captain Cook and his crew made their "discovery" of Hawai'i in 1778, Hawaiian music was represented solely by chants recited to the rhythm of the primitive hand-made instruments mentioned above. The sound of these chants, however, began to change with the introduction of foreign cultures and even the recordings collected by Helen Roberts in 1923 are probably different than those heard by Cook and his men.

It was during Cook's second visit that the Hawaiians got their introduction to Western instrumental music. In January 1779 several crewmembers entertained the natives with the sound of a French horn, a flute, and violin. Concerts were subsequently presented by other ship's crews that visited Hawai'i during the early years of European contact. When the Protestant missionaries arrived in 1820 they discouraged chanting and the hula. Christian hymn singing was introduced to the Hawaiians.

Foreign influences nearly destroyed traditional Hawaiian music and dance. Performers were forced to go underground to preserve their art. It was not until King Kalakaua took the throne in 1874, that Hawaiian music was allowed to step out from behind the shadows that had been cast by the missionaries. After a half-century of public silence it was time once more to shout, "let the dancing begin." ■

Above: Coconut knee drum, made of half a coconut shell, with striking cord. Nose flutes (bottom), were present throughout most of Polynesia when the Islands were discovered by Europeans.

The Hawaiian Language

Captain James Cook and his crew compiled the first list of Hawaiian words in 1778 during their initial visit to the Hawaiian Islands. The list of about 250 words was printed in Cook's *A Voyage to the Pacific Ocean,* published in London in 1785.

Hawaiian remained a spoken language until 1829 when the Calvinist-Christian missionaries selected 12-letter alphabet. They voted to establish the consonants as h, k, l, m, n, p, and w. It was also decided that the vowel sounds would be identical to the Italian a, e, i, o, and u.

The first Hawaiian-English dictionary, *A Vocabulary of Words in the Hawaiian Language,* was compiled by Lorrin A. Andrews and published in 1836 at Lahainaluna, Maui. Nine years later at Lahainaluna, the first English-Hawaiian dictionary was prepared by John S. Emerson and Artemus Bishop.

All words in the Hawaiian language end in a vowel and consonants do not occur without vowels between them. Words do not change to indicate tenses and there are no endings to indicate the plural.

Today a hamsa (') is used to mark the glottal stop. A macron, or line above a vowel (e.g., ā), is used to indicate long vowel sounds. The Hawaiian words used in *Celebration* are printed without the macron. Proper names of commercial businesses, institutions, and organizations are often spelled without diacritical marks.

Although the orthography of the Hawaiian language continues to be studied and debated, currently acceptable spellings and word meanings can be found in the *Hawaiian Dictionary* by Mary Kawena Pukui and Samuel H. Elbert. Also recommended is *Place Names of Hawaii* by Pukui, Elbert, and Esther T. Mookini.

The following pronunciation guide is taken, with permission, from the *Hawaiian Dictionary.* For more details consult section 2 of *Hawaiian Grammar,* also by Pukui and Elbert. All of the above books are published by the University of Hawaii Press.

Pronunciation Of Hawaiian

Consonants

p, k	about as in English but with less aspiration.
h, l, m, n	about as in English.
w	after *i* and *e* usually like *v*; after *u* and *o* usually like *w*; initially and after *a* like *v* or *w*.
'	a glottal stop, similar to the sound between the *oh's* in English *oh-oh.*

Vowels

Unstressed

a	like *a* in above	
e	like *e* in bet	
i	like *y* in city	but without off-glides.
o	like *o* in sole	
u	like *oo* in moon	

Stressed

a, ā	like *a* in far	
ē	like *e* in bet	
e	like *ay* in play	But without off-glides; vowels marked
i, ī	like *ee* in see	with macrons are somewhat longer
o, ō	like *o* in sole	than other vowels.
u, ū	like *oo* in moon	

Rising Dipthongs

ei, eu, oi, ou, ai, ae, ao, au these are always stressed on the first member, but the two members are not as closely joined as in English.

Stress (or Accent)

On all vowels marked with macrons; ā, ē, ī, ō, ū.

Otherwise on the next-to-last syllable and alternating preceding syllables of words, except that words containing five syllables without macrons are stressed on the first and fourth syllables. Final stress in a word (ʹ) is usually louder than preceding stress or stresses (ˋ): *hále, makáʻu, hòlohólo, ʻèlemakúle.*

Glossary

This list includes Hawaiian words which appear in the text as well as common words often used in everyday conversation. Most specific names of plants and animals have been excluded.

'ahu'ula	feather cape
'aina	land
akaku	vision, reflection
akamai	smart, clever
'ala	fragrant, perfumed
ali'i	chief or royalty
aloha	greeting, love, compassion
'anuenue	rainbow
aumakua	family or personal god
'auwana	to wander, modern
'apana	piece, land division
'auwai	ditch
ewa	unstable, wandering, westerly
halau	hula school, canoe house
hale	house, building
hana	bay, valley
hanai	adopted
haole	foreigner, white person
hapa	half
hapai	pregnant
hapa-haole	half-white
heiau	temple
hoku	star
holoku	long gown
holoholo	to walk
ho'olaule'a	celebration
hui	club, association
hukilau	net fishing
hula	a dance

'ili'ili	pebble
'io	hawk
'ipo	sweetheart
ipu	gourd
ipu hokiokio	gourd whistle
kahiko	old, ancient
kahuna	priest, sorcerer
kai	sea, sea water
kala'au	stick dance
kama'aina	native-born, longtime resident
kanaka	man, commoner
kanawai	law
kane	male
kapa	bark cloth
kapu	taboo, forbidden
keiki	baby, child
ki'i	picture, photograph
kilu	gourd, coconut shell
koa	endemic forest tree
kokua	help
kona	leeward
ko'olau	windward
kuhina	minister, premier
kumu	teacher
kupuna	grandparent, ancestor

lanai	veranda
lau hala	pandanus leaf used in plaiting
lei	flower wreath, necklace
limu	seaweed
lua	outhouse, toilet
lu'au	feast, party
luna	boss
mahele	portion, division
mahiole	feather helmet
mahimahi	dolphin fish
makahiki	ancient Fall festival
makai	toward the ocean
malihini	newcomer
malo	loincloth
makani	wind, breeze
mana	supernatural or divine power
mano	shark
manu	bird
mauka	toward the mountains
mauna	mountain, mountainous
mele	song, poem
menehune	Hawaiian elf or leprechaun
moana	ocean
mu'umu'u	loose gown
nane	riddle, puzzle, parable
nani	beauty, glory
nei	here, this place
nui	large, great, important
'ohana	family
'ohe hanoihu	nose flute
'okole	buttocks
'oli	chant not danced to
'ono	delicious, tasty
'opu	stomach

pahu	drum
palaka	indifferent, inactive, checked cloth
pali	cliff, precipice
paniolo	cowboy
papa hehi	treadle board
pau	end, finished
pele	lava flow, the volcano goddess
pikake	jasmine
piko	navel, umbilical cord
pili	to cling, grass used in house thatch
pohaku	rock, stone
poi	foodstuff made from taro
pua	flower
pueo	owl
pu'ili	bamboo rattle
puka	hole, gate, door
punee	couch
pupu	appetizer
pupule	insane
tutu	grandmother
ua	rain
'ukulele	string instrument
'uli'uli	gourd rattle with feather
wahine	female
wene	glow
wikiwiki	quick, hurry

Discography

Prior to forming The Brothers Cazimero, Robert and Roland recorded three albums with Peter Moon as a trio, the Sunday Manoa. These albums are *Guava Jam* (1972), *Cracked Seed* (1973) and *The Sunday Manoa 3* (1974).

In addition to their albums as The Brothers Cazimero, Robert has recorded one solo album, *Robert Cazimero.* Roland has recorded *Hokule'a* (with Keli'i Tau'a), and two solo albums, *Pele,* and *Warrior.*

The letters MOP below refer to the Music of Polynesia recording company. MAC is an abbreviation for Mountain Apple Company. Following the label identification is the company code number.

THE BROTHERS CAZIMERO (1976): Maunawili, Royal Hawaiian Hotel, Morning Dew, Maunaloa, Aloha Tower, Ocean of Memories, Rapid Transit, He Inoa No Pauahi, Kilakila 'O Haleakala, Ku'u Ipo I Ka He'e Pu'e One, No Ke Aloha Ana 'Ole (MOP 38000)

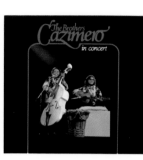

THE BROTHERS CAZIMERO IN CONCERT (1977): Ho'okele, Holo Wa'ape, Ua Noho Au A Kupa, Pauoa Liko Ka Lehua, Ku'u Ipo I Ka He'e Pu'e One, My Wahine and Me, Sanoe, Akaka Falls, Waikiki, Waikiki Hula, He Punahele, Christmas Wish, Kipikoa (Stevedore Hula), Morning Dew (MOP 47000)

THE BROTHERS CAZIMERO VOLUME II (1977): Kipikoa, Soft Green Seas, Tewe Tewe (Vickie II) Welina O'ahu, Holo Wa'apa, Kaneohe, Waika, Nani Koolau, Ku'u Ipo O Ke Aumoe, Punahou, Our Song (MOP 41000)

ROBERT CAZIMERO (1978): Mahai'ula, Maui Waltz, There's No Love, Poli Anuanu, Nani A'ala Wale, Skyflower (Pualani), Ho'onanea, Aloha no, Home Pumehana, Pane Mai (MAC 1001)

THE MUSICAL SAGA OF THE HOKULE'A (1977): Ho'onaniia (Praising the Hokule'a), La Ho'olana (Day of Launching), Na Pe'a O Hokule'a (The Sails of Hokule'a), Maxwell Namunamu (Complaining Maxwell), Oni Wa'a Kaulua (The Moving Double Hulled Canoe), Hokuli'ili'i (Little Star, the dog), The I'a Stew (The Fish Stew), Dreams (Moemoea), Doldrum Blues, Ho'okele (Steering), E O E Hokule'a (Announcing Hokule'a) (MOP 43000)

HO'ALA (1978): Nani Hanalei, Keala, The Beauty of Maunakea, Mu'olaulani I'a Stew (Fish Stew), Pua Hone, Ka Makani Ka'ili Aloha, Ka'Ulu La'au O Kai, Pua Mae'ole, Na Menehune, Ekolu, The Breeze and I, Pierre's Song (MAC 1005)

PELE (1979): I've Got to Find Me a Home, E Pele, Come Love Me Now, Hi'iaka's Pledge, Rebirth of Lohiau, Malama Pono, Kilu, Why Are We Apart?, I'm the One, A Promise Forgotten, Jealousy, Destiny, I Am, I Am (MAC 1003)

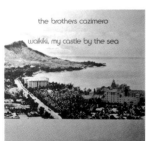

WAIKIKI, MY CASTLE BY THE SEA (1979): Talk With Me Waikiki/Sweet Memory, Kamamakakaua, Kalihi, I Lei'oe, E Ku'u Baby Hot Cha Cha, The Warmth of Our Love, Honolulu Skylark, Ka Wai Lehua, 'A'ala ka Honua, Kaimana Hila, Rainbow Connection, These Hidden Valleys (MAC 1101)

HAWAII, IN THE MIDDLE OF THE SEA (1980): Home in the Islands, Pehea Ho'i Au, E Hele Au Ma Ke Kai, One Small Favor, Haleakala, Na Kuahiwi 'Elima, Pu'u 'Ohu (Waimea Fantasy), Ka Wailele o Nu'uanu, Ho'okipa Hawaii, Waimea Lullaby, Lehua Hulu Mamo, Hawaiian Souvenirs, Dangers of the World (MAC 1013)

CAPTURED MAGIC (1982): Hello Honolulu, Nani Hanalei, Wahine Ilikea, Pua Hone, Home in the Islands, The Shores of Haleiwa, E Ku'u Baby Hot Cha Cha, Hilo Medley, My Sweet Gardenia Lei, Haleakala, Pualani (Skyflower) (MAC 1015)

HAWAIIAN HULA EYES (1982): Hawaiian Hula Eyes, Kapilimehana, Ka 'Iwa Hulu 'Ena Ki'i Makalei, Kuwiliwili Iho Au, Mai Lohilohi Mai 'Oe, Opae E, Hawaiian Spirits Live Again, He Beauty Wale 'Oe, Mapuna Ka Hala o Kailua, Mahina Hoku, Ka U'i E, Ka Manu (MAC 1017)

WARRIOR (1983): Warrior, A New Way of Life, Time and Again, Now I Know You, War, It's Not Easy, Follow Me, I'm Home, Struggle, Sit and Ponder, Warriors Lament, Move On (MAC 1016)

PROUD FAMILY (1983): Hana Chant/Pua Anaka Makani, Hanohano No 'O Hawai'i, Tropical Baby, Ka Hanu Pua Mokihana, My Beautiful Hawaii, Maui's Not the Same Anymore, Pueo, Tara and Me, Aloha Ko'olau, Maui On My Mind, The Lake/Mai Poina 'Oeia'U, Family (MAC 2001)

Hawaiian Monarchs

Kamehameha I, later called Kamehameha the Great, founded the Kingdom of Hawai'i and served as its first monarch. The following eight monarchs ruled Hawai'i from 1795 until 1893 when the monarchy was overthrown.

KING KAMEHAMEHA I: born, ca. 1758; began rule, 1795; died, May 8, 1819.

KING KAMEHAMEHA II (Liholiho): first son of Kamehameha I and Keopuolani; born, 1797; began rule, May 20, 1819; died, July 14, 1824.

KING KAMEHAMEHA III (Kauikeaouli): second son of Kamehameha I and Keopuolani; born, March 17, 1814; began rule, June 6, 1825; died, Dec. 15, 1854.

KING KAMEHAMEHA IV (Alexander Liholiho): grandson of Kamehameha I and adopted son of Kamehameha III; born Feb. 9, 1834; began rule, Dec. 15, 1854; died, Nov. 30, 1863.

KING KAMEHAMEHA V (Lot Kamehameha): older brother of Kamehameha IV; born, Dec. 11, 1830; began rule, Nov. 30, 1863; died, Dec. 11, 1872.

KING LUNALILO (William Charles Lunalilo): grandson of a half-brother of Kamehameha I; born, Jan. 31, 1835; began rule, Jan. 8, 1873; died, Feb. 3, 1874.

KING KALAKAUA (David Kalakaua): elected when Lunalilo died without naming a successor; born, Nov. 16, 1836; began rule, Feb. 12, 1874; died, Jan. 20, 1891.

QUEEN LILI'UOKALANI (Lydia Lili'uokalani): sister of Kalakaua; born, Sept. 2, 1838; began rule, Jan. 29, 1891; died, Nov. 11, 1917.

The Kingdom of Hawai'i came to an end when Queen Lili'uokalani was deposed on January 17, 1893. A provisional government, headed by Sanford B. Dole, was organized to work toward the annexation of Hawai'i by the United States.

Selected Readings

Acson, Veneeta
  Waikiki: Nine Walks Through Time. Honolulu: Island Heritage. 1983.

Baker, Ray Jerome, Robert E. Van Dyke and Ronn Ronck
  Hawaiian Yesterdays. Honolulu: Mutual Publishing, 1982.

Barrow, Terence
  Captain Cook in Hawaii. Honolulu: Island Heritage, 1976.

Barrere, Dorothy B.
  Kamehameha in Kona. Honolulu: Department of Anthropology, Bernice P. Bishop Museum, 1975.

Barrere, Dorothy B., Mary Kawena Pukui and Marion Kelly
  Hula: Historical Perspectives. Honolulu: Department of Anthropology, Bernice P. Bishop Museum, 1980.

Beckwith, Martha
  Hawaiian Mythology. New Haven: Yale University Press, 1940. Reprint 1970. Honolulu: University of Hawaii Press.
  The Kumulipo, a Hawaiian Creation Chant (ed.) Chicago: University of Chicago Press,1951.Reprint 1972. Honolulu:University of Hawaii Press.

Blanding, Don
  Vagabond's House. New York: Dodd, Mead, 1928.
  Hula Moons. New York: Dodd, Mead, 1930.
  West of the Sunset. New York: Dodd, Mead, 1966.

Bone, Robert W.
  Maverick Guide to Hawaii. New Orleans: Pelican. Annual.

Cox, J. Halley and Edward Stasack
  Hawaiian Petroglyphs. Honolulu: Bishop Museum Press, 1970.

Daws, Gavan
  Shoal of Time: A History of the Hawaiian Islands. New York: MacMillan, 1968. Reprint 1974. Honolulu: University of Hawaii Press.

Dodd, Edward
  Polynesia's Sacred Isle. New York: Dodd, Mead, 1976.

Elbert, Samuel H. and Noelani Mahoe, eds.
  Na Mele o Hawai'i Nei: 101 Hawaiian Songs. Honolulu: The University of Hawaii Press, 1970.

Emerson, Nathaniel B.
  Unwritten Literature of Hawaii: The Sacred Songs of the Hula. Washington, D.C.: Smithsonian Institute, Bureau of American Ethnology Bulletin 38, 1909. Reprint 1965. Tokyo: Charles E. Tuttle Co.
  Pele and Hi'iaka: A Myth from Hawaii. Honolulu: Honolulu Star-Bulletin, 1915. Reprint 1978. Tokyo: Charles E. Tuttle Co.

Finney, Ben R.
  Hokule'a: The Way to Tahiti. New York: Dodd, Mead, 1979.

Joesting, Edward
  Hawaii: An Uncommon History. New York: W. W. Norton, 1972.

Judd, Walter F.
  Kamehameha. Honolulu: Island Heritage, 1976.

Hoefer, Hans, Leonard Lueras and Nedra Chung, eds.
  Hawaii. Hong Kong: Insight Guides, Apa Productions. Annual.

Holmes, Tommy
  The Hawaiian Canoe. Hanalei, Kauai: Editions Limited, 1981.

Hopkins, Jerry
  The Hula. Hong Kong: Apa Productions, 1982.

Kanahele, George S., editor
  Hawaiian Music and Musicians. Honolulu: The University Press of Hawaii, 1979.
  Hawaiian Renaissance. Honolulu: Project Waiaha, 1982.

Kane, Herb Kawainui
  Voyage: The Discovery of Hawaii. Honolulu: Island Heritage, 1976.

Kasher, Robert K. and Burl Burlingame
  Da Kine Sound: Conversations with the People who Create Hawaiian Music. Honolulu: Press Pacifica, 1978.

Kaeppler, Adrienne L.
  Polynesian Dance. Honolulu: Alpha Delta Kappa, 1983.

Lewis, David
  We, The Navigators. Honolulu: University Press of Hawaii, 1972.

Mcdonald, Gordon, Agatin Abbott and Frank L. Peterson
  Volcanoes in the Sea: The Geology of Hawaii. Honolulu: University of Hawaii Press, Second Edition, 1983.

McDonald, Marie
  Ka Lei: The Leis of Hawaii. Honolulu: Topgallant Publishing Co., 1978.

Pukui, Mary Kawena, and Samuel H. Elbert
  Hawaiian Dictionary. Honolulu: University of Hawaii Press, 1971.

Pukui, Mary Kawena, Samuel H. Elbert, and Esther T. Mookini
  Place Names of Hawaii. Rev. ed. Honolulu: University of Hawaii Press, 1974.

Rose, Roger G.
  A Museum to Instruct and Delight. Honolulu: Bishop Museum Press, 1980.

Todaro, Tony
  The Golden Years of Hawaiian Entertainment, 1874–1974. Honolulu: Tony Todaro Publishing Co., 1974.

Youngblood, Ron
  On the Hana Coast. Honolulu: Emphasis International Ltd. and Link Inc., 1983.

Photo/Art Credits

Cover	*Douglas Peebles; Airbrush work by Ron Hudson; Calligraphy by Leo Gonzalez*
Endpapers, front and back	*Early 19th century Pa'u kapa courtesy of Bernice P. Bishop Museum, Ethnology collection; photographed by Douglas Peebles*
2	*Frontispiece, Douglas Peebles*
8	*Allan Seiden*
10–11	*Framed photo from Cazimero family collection; photographed by Douglas Peebles*
11	*Top, Cazimero family collection*
12	*Cazimero family collection*
13	*Cazimero family collection*
14	*Both Baker-Van Dyke collection*

Index

Song Acknowledgments continued

WENDELL AND ALLAN DAVIS: My Beautiful Hanalei by Kai Davis.
WENDELL ING: The Lake by Wendell Ing © 1974.
JEBSEY MUSIC: My Beautiful Hawaii by Sonny Kamahele © 1975.
HENRY KAPONO KAAIHUE: Home in the Islands by Henry Kapono Kaaihue © 1980.
MOKIHANA: The Breeze and I by Mokihana © 1954.
MAKANI PUBLISHING: Hello Honolulu by Doolin Samuels and John Spencer © 1981.
MAUNA KEA PUBLISHING: Talk With Me Waikiki by Ron Kaipo © 1976.
KEN MAKUAKANE: Maui on My Mind by Kenneth Makuakane © 1982.
MRS. DON McDIARMID, SR: My Wahine and Me by Don McDiarmid, Sr.
PEER INTERNATIONAL CORPORATION: My Sweet Gardenia Lei by Danny Kuaana and Bernie Kaai © 1949, Peer International Corporation. Copyright renewed by Peer International Corporation. Used by permission. All rights reserved.
POCHOLINGA PRODUCTIONS: Waimea Lullaby by Patrick Downes © 1979.
WELK MUSIC GROUP: Soft Green Seas by R. Alex Anderson, Leonie Weeks and Ted Fio Rito © 1934, Harms, Inc. Copyright renewed and assigned to Bibo Music Publishers and Harms, Inc. (c/o The Welk Music Group, Santa Monica, CA 90401). International copyright secured. All rights reserved. Used by permission.
UNIVERSITY OF HAWAII PRESS: Royal Hawaiian Hotel by Mary Pula'a Robins © 1970.

© THE MOUNTAIN APPLE COMPANY/MUSIC OF POLYNESIA: Ka Wailele o Nu'uanu; He Beauty Wale 'Oe; There's No Love; No Ke Aloha Ana 'Ole; Ho'onani Ia Hokule'a; La Ho'olana; Na Pe'a O Hokule'a; Oni Wa'a Kaulua; I'm The One; Hokuli'ili'i; The I'a Stew; Dreams; Doldrum Blues; Ho'okele; E O E Hokule'a; Pane Mai; Kai Hanupanupa; Oceans of Memories; Kapilimehana; Ka'Iwa Hulu 'Ena Ki 'i Makalei; Hawaiian Spirits Live Again; Ka'U'i E; One Small Favor; Tropical Baby; I've Got To Find Me A Home; E Pele; Come Love Me Now; Hi'iaka's Pledge; Rebirth of Lohiau; Malama Pono; Why Are We Apart?; A Promise Forgotten; Jealousy; Destiny; I Am, I Am; These Hidden Valleys; The Beauty of Mauna Kea; He Beauty Wale 'Oe; Haleakala; He Inoa No Pauahi; Ho 'Okele; Ho'okipa Hawai'i; I Lei 'Oe; Ke'ala; Maui's Not the Same Anymore; Our Song; Pueo, Tara and Me; Rapid Transit Hula; The Warmth of Our Love; Warrior; I'm Home; Ka Hanu Pua Mokihana.
© TRANSLATIONS BY LARRY LINDSEY KIMURA: Aloha Tower; Eku'u Baby Hot Cha Cha; He Inoa No Pauahi; He Punahele; Holo Wa'apa; Kai Hanupanupa; Ke Alii Hulu Mamo; Kilakila 'O Haleakala; Ku'u Ipo I Ka He'e Pu'e One; Ku'u Ipo O Ke Aumoe; Kuwiliwili Iho Au; Mahina 'O Hoku; Mai Lohilohi Mai 'Oe; Maunawili; Mu'olaulani; Na Kuahiwi 'Elima; Nani Hanalei; Nani Ko'olau; No Ke Aloha Ana 'Ole; 'Opae E; Pua Mae'ole; Rapid Transit Hula; Royal Hawaiian Hotel; Tropical Baby; Waikiki Hula.
CRITERION MUSIC CORP./WEBLEY EDWARDS DIVISION: Nani Ko'olau by John Kalapama © 1962
COLUMBIA PICTURES PUBLICATION: Kilakila 'O Haleakala by William J. Coelho © 1937 (renewed 1964), Miller Music Corporation. All rights assigned to CBS Catalogue Partnership. All rights controlled and administered by CBS Miller Catalog. International copyright secured. All rights reserved. Used by permission.

Concept and text: Ronn Ronck
Art direction and design: Bill Fong and Leo Gonzalez
Design assistants: Pam Suzuki, Gregg Ichiki
Editorial assistant: Jay Hartwell

Display type: Torino
Text type: Torino Normal and Century Oldstyle/Italic
Song titles: Palatino Swash Italic (Display)
Song text: Palatino Bold Italic
Captions: Century Oldstyle Italic
Typesetting by Innovative Media and Ad Type

Printing/Materials:
Text, 4 color plus spot varnish/Espel, matte coated, 128 GSM
Endpaper, 4 color/Woodfree, 157 GSM
Jacket, 4-color plus film lamination/Coated stock, 128 GSM
Cover-T-Saifu over 2000 GSM board
Printed and bound in Tokyo, Japan, by Toppan Printing Co., Ltd.

Mutual Publishing of Honolulu